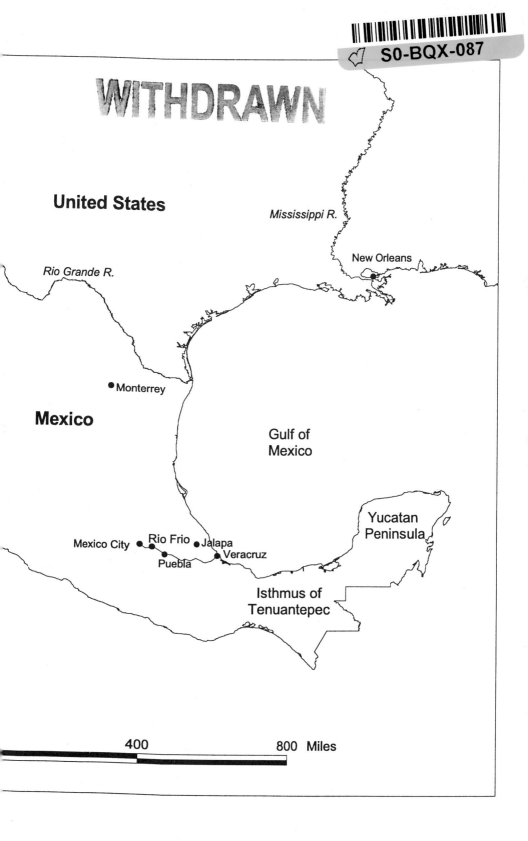

United States

*Mississippi R.*

New Orleans

*Rio Grande R.*

●Monterrey

**Mexico**

Gulf of
Mexico

Yucatan
Peninsula

Mexico City ● Rio Frio ● Jalapa
● Puebla ● Veracruz

Isthmus of
Tenuantepec

400          800  Miles

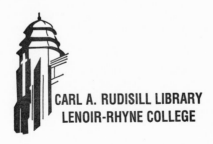

For
Honor
Glory &
Union

# For Honor Glory & Union

The Mexican & Civil War Letters
of Brig. Gen. William Haines Lytle

Ruth C. Carter, Editor

THE UNIVERSITY PRESS OF KENTUCKY

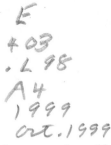
Publication of this volume was made possible in part by a grant from the National Endowment for the Humanities.

Scholarly publisher for the Commonwealth,
serving Bellarmine College, Berea College, Centre
College of Kentucky, Eastern Kentucky University,
The Filson Club Historical Society, Georgetown College,
Kentucky Historical Society, Kentucky State University,
Morehead State University, Murray State University,
Northern Kentucky University, Transylvania University,
University of Kentucky, University of Louisville,
and Western Kentucky University.

*Editorial and Sales Offices:* The University Press of Kentucky
663 South Limestone Street, Lexington, Kentucky 40508-4008

03 02 01 00 99   5 4 3 2 1

*Frontispiece:* Brig. Gen. William Haines Lytle.
(Courtesy of the Cincinnati Historical Society)

Library of Congress Cataloging-in-Publication Data

Lytle, William Haines, 1826-1863
    For honor, glory, and union : the Mexican and Civil War letters of
Brig. Gen. William Haines Lytle / Ruth C. Carter, editor.
        p.    cm.
    Includes bibliographical references and index.
    ISBN 0-8131-2108-6 (cloth : alk. paper)
    1. Lytle, William Haines, 1826-1863—Correspondence. 2. Mexican War,
1846-1848—Personal narratives. 3. United States—History—Civil War,
1861-1865—Personal narratives. 4. Generals—United States—Correspondence.
5. United States. Army—Biography. I. Carter, Ruth C. II. Title.
E403.1.L98A4    1999
973.6'2—dc21                                                        98-37536

This book is printed on acid-free recycled paper meeting
the requirements of the American National Standard
for Permanence of Paper for Printed Library Materials.

*To John*

Sunday morning

Dear Uncle

In the desk by my bedside are those papers I value most.

I want them all carefully preserved. they contain many of the fruits of the latter portion of my life in the shape of speeches—poems—translations—essays &c. In case of any accident (which for my friends and sisters' sake God avert) if submitted to the inspection of some suitable person it is possible some few might be thought worthy of publication— At any rate they are all, so far, that in the event of my death (which it is well for a brave & wise man always to be prepared for) will aid in grappling my name to the memories of my friends.

Aff$^{ly}$ yours
WH Lytle

Letter from William Haines Lytle to Elias H. Haines [1847], Lytle Papers, Mss qL996P, box 30, no. 9, Cincinnati Historical Society, Cincinnati Museum Center. Lytle sent this undated letter to his uncle when he entered military service in 1847. Lytle's desire to leave a record for his friends and future generations would have been similar when he entered military service during the Civil War.

# Contents

*Illustrations follow page 114*

# A Note on the Editing

Whenever possible, the letters are presented using William Haines Lytle's punctuation, superscripts, and emphasis. In a few cases where it was not clear whether he intended to show superscript for an abbreviation, I used a regular font. Lytle wrote in paragraphs but often omitted periods. I added periods for clarity. When I could not decipher a word or words, I used brackets with my best guess at the word or phrase, or ellipses if I could not make a reasonable determination. I tried to preserve Lytle's capitalization and spelling but employed modern usage when necessary for clarity. Various inconsistencies and misspellings as made by Lytle remain in the letters. Italicized words in the letters were underlined by Lytle.

# Acknowledgments

In preparing this book I am indebted to many people, including, first and foremost, those who wrote and saved the wonderful collection of letters and other documents known as the Lytle Papers. Their existence is a tribute to William Haines Lytle and his sisters, ancestors, and heirs. Without the Lytle family's sense of history and the value they placed on each other, this publication would not be possible. Lily Foster and Charles Livingood, Lytle's niece and her husband, preserved the letters so carefully saved by the general's sisters, Elizabeth Lytle Broadwell and Josephine Lytle Foster. After Livingood's death, his children gave the collection to the Cincinnati Historical Society, where it is located today. Virginius Cornick Hall, a great grandson of Josephine Lytle Foster, has enthusiastically supported this effort, supplying me with family lore that is not available anywhere else and reviewing portions of the manuscript.

Anne Shepherd, from the Cincinnati Historical Society Library, deserves special mention for she took my project as her own and provided unstinting help and persistence in locating material. We share an appreciation for the many contributions the Lytles made to Cincinnati and are happy to have that distinguished family receive recognition for its achievements. I am also grateful to all the staff at the Cincinnati Historical Society who have helped me over the years.

Wendy Mann, of the reference department in the University Library System at the University of Pittsburgh, provided extensive help in creating maps for this book. James Ogden III, historian at the Chickamauga and Chattanooga National Military Park, took me behind the scenes into the park library and furnished copies of material from the park's collection.

Van Beck Hall, professor of history at the University of Pittsburgh, read an early draft of the book and made many helpful suggestions. Edward Shanahan, a friend, librarian, and Civil War enthusiast, has read almost every version of the manuscript and served as a sounding board for some ideas. Rush G. Miller, director of the University Library System, supported my work in several ways and generally encouraged this undertaking.

I am grateful to the reviewers selected by the University Press of Kentucky. Their suggestions dramatically improved the book. Any remaining errors and inconsistencies are my responsibility alone.

My sister Mary Matsi read part of an early draft and has cheered my efforts. My cousins Eileen and Floyd Hastings and lifelong friend Jo Ann Ruppanner took turns providing me with places to stay during my research trips to Cincinnati. Most of all my husband, John, deserves my gratitude. He accompanied me to Chickamauga and Bardstown, took photographs included herein, accepted those times when I made the book a priority, and provided support in countless ways. And though my parents, Helen and Raymond Brill, are not here to enjoy this publication, I will always be grateful for their love and encouragement.

# INTRODUCTION

BRIG. GEN. WILLIAM HAINES LYTLE, the poet-general killed at the battle of Chickamauga on September 20, 1863, was a fearless commander and highly respected volunteer officer in the United States Army. Like so many other Federal officers, he entered his country's Civil War from a desire to preserve the Union.[1] His Civil War letters resonate with his overwhelming commitment to the Union. Lytle's fervent desire to join the fighting to save the Union overrode his upper class background, Democratic ideology, and close connections to Kentucky. He fought and was wounded—the last time fatally—in three battles during the Civil War: Carnifex Ferry, Perryville, and Chickamauga.

His letters written during the Mexican and Civil Wars reveal much of his character—his strengths and weaknesses. They shed light on his interests and values and the reasons he fought. At the same time the extant letters, mostly to close family members, illuminate his perspective on activities of the Army of the Ohio and Army of the Cumberland. Lytle's correspondence is also valuable for his frequent mention of the officers with whom he served, including Generals William S. Rosecrans, Ormsby Mitchel, and Philip Sheridan.

Although this narrative provides biographical information on Lytle, his letters constitute the core of this book. They are divided into two sections: the Mexican War letters and the letters from Lytle's three years of service in the Civil War (1861, 1862, and 1863). This correspondence allows us into his heart and mind as he shared his experiences and observations with his sisters and other close family members. All but three of the 106 letters are held in the Lytle Family Papers, Mss qL996P, in the collections of the Cincinnati Historical Society, Cincinnati Museum Center. The remaining letters are in the collections of the Historical Society of Pennsylvania and are so noted.

Lytle's childhood and education contributed to the formation of his values and ideals, including leadership, honor, bravery, the importance of social graces, Democratic ideology in the Jackson tradition, and a strong, vigorous Union. Although a native son of Ohio, Lytle had a personality and temperament more akin to that of a southern cavalier than a Yankee. By illuminating the factors that made Lytle want to fight in April 1861, we gain some understanding of why he and other midwestern Democrats put aside close southern associations, either business or heritage, to fight for the Union. Along with his intrinsic abilities and intelligence, Lytle's values shaped him as he reached maturity during the years when the United States debated not just slavery but the nation's very future.

William Haines Lytle was born in Cincinnati, Ohio, on November 2, 1826. On September 20, 1863, six weeks before his thirty-seventh birthday, he died during the battle of Chickamauga. Throughout his life, Lytle's attitudes and values often differed from those of most Cincinnatians and residents of other northern cities. His zest for military service, disdain for money as an end in itself, political activism, and romantic nature characterized a Southern rather than Northern ideal. From earliest childhood he was schooled in social graces, civic responsibility, and love of country. Lytle thought of himself as of the West and knew well not just Cincinnati, his lifelong home, but most of Ohio and northern and central Kentucky, including Bardstown and Louisville. His Kentucky ties gave an extra dimension to his Civil War service when in 1862 Lytle traveled through and was stationed in locations where he played as a child and socialized as a young man. To some extent in his Kentucky-based service, culminating in the battle of Perryville, Lytle was defending his second home from Confederate advances. Though Lytle also had family in the East and spent time in central Pennsylvania, Philadelphia, New York, and Washington, the eastern cities were more difficult to reach. More important, the East and its urban centers did not hold as much appeal to Lytle as the West.[2]

Lytle flourished during Cincinnati's golden age when the city's future seemed limitless and the population grew rapidly. By 1860 the city had 161,044 residents, making it the largest city in the Midwest and seventh largest in the United States, just behind New Orleans and ahead of St. Louis. Cincinnati was also one of America's most densely populated cities.[3] Many immigrants, mostly German and Irish, flooded into the city. Known as the Queen City of the West, antebellum Cincinnati was located at America's center,[4] where men and women of all sections and classes came together. Both refinement and rawness were present in extremes.[5] Cincinnati had the further distinction of being the largest Northern city that directly bordered a Southern slave state. Despite the absence of a bridge over the Ohio River, both economic and social intercourse between Cincinnatians and their Kentucky neighbors prospered from the city's inception. Geography and economics combined to turn Cincinnati's face toward the South.

Dependent on the South for commerce, Cincinnati businessmen and politicians feared alienating it. Consequently, despite the presence of leading abolitionists, including James G. Birney, publisher of the abolitionist newspaper *The Philanthropist,* and Harriet Beecher Stowe, a resident for almost twenty years during the 1830s and 1840s, many of the city's most influential citizens argued against abolition until well into the 1850s. Cincinnati at mid-century was out of step with most of Ohio, yet inherently different from its slave-state neighbor Kentucky.

In 1860, on the eve of the Civil War, Kentucky literally was caught between the North and South, for three slave and three free states touched its borders. Slavery allied it with the South, yet commerce bound it to the midwestern states. Like Ohio, Kentucky had a Whig rather than Democratic tradition; its political history through mid-century was dominated by Henry Clay, three-time presidential candidate and shaper of sectional compromises. Abraham Lincoln, 1860's victorious presidential candidate, had Kentucky roots but lost his native state to John C. Breckenridge, also from Kentucky. Jefferson Davis, the Confederate States president, too was born in Kentucky.

When the war to save the Union erupted, Kentucky residents were split. With most citizens in favor, Kentucky adopted a policy of neutrality. Meanwhile, Kentucky men signed up with both Confederate and Union forces. About two-fifths, including Lytle's second cousins William Lytle Rowan and William Lytle Blanchard, joined the Confederate army.[6] The state's coveted neutrality could not continue indefinitely; early military campaigns in Kentucky and Tennessee were waged in attempts to secure Kentucky support.[7] The battle of Perryville in October 1862 had significance far beyond the Union victory. Excluding brief raids, the battle represented the northernmost advance of the Confederate army in the West and put to rest any possibility that Kentucky would leave the Union.

William Haines Lytle, the general, is inseparable from his background. Born into an upper class Cincinnati family with a Kentucky heritage and continuing strong ties to elites in the Bluegrass State, he lived during a period of geographic expansion and rapid social change in America. The Lytles played a prominent role in the development of the West. Their presence in Ohio and Kentucky began with William H. Lytle's great grandfather Capt. William Lytle (1728-1797). A Pennsylvania native of Scots-Irish ancestry and veteran of the French and Indian Wars, Captain Lytle received his introduction to the Ohio Valley when he commanded Fort Pitt prior to the Revolutionary War.[8] After receiving lands in the Virginia Territory as a reward for his military service, Captain Lytle took his family to Kentucky in 1781 and soon settled permanently near Lexington, Kentucky. The first Kentucky census in 1790 lists both Capt. William Lytle and his son William (1770-1831); the second census of 1800 gives the younger William Lytle as a resident of Fayette County, near Lexington.[9] When Captain Lytle's daughter Ann married John Rowan in 1794, Lytle gave the newly married couple the land on which they built their home, Federal Hill, near Bardstown.[10] His oldest son, William, received from his father lands and training as an Indian fighter and surveyor. Adept at survival in the early rugged West, William Lytle (the younger), grandfather of the Civil War hero, became an entrepreneur and philanthropist in Cincinnati.

Though Captain Lytle's two sons, William and John, both settled in Ohio, other family members remained in Kentucky. Ann Lytle and another of William Lytle's sisters married and raised families in Kentucky. Federal Hill, the home of Ann Lytle and John Rowan, became famous from the long-held, if erroneous, belief that it inspired the song "My Old Kentucky Home," written by Stephen Foster, a distant relative. Foster, coincidentally, became a friend of William Haines Lytle during Foster's residency in Cincinnati from 1846 through 1850.[11] Mary (Polly) Lytle (1764-1808) married David Blanchard. The Blanchards raised three sons, Robert, John, and William, while living on a farm near Washington, Kentucky. John and William Blanchard died young, but before William's death he often served as a sales agent for his uncle William Lytle.

When William Lytle, grandfather of the Civil War general, first moved to Ohio in 1801, he established Williamsburg in Clermont County. However, he soon realized the best development opportunities were in Cincinnati. In 1806 he bought the site of the future Lytle mansion, then on the outskirts of the rapidly growing frontier city, and moved his family there in 1809. When the Lytles settled in Cincinnati, the family consisted of William, his wife, Eliza Stall Lytle, and five children who grew to adulthood: John Stall (b. 1800), William Henry (b. 1802), Robert Todd (b. 1804), Eliza Ann (b. 1806), and Edward (b. 1808). Although the Lytles had additional children, none survived childhood. Of the five Lytle children who reached maturity, all except Edward died before reaching forty years of age. John, William Henry, Robert (William Haines Lytle's father), and Eliza, like their parents, succumbed to that scourge of nineteenth-century cities—tuberculosis (then known as consumption).

Even before William Lytle moved his family to Cincinnati, he had established himself there as a leading entrepreneur. His wealth and leadership abilities kept him in the forefront of Cincinnati society. In 1819 when leading citizens united to found Cincinnati College, William Lytle made the initial and largest contribution to the project—$11,500.[12]

The emphasis on education constituted one aspect of Cincinnati's flourishing intellectual and cultural life. During the three decades preceding the Civil War, the Queen City claimed the title "Athens of the West." The city's elites set the tone for the pursuit of culture.[13] William Lytle was among the most active civic- and culturally minded citizens. He and his sons, Robert and John, took active roles in establishing and promoting the arts and intellectual life. For example, in 1820 William Lytle commissioned the young artist John James Audubon to paint portraits of himself and his first wife, Eliza.

The Lytles, however, held atypical political views compared to the business-oriented Whigs who comprised most of Cincinnati's elites. William Lytle, his son Robert, and his grandson William Haines Lytle all were Jacksonian Democrats. Nonetheless, they found common ground with other city leaders, at least for most of the antebellum period, on the rights of slave owners.

Despite Robert Todd Lytle's short life of only thirty-five years, he was a lively, charismatic man, who left a strong impression on his son, William Haines Lytle. Robert Lytle attended Cincinnati College. Afterward he left his hometown to study law in Louisville and Bardstown with his uncle John Rowan from 1822 to 1824. Returning to Cincinnati, Lytle practiced law for several years and served for a time as county prosecutor. In November 1825 he married his stepsister, Elizabeth Smith Haines, the daughter of his father's second wife, Margaret Haines Lytle.[14] Meanwhile, law did not hold Robert's heart. Rather, this outstanding orator thrived on politics. Despite being slightly under age, in October 1828 he won election to the Ohio House of Representatives. When separation from his wife, two-year-old son Will, and baby Margaritta proved painful, Lytle decided not to run for a second term.

After his father died in March 1831, Robert Lytle spent much of the remainder of that year handling complicated estate matters in Kentucky, where his father had invested heavily in land. The following year "Orator Bob" easily won election as a Democrat to the United States House of

Representatives. There he formed strong friendships with fellow first-term congressional Democrats Franklin Pierce of New Hampshire and Thomas Hamer of Ohio.[15] On a later trip to Washington in 1837, Elizabeth and Robert Lytle shared a boarding house with James K. Polk and his wife.[16] The Lytle family's respect for the Polks continued into the 1860s, when William Haines Lytle called several times on the widowed Sarah Childress Polk while he was stationed close to her home near Murfreesboro, Tennessee.

A strongly pro-Jackson Democrat, Robert Lytle lost political favor with Cincinnati businessmen over his support for the president's policies that were hostile to the Bank of the United States. After Robert Lytle narrowly lost his re-election bid to Bellamy Storer, the Whig candidate, President Jackson rewarded the son of his old friend by recommending Lytle for the position of surveyor general of the United States, a position to which he previously had appointed William Lytle in 1830.[17] Robert Lytle retained the surveyor general's office until June 1838, when poor fiscal management forced his resignation. Meanwhile, Robert also followed in his father's footsteps by holding the position of major general in the Ohio Militia. In late 1838 he made an unsuccessful attempt to gain the Democratic nomination for United States senator from Ohio. A victim of frequent poor health throughout the 1830s, the handsome, intelligent Robert Lytle lived only a year after his last attempt to gain public office. Consumption claimed both Robert and his older brother, John, in December 1839.

Robert Lytle left social position and a tradition of leadership to his only son, William Haines. This third-generation male of Cincinnati's Lytle family received a college education, exposure to arts and literature, opportunity to travel, and a network of connections among the nation's elites. With so many advantages and a display of intelligence early in life, it is not surprising that much was expected of this heir to the family's proud legacy.

On his deathbed in March 1831, patriarch William Lytle expressed the family's outlook: "Thank God I have now a boy who will keep up the name of Lytle when the rest of us are laid in the dust."[18] That precious boy, William Haines Lytle, became a talented man who combined the warrior and the poet, the man of action and the dreamer, and a tender heart with fiercely held principles. The oldest child and only son of Robert and Elizabeth Lytle, Will was a prodigy, marveled over by his parents and other relatives. The family's lofty hopes and ambitions focused on the heir to the family name, creating tremendous pressure and high expectations. Will's youngest sister, Lily, even expected him to become president of the United States.[19] During his brief life Lytle displayed many flashes of brilliance. Yet his failure to channel his energies consistently frustrated those who knew him best. When the Civil War erupted, Lytle became motivated and focused. With his beloved Union in jeopardy, he dedicated himself to the struggle to save it. In doing so, he more nearly realized the substantial potential that had often gone unfulfilled in happier, easier times.

Robert and Elizabeth Lytle had four children: William Haines (b. 1826), Margaritta (b. 1828), Josephine Roberta (b. 1830), and Elizabeth Haines (b. 1835). Margaritta died in 1832 from measles. When their mother, Elizabeth, died in December 1841, the three remaining children became orphans. Responsibility for their welfare fell to Elizabeth's mother, Margaret Haines Lytle. Elizabeth Lytle's sister, the widowed Joanna Haines Reilly, also lived in the Lytle mansion and contributed greatly to the household's daily activities.

The family's letters from the late 1820s and 1830s often mention Will. Even as a toddler of thirteen months, Will picked up the family's political enthusiasms, shouting "Jackson" from morning to night. Five months later, in May 1828, his grandmother observed that he said almost everything and was "an uncommon child." Soon Will's father described his son as fat, full of activity, and eating corn and potatoes every day. His parents continually evinced pleasure at their smart little boy. By the time he turned two in November 1826, Will was renowned for his intelligence and ability to speak. Those two traits characterized the man as well as the boy.[20]

As a young child, William Haines Lytle not only showed flashes of brilliance and a propensity for speaking, but he also developed a keen interest in riding horses and being a soldier. Military pursuits had constituted a continuing passion for the Lytle men through the generations. Gov. Edward Tiffin appointed Will's grandfather William Lytle, an Indian fighter in his youth, lieutenant colonel in the Ohio Militia on August 10, 1804. He received a promotion in February 1808 to major general. Though his duties were largely administrative, Lytle participated in the War of 1812 in maneuvers near Detroit. Robert Todd Lytle, although less actively militaristic than his father, also held the position of major general in the Ohio Militia. Both elder Lytles took part in parades and military ceremonies, filling the Lytle home with uniforms, swords, and arms. This exposure from earliest childhood to military exploits and displays greatly influenced the development of William Haines Lytle.

When only three years old, Will was painted in full uniform with a sword hanging at his side.[22] Also at three he began training on horseback[23] and at four requested a gun.[24] From his earliest days Will was energetic and high spirited. Yet his interests in horses and guns did not diminish his interest or abilities in more academic learning. At four years of age, Will seemed to his father to possess "matchless inteligence & *all* other manly attributes."[25] In March 1831 Will and Margaritta began attending an all-day school.[26] The next year Robert Lytle bragged that Will could *"positively read."*[27] When Will was seven years old in July 1834, his mother described his progress on his lessons: "I was surprised . . . to see the wonderful memory he has—The hard names of Asia gave him no trouble to commit." By winter she expected his English would be strong enough that he could begin to study French.[28]

Growing up in the early nineteenth century, Will inevitably encountered sickness and death at an early age. In March 1831, his grandfather Lytle died in the family home following a long bout with consumption. Later that year the young boy was "disconsolate" over the death of a great aunt who had lived in the Lytle household. Most shocking, his sister Margaritta died from measles in April 1832 at age three. Will contracted the disease also and was slow to recover.[29] Meanwhile, his mother had complained for months of poor health. Her own malaise, combined with Margaritta's death, prompted her to leave the remaining children and venture east for what she hoped would be a restorative visit to relatives.

Will's early separation from his mother lasted almost six months. Although her return date is not clear, Elizabeth was probably back in Cincinnati for Will's sixth birthday, November 2, 1832. Meanwhile, Will gloried in the excitement connected with his father's successful race for the United States Congress. Accompanied by his aunt Joanna Reilly, the five year old sat in the gallery in high spirits during a parade in honor of Robert's nomination. Robert described Will as "very fat," very manly, and dressed in a "roundabout and jacket with pockets."[30]

Robert Lytle's election to Congress separated the family again. He left for Washington in January 1833. Late that summer, Elizabeth, accompanied by her mother, took Will and his sister Josephine east to be closer to Robert. During her extended stay in the East, Elizabeth gave birth to her last child, Elizabeth Haines Lytle, commonly known as Lily or Bessie. Lily was born January 10, 1835, in Princeton, New Jersey. In early February, as soon as she could travel, Elizabeth took the new baby and Will to Washington so they could travel back to Cincinnati in March with Robert.

These early travels contributed to Will's spirit of adventure. Once safely in Washington, the young boy delighted in his privileged visits with

President Jackson. He also enjoyed his playmate William Calhoun, presumably the son of John C. Calhoun, who resided in the boarding house next door. Elizabeth noted that she had to direct Will not always to talk politics.[31] From his early days Lytle became accustomed to being around famous and powerful individuals and grew quietly confident in his social graces.

Back in Cincinnati and the West, the youth engaged in studies and active outdoor pursuits. By age eleven Will was an avid hunter, putting all his money into powder and shot and shooting fourteen quail in one day.[32] On one occasion, in late summer 1837, Margaret Lytle took Josephine and Will to visit their Blanchard relatives on their large farm near Washington, Kentucky. There Will became pals with his second cousin William Lytle Blanchard. The two boys would hunt before breakfast and afterwards bathe and fish.[33] Will gave his parents a major scare the following year when they visited the Blanchards together. According to Elizabeth Lytle, a horse Will was riding ran away with him. When the horse raced by on the turnpike, its saddle was turned as hard as it would turn. By the time the men caught up with Will he had dismounted after being dashed against a stone wall and letting the horse run. Will, then eleven, was lauded for his coolness and judgment in managing the horse. Fearing that the horse might kill someone someday, the Blanchards sold the mount for fifty dollars.[34] Will's playmate and second cousin William Blanchard joined the Confederate Army during the Civil War, serving at one point on Gen. Albert Sidney Johnston's staff. Lytle took pride in his cousin's accomplishments and mentioned them in several letters.

Not all of Will Lytle's early visits to Kentucky had recreational purposes. In 1841 Lytle accompanied his widowed mother when she went to Kentucky in conjunction with Robert Lytle's estate. Unfortunately for the financial well-being of the Lytles, John Rowan, Will's great uncle, provided little satisfaction in Elizabeth's attempt to secure favorable property settlements. When writing home, both Elizabeth and Will mentioned the judge's house as being small and crowded, so this was likely the Louisville home rather than Federal Hill. The Rowans, nonetheless, were gracious hosts.[35] Also in 1841, just six months before her death from consumption, Elizabeth Lytle described Will as taller than she and "remarkably manly and thoughtful." Elizabeth trusted that he would "make a good and useful Man— He has been a peculiar blessing thus far—& I trust, the grace of God, will sustain him thro Life—whether he wills it—to be a long—or a short one."[36] Elizabeth Lytle, when she wrote those words, could not have foreseen the violent sectional conflict that took her son's life at the young age of thirty-six.

Lytle entered Cincinnati College in August 1840 at the early age of thirteen. There he made a number of close friends, one of whom was Findlay Harrison, a grandson of William Henry Harrison. Though the two boys were nearly inseparable, they managed to avoid the topic of their opposing politics during Tippecanoe's 1840 presidential campaign as the Whig nominee. Their restraint showed good sense on both sides, commented Lytle's grandmother.[37] Lytle's earliest extant poem, called "The Soldier's Death," was written in 1840. Almost prescient, the poem describes the death of a soldier on the field of battle.

His own battlefield fatality more than two decades in the future, the young student wrote Findlay Harrison in January 1842 about his mother's death and his progress at school. Noting that he expected to be among the leaders in his class in the examinations beginning the next week, Will confessed, "I dislike much to be any wheres but 1st."[38] Ten months later Will explained that he was studying very hard because he desired "to come off with flying colours." Although his senior class was not large, Will, terming them all "first rate students," noted that competition was intense. He also reported having "the pleasure of using my lungs and throat" one night in a debate.[39]

In early 1843 as Lytle's graduation from Cincinnati College neared, uncles on both his mother's and his father's sides corresponded with their nephew about future educational options. Edward Lytle advised Will to complete his studies at one of the best eastern colleges and to pay less attention to public speaking and more to such academic pursuits as history or science; "until our minds are matured," he counseled, it is better to spend time and energy acquiring rather than disseminating knowledge.[40] In contrast, Elias Haines urged Will to graduate from college in the city where he expected to pursue his professional career. Cincinnati College also was his father's alma mater. Elias conceded, however, that Elizabeth Lytle might well have wished that her son attend Princeton. Elias also applied emotional pressure by urging Will to stay in the household with his grandmother, Margaret Lytle, for "it is very uncertain how long this last and only parent may be preserved to us."[41] Bowing to Haines family entreaties, Will ultimately stayed in Cincinnati, where he graduated first in his college class. Following graduation, the sixteen-year-old youth elected to read law in Cincinnati with his maternal uncle Ezekial Smith Haines.

Will attacked his legal studies with great enthusiasm. In a self-imposed schedule he studied law from 5:00 A.M. until 2:00 P.M. and Latin from 3:00 to 6:00 P.M. By adhering to this schedule, young Lytle expected to finish his law studies in two and a half years. Despite his interest in a social life as well, he confided to Elias Haines, "The town is dull as a meat axe. There has scarcely been a single party among the elite since you left."[42]

In May 1845, after almost two years of reading law, Will sought Elias Haines's opinion about attending the Lexington Law School the following winter. At his young age he would not be allowed to practice law in Cincinnati for almost three years, and, if he had training in Kentucky, he could help with Lytle family legal matters in Louisville.[43] There are also indications in newspaper obituaries, though not in existing correspondence, that Lytle had hopes at one time of attending West Point. In any event, although he had the connections to make a West Point or Lexington Law School education possible, he received all his college education and legal training in Cincinnati.

By staying in Cincinnati for college and the study of law, William Haines Lytle spent his teenage years in an all-female household headed by his grandmother. Not unexpectedly, the spirited youth became eager to establish his independence. The Mexican War came at a critical point in his development. The conflict excited his nationalistic pride, provided a chance to support Polk and the Democratic tradition, and offered the perfect opportunity for travel and adventure. Despite strenuous family protests, Lytle could not be held back. Having begun active service in October, he sailed from New Orleans for Vera Cruz, Mexico, on November 2, 1847, his twenty-first birthday.

Like many other volunteers, William Haines Lytle entered military service in September 1847 with high hopes of achieving honor and glory in the service of his country.[44] An ardent nationalist and partisan Democrat, Lytle supported President Polk's policies to protect Texas and expand United States territory. And he had long admired and romanticized soldiers. Elected lieutenant on entering the Second Ohio Volunteer Regiment's Company L, also known as the Montgomery Guards,[45] Lytle was voted captain three months later when a vacancy occurred.

By the time Lytle reached Mexico in November 1847, most of the fighting had ceased. The young officer had no opportunity to participate in battle. Instead, garrison duty highlighted this period and often resulted in boredom for Lytle. Though he failed to gain the glory he sought, Lytle's service in Mexico laid important groundwork for his Civil War experiences. Caring for and feeding volunteer troops as opposed to the more rigorously trained and disciplined regulars served him well in campaigns to come. He learned war was not all glamour: it included long marches, unpleasant weather, and short periods of action between long intervals of routine. As part of the Second 2d Ohio, Lytle also experienced firsthand the death of soldiers. Seventy-five members of the Second 2d Ohio died either from disease or in skirmishes with guerrilla bands.[46] Despite witnessing the loss of life and enduring hardships, Lytle was inspired by his Mexican War service to write many of his best poems, including "The Volunteers" and "Popocatapetl."

Although Lytle had eagerly joined the army and gone to Mexico, he was equally enthusiastic to return home once it became clear in early 1848 that peace was imminent. During that spring Lytle's family hoped he would return from Mexico in time to escort his sister Josephine from New York back to Cincinnati. He did not reach home until mid-July, however, by which time Josephine had started her return journey accompanied by their uncle Elias Haines. To her great joy, Will, now "rather thinner than when he left home," met her at Milford, Ohio. Soon Will, Josephine, and their sister Lily were reunited at home in Cincinnati in what Josephine called "a grand scene."[47]

In early October after a few months at home, Lytle left for a five-week visit with his uncle Edward Lytle near Martinsburg, Pennsylvania. When Lytle returned, he focused his attention on his legal studies and settled into daily life in Cincinnati. On November 26, 1848, he happily observed that his grandmother was enjoying life again. His father on his mind, Lytle wrote to the famous sculptor Hiram Powers[48] in December 1848 about putting Powers's bust of Robert Lytle in marble. The young Lytle noted that having the bust of his father had been his mother's "long cherished hope." As no good portrait of Robert Lytle survived, the bust would be invaluable.[49] On January 26, Powers wrote back saying the bust existed and he would undertake the project gladly, as Robert Lytle had been a "kind and true friend."[50] When the bust arrived two years later, Will delighted in "the truthful likeness," even placing it for a short time in the Arts Union gallery where his father's many friends could view it.[51]

Early 1849 was peaceful and beautiful, but the pleasant spring did not last long. By mid-May Cincinnatians were in a panic as cholera had struck the city. Both Lily Lytle and Joanna Reilly contracted severe cases. Lytle's great aunt, Ann Lytle Rowan, died while visiting her daughter Ann Rowan Buchanan in Cincinnati. Though he survived Cincinnati's dreadful cholera epidemics, Lytle became so ill from the disease in 1850 that doctors did not expect him to live.[52]

Shortly after the Rowan matriarch's death, the Lytles' renewed claims against the Rowans over the estate of William Lytle set off a period of friction between the two families. With Edward Lytle's blessing, Will engaged in efforts in the early 1850s to gain additional benefits from his grandfather's estate. John Rowan had often provided legal services for his brother-in-law and had played a major part in settling William Lytle's estate. After the latter's death in 1831, his heirs contested parts of the estate for more than two decades. At least one of the claims involved property at Lake Erie.[53] Considerable property in Kentucky, especially in the Louisville area, also entered into claims spanning many years.

Though relations between the two families did not cease entirely, after 1851 angry feelings existed particularly between Will and Joseph R. Buchanan, John Rowan's son-in-law and Cincinnati physician. In 1850 Buchanan was among the physicians who helped treat Lytle when he nearly died from cholera.[54] By June 1851 Lytle and Buchanan had evidently exchanged words concerning the memories of William Lytle and John Rowan. On June 18, 1851, Buchanan noted that he and his wife were removing to Louisville where they would now be separated by distance as well as consciousness from the Lytles.[55]

Margaret Lytle's death on June 14, 1851, brought much sadness to Will and his sisters. Their grandmother had doted on them and for almost ten years had held the family together. Although death was nothing new to the young attorney, the passing of Margaret Lytle effectively closed an era.

In 1851, the same year his grandmother died, Will accepted a nomination to run for the Ohio legislature on the Democratic ticket. His election by a wide majority delighted Lily, who enthusiastically described the Democrats' torchlight procession with two thousand horsemen and many others on foot. At least seven or eight banners recognized Lytle: "'W^m H. Lytle—the worthy son of a noble sire' 'Small in body but big in soul' 'William the conqueror'" Even the Whigs considered Lytle's speeches to be the best of the campaign,[56] despite his radical Democratic positions, including support for the rights of slaveholders. Accustomed to the adoration of his family, Lytle feasted on this public admiration. His purposes, however, he explained to Edward Lytle, were entirely noble: "my political career at least shall be free from all impurity and have but one guiding star a sincere and holy ambition to promote the true interest of the people—."[57]

Will Lytle spent the winters of 1851-52 and 1852-53 fulfilling his responsibilities in the Ohio House of Representatives. That first winter, Lily must have expressed a hope that Will would soon make a speech in the legislature. He wrote back that she shouldn't be in a hurry to have him speak as "it requires sometimes more intellect to keep the mouth shut than to keep it open."[58] Finally, shortly before the session ended, Will ventured his maiden speech in April 1852. Though his friends seemed pleased with his effort, his poor health (including a bad cough) marred the occasion for him.[59]

After the legislative session concluded, Lytle participated in Cincinnati's commotion over the funeral of Henry Clay in July 1852. Lytle's uncle Ezekial Smith Haines was among the men appointed to meet Clay's remains at Cleveland and escort the cortege to Cincinnati on the way to Clay's final resting place in Lexington, Kentucky.[60] The procession in the Queen City lasted more than two hours. Will Lytle was among the marshals, the only young man elected. According to Lily, everyone talked about how handsome he looked astride a pure white horse on a borrowed Mexican saddle that he covered with massive silver. The saddle cost her brother five hundred dollars but was well worth the price, Lily said, because his uniform became him and he could display his horsemanship, a point of great pride.[61] Once again, Will found himself drawn to the excitement and glamour of uniforms, parades, and horses.

In 1852 Will and Edward Lytle, ardent Democrats, exchanged letters about the forthcoming presidential election. Edward strongly supported Franklin Pierce, a devoted friend to Robert Lytle when they were first-term United States Congressmen from 1833 to 1835. Terming Pierce "an honest man, and accomplished statesman—a fair man withal," Edward considered Pierce certain to be successful.[62] In December 1852, with Pierce's election accomplished, William H. Lytle began his second session as a representative in the Ohio legislature. Shortly after he returned to Columbus, Will wrote to Lily the news that Perry County delegates had been instructed to vote for him for Ohio's secretary of state. But, because he wanted to return to his legal practice in the spring of 1853, he declined. At least for a few years, he believed, he could achieve "more brilliant triumphs at the bar than in any other arena." He also wanted to spend more time with his aunt and younger sister. Meanwhile, Josephine was preparing for marriage with Dr. Nathaniel Foster in April 1853.

Devoted to both his sisters, but with an almost fatherly affection for the younger, Will shared his views on education with Lily and in doing so revealed much of himself. Study, he considered, is a pleasure for an active and healthy mind. History and philosophy had many "eloquent facts" and "fascinating secrets" and "rich and glorious thoughts, which are most valuable & shed on our lives more real happiness than the triumphs of the fleeting incense of the parlour or the ball room." Will, then age twenty-seven, continued this emotional letter to Lily with a further statement of his optimistic yet melancholy philosophy of life:

> "My own life dear Bessie has been—though so young—crowded with much experience. I know something of the folly & something of the true beauty of Life. I have had my troubles. I have sat on the sunny & shaded side of the amphitheater. Troubles crush some men, others they make. . . . Do not think dear Bessie that I am involved in any serious trouble or difficulty. Like all other men I have had my dark days. All I mean to say is that a firm & resolute heart can not be subdued & that He who spoke the universe into being has not been so cruel as not to give even the meanest of his creatures power & fortitude to overcome or endure their misfortunes."[63]

Before returning to Cincinnati and his legal practice, Lytle also had decided against another career option. About December 1852, he consulted Edward Lytle regarding the possibility of seeking a position in the United States mission to Naples. The elder Lytle replied that Will should not think "of going abroad and particularly to such a post as Naples." Edward gave many reasons why Will should decline the offer, including insufficient salary, the potential for becoming an alien at home, and the destruction of his prospects both professionally and politically. Edward advised him to stick with the law for at least a few more years and then find a "clever woman with sound constitution, good sense, domestic habits, and a *fourth rate consideration, some funds*" and marry her. Then Will would have the best friend and adviser ever.[64]

Lytle's aunt Charlotte Haines, a bright, cultivated woman, also offered him advice. Haines, like the rest of his family, expected Lytle to achieve distinction. However, she feared he lacked sufficient opportunity to read in his current lifestyle and suggested to him that by reading German metaphysicians and French sophists who tended to make things in life appear unreal, he would underestimate the value of the exertions necessary to "make men great or distinguished."[65] Although he lacked parents, William Haines Lytle clearly had intelligent, sophisticated aunts and uncles who provided him with practical advice and attempted to bring out their nephew's better qualities.

The year 1853 was eventful for Lytle. He followed through on his intent to leave the Ohio legislature and resumed the practice of law in Cincinnati. Before returning home, however, he went to Washington, D.C., to celebrate Franklin Pierce's inauguration. His trip also had another purpose, to secure Elias Haines's appointment as a consul. Lytle presented his uncle's papers along with a letter of recommendation signed by several luminaries, including Senator Salmon P. Chase. Although President Pierce received Lytle cordially, they shared no time alone.[66] Ultimately, Haines failed to receive either a consulate or appointment as a port collector. Lytle received, however, an offer to serve as the secretary to the Chile legation. He declined, saying the law offered "as brilliant a field as diplomacy" and that he would "eschew politics" for a few years at least. In June 1853 Lytle demonstrated his serious intentions regarding the practice of law by joining a copartnership with his friend Alex Todd and his uncle Ezekial Smith Haines.[67] The trio's law firm, Haines, Todd, and Lytle, remained intact until Lytle's death at Chickamauga ten years later.

Lytle spent the rest of the 1850s and 1860 alternately engaged in his legal practice and participating in the political process. In 1854 he turned down the opportunity to run for the United States Congress. Louisville friend Judge Henry Pirtle supported his decision on the grounds that Washington was not a good place for a young man and, besides, few had his exceptional prospects for becoming a prominent lawyer.[68] But Lytle became easily bored and did not take to routine. One of his efforts to create excitement occurred in the mid-1850s while he served as Hamilton County recorder. On that occasion the free-spirited public official attracted attention "by riding his horse up the Courthouse steps into the Recorder's office."[69]

During August 1855 Lytle visited Kentucky to take care of legal business. By a quirk of fate he was in Bardstown, Kentucky, the day his second cousin John Rowan Jr. died. In shock, Lytle wrote home commenting that Rowan "was a very handsome young man—much like his father—the main stay of his family." The two had visited together just a few days previously.[70] Whatever tensions had existed between Lytle and the Buchanan branch of the Rowan family did not exist between Lytle and John Rowan Jr. Yet, after the latter's death, Lytle apparently had no occasion to return to Bardstown and Federal Hill until stationed there in the Union Army in January 1862.

In 1856 both Lytle and Ezekial Haines participated in a rally of the First Ward Democrats for the purpose of endorsing the candidacy of James

Buchanan for president. Lytle gave the evening's main speech on the great issues facing the country. England, he said, was responsible for slavery in the United States. "Slavery was the misfortune rather than the fault of the South." Further, the abolitionists were to blame for the failure of the Missouri Compromise as they effectively abolished it during the Oregon dispute in 1847. Lytle also paid eloquent tribute to the courage and patriotism of the southern people but noted that, despite their fidelity to the Union, southerners would leave the Union "instantaneously in case of the success of the Black Republican party. Their self respect will not permit them to remain."[71]

With politics in his blood, Lytle could not pass up his own candidacy for political office indefinitely. In 1857 he accepted the Democratic nomination for lieutenant governor of Ohio. Henry B. Payne of Cleveland faced incumbent Salmon P. Chase for governor. The Democratic platform endorsed the Supreme Court's decision in the Dred Scott case and its rejection of Negro citizenship.[72] Both Democrats waged vigorous, highly partisan campaigns, stumping in every corner of the state to voice support for the Dred Scott decision. On a swing through northwest Ohio, Lytle spoke at Port Clinton, Toledo, and Sandusky.[73] One report of Lytle's campaigning described him as one of the cultivated young men of the state with the "polish of the accomplished gentleman" combined with "good sense and high principle." Foreshadowing his future martial exploits, Lytle was described as having "the patriotism that eagerly embraces the opportunity of serving his country in her warlike contests."[74] Lytle got further good marks after a two-hour speech during which he held his audience rapt. A Sandusky correspondent noted that he was "a young man of excellent talent, a good reasoner and orator."[75]

When the dust settled and all the votes were counted, Chase outpolled Payne by the slim total of 1,503 votes. Lytle also lost narrowly. By 1858 support for slavery and disunion had diminished in Cincinnati. In 1860 Lytle made an attempt to gain the Democratic nomination for the United States House of Representatives, but George H. Pendleton, the Democratic incumbent, gained renomination. In a letter reporting his defeat to his brother-in-law, Sam Broadwell, Lytle indicated that he was *"sold out"* and that "great dissatisfaction" existed among local Democrats.[76] His personal defeat notwithstanding, he campaigned vigorously in 1860 on behalf of Stephen A. Douglas for president. He believed abolition would result in huge social and economic problems and criticized Republicans for asserting that abolition could be accomplished by peaceful or legal means. Although Lytle did not have another nomination for elective office, he was approached and urged to run during the Civil War. But he ultimately rejected pursuit of a political career while the war continued.

Lytle also pursued his military interests during the mid-1850s. On July 26, 1855, Governor William Medill appointed Lytle to the position of lieutenant colonel in the First Division, Ohio Volunteer Militia. He was elected major general of the division September 19, 1857, in the midst of his campaign for lieutenant governor. Governor Chase confirmed the election by commissioning Lytle major general on October 5, a post he still held in April 1861 when the hostilities at Fort Sumter reverberated throughout the nation.

While Lytle enjoyed the masculine worlds of politics and the military, his softer side, that of the poet and tender older brother and devoted nephew and grandson, was always present. Much of this came out in his poetry, an interest which he acquired from his mother. Though only two of Elizabeth Lytle's poems remain, she undoubtedly influenced her son through her personal interest in writing and literature. Will also loved music. When at home he often sang while Josephine played the piano.[77]

Lytle wrote many of his published poems in the interval between the Mexican and Civil Wars. By the time the latter broke out he was famous in cultivated circles for his stirring poetry, especially "I Am Dying, Egypt, Dying," written in 1858. Often ballads with a military theme, Lytle's romantic poetry reflected his cavalier's values as did his superb social graces and conscious behavior as a gentleman.

The cultivated Lytle had the gentleman's weakness for drinking. Living in times when heavy drinking was common, and often learned from childhood,[78] Lytle was no exception. That Lytle sometimes drank to excess is documented on several occasions. This propensity for alcohol on Lytle's part affected his relationships with his romantic interests, his sisters, and his professional interests. Nonetheless, it must be noted that Lytle typified many of his era. Further, Lytle was a connoisseur of fine wines, many of which were produced in Cincinnati. Certainly, many other Civil War officers were also cited for immoderate drinking at one or another points in their lives, including Ulysses S. Grant and William S. Rosecrans. And, except for one mention by Lily Broadwell of a lapse on Lytle's part at the end of his two-month command at Bardstown in early 1862, there is no indication that he indulged excessively during the Civil War. Rather, Lytle understood the importance of restraint. He worried about his longtime friend and cousin-in-law Findlay Harrison by making the latter "take the pledge" and giving him a second and even third chance to serve as his volunteer aide during 1863.[79]

His love of the arts and literature extended beyond music and poetry. Lytle relished visiting art museums.[80] He attended operas and even participated in plays; on one occasion he took the role of the Ghost in Hamlet in an amateur dramatic performance.[81] On a less intellectual note, he played billiards and spent time with friends in the Irish part of town, a less staid area than the central portion of town where the upper-class families lived.[82]

Lytle enjoyed parties and other social events. He participated in upper-class society on a regular basis not only in Cincinati but in Kentucky, particularly Louisville. Shortly before his twenty-sixth birthday, Lytle attended the wedding of one of his Kentucky cousins, Mary Blanchard, near Maysville. In telling the story of the party, which took place several days following the wedding due to commotion caused by the bride's very unhappy former suitor, Lytle revealed the nature of the gala event along with his own pleasure in helping to host the celebration. After enjoying the Kentucky portion of the party, "a glorious night," Lytle brought a number of the wedding guests to Cincinnati, where the festivities continued until the next day.[83] On another Kentucky visit, however, Will wrote that he had gone out very little for he had been "low in spirits" and did not feel like "mingling in society."[84] Yet, overall, Lytle believed that Cincinnati was droll and stupid compared with gay Louisville. He described his home city as nothing but a "perpetual hunt after the 'dollar' & the d———l take the hindmost."[85]

Although he never married, Lytle had at least two serious relationships and numerous flirtations. At the time of his election to the state legislature in October 1851, news of his interest in Therese Chalfant had even reached Edward Lytle in central Pennsylvania. Though Will said, on learning of Chalfant's engagement, "I might contest the prize if I were home," he took no action.[86] Any disappointment on Lytle's part did not last long. By late 1852 he had fallen in love with his first cousin Lily Macalester.[87] No letters between the two survive, but letters from Will's sisters, Charlotte Haines, and Edward Lytle discuss the couple. Charles Macalester, Lily's father, disapproved of the marriage for at least two reasons: his daughter and Will Lytle were first cousins in a family where consumption flourished and, according to a Columbus friend of Macalester's, Will's habits had been unacceptable.[88] The engagement collapsed in June 1853.

Lytle's next serious romance was with another relative, this time a distant cousin, Sed Doremus. Although evidence is scant, fragments of an

1855 letter from Lily Broadwell confirm the family lore that Lytle asked Doremus to marry him in early 1855. Apparently Doremus expected to be asked a second time, but the proud Lytle, not accepting rejection, instead broke off the romance. Vowing never to marry until after Lytle did, Doremus devoted herself to study. Broadwell expressed disappointment, saying that she "had never seen any one whom I would so love to have as a sister."[89] As early as July 1858 Lytle commented that in regard to *"love,* that star with me has set—forever, most probably."[90] Yet, as the years passed, Lytle and Doremus maintained interest in each other and as the dreadful war progressed again expressed their mutual devotion. In late August 1863, just weeks before his death, Lytle told his aide Alfred Pirtle that should he ever meet Doremus he should relay Lytle's devotion: "tell her that never was [k]night truer to his lady love than I am to her never have I thought of another woman. That I shall go on loving her. . . ." Sed Doremus kept an all-night vigil by Lytle's casket the evening before his funeral and remained single for the rest of her life from devotion to her fallen lover.[91]

Between the Mexican and Civil Wars, William Haines Lytle scattered his energies and failed to achieve either the satisfaction of sustained professional excellence or the stability in his personal life that marriage might have brought. Lytle, given to melancholy moods, even destroyed many of his best poems to the dismay of friends and colleagues. On occasion though, they took matters out of his hands and arranged for publication.[92] Yet, despite receiving renown as a poet and admiration for his many talents, Lytle frequently seemed bored and restless. On one occasion, he wrote Lily Broadwell that he was "bored to death with several perplexing questions growing out of [his] official position as Major Gen$^{l}$, besides other matters!"[93] In 1858 he commented that he had accepted an invitation to make a Fourth of July speech in Clermont County, but "What a bore!"[94]

Lytle's trouble reaching his full potential and his occasional improprieties disappointed his family, including Edward Lytle and Lily Broadwell. In January 1858 Lytle apparently caused Lily Broadwell some form of injury that required medical treatment months later, though the nature and the circumstances are not clear. Broadwell wrote that she had endured pain for her brother's sake for many long, weary months and that if it would do any good she would "gladly" die for him. If Lytle loved her as much, he should prove it, for he had it in his power to make her and all those who loved him "either *perfectly happy* or *entirely wretched.*"[95]

Edward's anguish over his nephew resulted from a newspaper clipping that reported Will's disreputable conduct in public. On July 25, 1858,

Edward told Will, whom he had "loved as a son or brother," that if the "foul publication" contained even "a shadow of truth" Will should leave Cincinnati forever. "If *true,*" Edward wrote, "I would ten thousand times sooner have heard of your death— My scorn of rowdyism, and vulgar debauchery is and always has been *inexpressable.*"[96] Will's reply, apparently attributing the account to political rivals, relieved Edward's anxiety. The elder Lytle then urged his nephew to visit. Although there is no record of Will traveling to Pennsylvania to see Edward Lytle until 1860, their warm relationship continued unabated.

Will's description of his travel to Pennsylvania to visit Edward Lytle in April 1860 reveals both his sense of humor and a bit of hauter. After a frightful trip with many delays due to heavy rains, Will finally got to Pittsburgh from Wheeling via a steamer. Dismayed at the prospect of the clothes in his trunk being exposed to rain and sleet on the steamer's deck, Will covered it with the trunks of the other passengers. "I did not hesitate to do this, as I thought their apparel would probably be benefitted by a little washing."[97]

Later in 1860, when Will failed to secure his district's Democratic nomination to the U.S. House of Representatives, Lily delighted that he took the disappointment so well. She counseled her brother that he was at a turning point and should try to rally all his energies toward "loftier aims & higher purposes in life than hitherto." He should learn to work hard and be patient. Why should he not try for some of the big legal cases? Not only did they bring in big money, but more importantly they would require hard work, the best thing for Will who's worst enemy was *"laziness!"* Lily urged Will to reform by getting to the office early and being regular in his attendance both at the office and the court house. If he willingly took on little cases he would soon get big ones. Lily considered Will to be impatient but thought the slow, steady way was sure. His loving sister felt that "such a systematic, busy life" would give him "a lighter happier heart" than he had had in recent times.[98]

The picture, then, of William Haines Lytle shortly before the outbreak of the Civil War is one of a gifted yet less than happy or fulfilled individual. His sisters were both married and, though they still doted on their idol, had busy personal lives to lead. Bright, quick, and multitalented but sometimes impulsive and impatient with routine, Lytle had not become absorbed with either his legal career or political interests. Poetry was an avocation only. Even when giving speeches or participating in his Ohio Militia duties, Lytle often described himself as bored. He was a man without a fixed purpose in life when the Civil War and the call to his country's duty touched a deep need to devote himself to a cause.

When hostilities erupted at Fort Sumter on April 12, 1861, William Haines Lytle held an appointment as major general in the Ohio Militia. Three days later, while in Columbus, the state capitol, Lytle learned of President Lincoln's call for fifteen thousand three-month troops.[99] That day Lytle returned to Cincinnati carrying orders to set up an assembly for Hamilton County troops. He selected the Cincinnati Trotting Park, located seven miles outside the city on the Cincinnati, Hamilton, and Dayton Railroad line, as the site for Camp Harrison.[100] Lytle worked tirelessly over the next several months organizing the camp and gaining recruits.

Despite sympathizing with states' rights and those of southern slave owners, Lytle held a national view and strong pro-Union sentiments. His father and grandfather had ardently supported Andrew Jackson, who believed in the Union above all. In 1860 Lytle had campaigned hard for Stephen Douglas, who on the outbreak of war called for national unity, saying there could be only patriots—or traitors.[101] Neither neutrality nor a position away from the front was an option for Lytle. Desperately wanting to serve his country in action, the thirty-four-year-old officer gave up his position in the militia to accept a commission on May 6, 1861, as colonel, Tenth Ohio Volunteer Infantry, a mostly Irish regiment from the Cincinnati area.[102]

Supplying, training, and disciplining troops occupied most commanders at Camp Harrison. While inexperienced commanders often had difficulty controlling their men, seasoned veterans like Lytle did not. Jacob Cox recalled that "the brilliant Lytle" gained control over his feisty, hard-drinking regiment right away. The Tenth "had fallen into competent hands."[103] Lytle's Mexican War experience proved its value early in his Civil War assignments.

Townsmen not rushing to military service sought to recognize the bravery of fellow citizens. The Cincinnati Bar presented Colonel Lytle with a sword on May 16. Thomas Gallagher's presentation speech noted that the offering was spontaneous and a tribute from "your brother lawyers who appreciate and understand your character as a gentleman and as a soldier."[104] Other friends gave him a handsome black horse with an Irish name, Faugh-a-Ballaugh, meaning "clear the way." In June, before departing for Virginia, Colonel Lytle accepted a stand of regimental colors presented to the Tenth Ohio by the patriotic women of Cincinnati. Remarking that the Tenth would bring the colors back to "the Queen City of the West, without spot or blemish," he thanked the women and bid them good-bye. Lytle shouted "Faugh-a-Ballaugh," and the Tenth rode away.[105]

Governor William Dennison of Ohio and Governor Oliver Morton of Indiana had raised troops rapidly, placing them under the command of West Point graduate Maj. Gen. George B. McClellan with directions to secure the Baltimore and Ohio Railroad near Grafton, Virginia. Lytle's regiment was first ordered to western Virginia in June 1861 to help protect Ohio and critical transportation routes. Long marches in bad weather over mountainous terrain characterized the movement of Union troops that summer in western Virginia. As McPherson points out, the marches in drenching rain would have done credit to veteran troops much less new recruits.[106] The Union needed this Virginia border territory both politically and strategically.

After seemingly endless marches, Lytle and the Tenth experienced battle for the first time on September 10 at Carnifex Ferry. For thirty to forty-five minutes during the fighting, Lytle's command alone had to sustain the battle. Finally, Lytle decided to make an independent assault on the Confederate entrenchments and to carry forward the Tenth Ohio's colors as an incentive. His men followed his charge across a cornfield and over rugged terrain. The rebels opened fire with a savage volley. Although telling his men to fall flat, Lytle, on horseback, was struck by a Minié ball in the calf of his left leg. When Lytle fell to the ground, where he continued to direct his troops, Faugh-a-Ballaugh ran briefly and then died from the same ball that had struck his master. Lytle's wound was serious. The ball went through his calf just between the main arteries, scraping bone on the way. Incapable of further active duty until his wound healed, Lytle returned to Cincinnati to recuperate for almost four months. Others were not so lucky. Sustaining ten of the twenty-seven Federal casualties, the Tenth became known as the "heroes of Carnifex" and gained the sobriquet "The Bloody Tenth." Its colonel earned praise from both Union and Confederate soldiers for his bravery.[107] Although Lytle solidified his reputation for gallantry and bravery, some believed he had a propensity for unnecessary risk taking.[108]

In late November 1861, the Tenth returned briefly to Cincinnati, where the regiment had a joyful reunion with its wounded colonel. Disembarking at the wharf, the regiment, preceded by its band, marched past Lytle's house at Third and Broadway where he stood in the door. "The boys had not seen him since the battle of Carnifex and they needed no command to salute him. As each company passed, they sent up vociferous cheers for Colonel Lytle, waving their stained caps high in the air." Still unable to mount his horse, Lytle took a seat in an open barouche in the company of the chaplain, Father O'Higgins. For the duration of the parade Lytle commanded his regiment. Together they basked in Cincinnati's enthusiastic welcome ovation to the brave heroes of the Tenth.[109] The Tenth's flag, given so proudly by Cincinnati women, survived in tatters to be brought home with the wounded, where it was displayed in the windows of Shillito's department store for all to see.

As the new year dawned, Lytle returned to active duty to a series of commands that culminated in October 1862 at the battle of Perryville. Recognizing that the colonel needed more time before assuming duties that were physically taxing, Gen. Don Carlos Buell assigned Lytle to command Camp Morton at Bardstown, Kentucky. A site for training and assembly, Camp Morton averaged ten thousand troops at any given time. While stationed at Bardstown he enjoyed the community's social life and visited Federal Hill, the nearby home of his Rowan cousins. Despite earlier strained relations between the Lytles and the Rowans, in his letters of January and February 1862 Lytle described pleasant interaction with Rebecca Rowan and her children. His social calls on the Rowans went beyond mere courtesy. They signified, in part, an earnest effort to reestablish the family ties between the Lytles and the Rowans.

Although Kentucky was divided between Union and Confederate sentiment, most Bardstown residents favored secession as Lytle found out when he was stationed there in early 1862. Lytle's observance of the social graces of a gentleman and his appreciation of many southern values earned him praise even from the secessionist Bardstown residents. A Bardstown newspaper evinced enthusiasm over Lytle's assignment as Camp Morton's commander. Noting Lytle's "stern justice and sterling integrity," the paper termed him "one of the best officers" currently in Kentucky and commented that the Union would be in safer hands if only all Federal officers were like Colonel Lytle.[110]

Yet, despite enjoying the pleasures of Bardstown society, Lytle chafed at the lack of action. Never one to sit on the sidelines, he soon was allowed to return to the Tenth Ohio, then stationed in Tennessee. He arrived in Nashville in mid-March, just after Federal forces occupied the city, and was given command of the Seventeenth Brigade, Third Division of the Army of the Ohio, under Gen. Don Carlos Buell.

Lytle spent most of April 1862 near Murfreesboro, where he formed a friendship with a wealthy local family headed by a David Lytle who claimed kinship. He also called upon the widow of President James K. Polk, whom his parents had known in Washington during the mid-1830s.[111] For most of the spring and summer, however, Lytle and his brigade helped secure supply lines through Nashville and Huntsville, Alabama. During that period, Lytle's correspondence reflects the concerns of the Union forces about Confederate movements following the battle of Corinth.

From early May 1862 until the end of August, Lytle was on garrison duty at Huntsville, Alabama, after which he received orders to march with Buell to Kentucky. During September Lytle's brigade and the rest of Buell's forces made long grueling marches in an effort to contain Braxton Bragg's Confederates. The two armies finally clashed in Kentucky in the battle of Perryville on October 8, 1862. Like the even bloodier battle Antietam, Perryville marked a halt to a Confederate offensive aimed at Northern territory. The invasion also failed in its aim to bring Kentucky into the Confederacy. Tactically a draw, Perryville was the Confederacy's northernmost large-scale initiative in the West.

The battle of Perryville took place over three thousand acres of rolling farmland interspersed with woods. Lytle's Seventeenth Brigade was part of the Third Division under Lovell Rousseau. By four o'clock in the afternoon, Union units were falling back. The Ninth Brigade's Col. Leonard Harris rode to Lytle to tell him the grim situation. When Lytle realized the Eighty-eighth Indiana could not reach his line in time, he ordered the Third Ohio to retire. Lytle then tried to hold the Fifteenth Kentucky, commanded by Col. Curran Pope, against a Confederate surge. The regiment broke for the rear as Lytle, then in front, was hit.[112] Shot in the head behind the ear he fell to the ground and insisted that his retreating troops leave him. Confederates captured Lytle and took him behind their lines. His telegram dated October 13, 1862, relieved his family who had feared he was dead, based on newspaper reports.[113] Lytle said he had been wounded, not dangerously, and captured, but expected to go home soon on parole.[114] Within days he received parole with the understanding that he could not return to active duty without a suitable exchange. Lytle spent the winter months in Cincinnati, where he celebrated his thirty-sixth and final birthday, presumably in the loving company of his family. That birthday occasioned one of Lytle's last poems, the melancholy "Lines on My Thirty-Sixth Birthday."

In late November 1862, the army began an investigation into General Buell's actions in the campaign that ended with the battle of Perryville.

The Buell court of inquiry took place in Cincinnati with Col. William Haines Lytle as the government's first witness. Lytle's testimony began on December 1 and continued through December 4. Investigators wanted his testimony regarding Buell's abilities as a commander and were interested in his own insights concerning Confederate strengths and plans based on his time behind enemy lines. Lytle replied as briefly as possible. In keeping with the terms of his exchange, he refused to provide any information about the Confederates. To satisfy the court, Lytle produced the parole agreement which included the following: "I will not bear arms against the Confederate States, nor will I in any way aid or abet its enemies, until I am regularly exchanged, under the penalty of death; nor will I disclose anything that I have seen or heard in said Confederate States Army to its prejudice."[115] (See Appendix A.)

The year 1863 was filled with much sadness on both the homefront and the battlefront for Lytle. Early in the year he received news of the bloody battle of Stones River and the heavy losses suffered by the Tenth Ohio. Then, on the day after his departure from Cincinnati in late March, his ailing aunt Joanna Reilly died. A grieving Lytle telegraphed Rosecrans for permission to attend the funeral, but a communications delay kept him from receiving approval in time. His grandmother's sister Sarah Bullock and several other relatives and close friends of the family also died that spring. At one point an anguished Lytle wondered if he would ever again receive a letter without sad news.

In contrast to the disasters 1863 brought Lytle, the year proved to be a turning point for the Union. Union forces won key victories at Stones River, Gettysburg, and Vicksburg. Stones River forced the Confederates out of central Tennessee toward Alabama and Georgia. Lee's invasion of Pennsylvania was repelled at Gettysburg in early July, and in the West, Grant captured Vicksburg. Though many considered Chickamauga a Confederate victory, that September battle proved costly to both sides and with elusive benefits for the victor. Two months later, in November 1863, Union forces gained victory at Missionary Ridge just outside Chattanooga. By the end of the year northern troops controlled Chattanooga; the critical railroad and river transportation centers of northwest Georgia, northeast Alabama, and eastern Tennessee; and the entire Mississippi River. Even though further battles lay ahead, the Union forces had turned the corner.

Lytle's final year had some bright spots as well. On March 17 he was promoted to brigadier general, with rank dated back to November 29, 1862. Notwithstanding his attachment to his first command, Lytle rapidly adapted to his new one, the First Brigade, Third Division, Twentieth Army Corps of the Army of the Cumberland. Most of the spring and early summer of 1863 he spent in and around Murfreesboro. His immediate superiors, General Rosecrans and General Sheridan, commander of the Third Division, thought well of his abilities. In assigning him to command the Third Division's First Brigade, they implied he could ultimately receive command of a division. During his strenuous last six months, Lytle was kept busy with marches, outpost duty, oversight of bridge construction, and other necessary activities as the Army of the Cumberland pursued Braxton Bragg and the Army of Tennessee into south central Tennessee and the tri-state corner of Tennessee, Alabama, and Georgia.

Throughout this difficult year Lytle, like many Union soldiers, maintained his patriotic fervor and his conviction that fighting for the Union was a higher endeavor than protecting his life.[116] Nonetheless, he hoped for an opportunity to command a new division of Ohio troops rather than his current assignment. As the summer progressed, he spoke repeatedly in his letters of references to his generation's burden, his longing for peace, and his hopes that the president would declare amnesty for all rebels who would lay down their arms and return to allegiance.

In August Lytle received orders to march to Bridgeport, Alabama, and build a bridge across the Tennessee River. On August 9 at Bridgeport the officers from his former regiment, the Tenth Ohio, presented him with a Maltese cross. Six weeks after the happy ceremony, the Army of the Cumberland and the Army of the Tennessee finally collided near Chickamauga Creek on September 19, 1863. The fierce fighting lasted two days, but before the firing stopped Lytle lay dead. After a successful stand at Gordons Mills on September 19, Lytle was up all night under orders to move to a new position. He also suffered from a severe cold. When his servant, Guthrie, urged him to stay out of the fight on September 20, Lytle replied, "No Guthrie I never shrink from my duty but if I fall I want you to carry me off the field—& take care of my poor horse."[117] Around noon on the second day, Lytle led his brigade in a valiant but futile counterattack to stop the Confederate troops who stormed through an opening in the Union lines. General Lytle's final moments display his keen sense of duty, leadership style, and heroism along with his upbringing as a gentleman. Sensing that he would not survive this battle, when pulling on his gloves he reputedly noted, "I was raised as a gentleman, I will die as a gentleman." He also was heard to say, "We can only die once. Now is our time." Lytle, on horseback, led his men, urging them to be calm and steady.

Confederate bullets hit Lytle several times before he was pulled from his horse and motioned for his sword to be carried away. As Lytle was falling off his horse, a sergeant from the Twenty-fourth Wisconsin heard his last words, "Brave boys, brave boys."[118] Some controversy exists regarding the wisdom of Lytle's call for the charge directly into enemy gunfire.[119] Yet, given his position when the hole in the Union lines was created, he had little choice.

Confederate officers recognized their fallen enemy and voiced regrets over his death. One termed Lytle "as good a man as ever lived, [even] if he did have on Yankee clothes."[120] They provided temporary burial on the field and later gave safe passage to an officer from the Tenth Ohio who identified the body.[121] Lytle's immediate commander, Philip Sheridan, also paid tribute: "Among those killed early in the engagement of the 20th was Brig. Gen. W.H. Lytle, who was three times wounded, but refused to leave the field. In him, the country has lost an able general and the service of a gallant soldier."[122]

William Haines Lytle ranks among the best Union volunteer officers for his leadership skills and abilities. Small in stature with dark brown hair, gray-brown eyes, and a long flowing beard, Lytle inspired his men with his personal bravery and concern for their welfare. A true son of the West and third generation Cincinnati elite, Lytle's inherited wealth and social position differentiated Lytle from many of his Ohio contemporaries. In his devotion to duty, military leadership, honor, courage, and gallantry toward women, he resembled a Southern cavalier more than a northern Yankee.[123]

The aristocratic Lytle, with his emotional, passionate nature, was guided in his actions by a romanticized ideal. In 1862 he termed the famous rebel guerrilla leader John Hunt Morgan "a gallant gentleman," adding that Morgan was a man quite after his own heart.[124] Morgan, a folk hero in his own lifetime, epitomized his Confederate countrymen's belief in the South's code of honor and system of ethics, calling for the defense of personal and family honor, personal courage, and valor.[125] Lytle's admiration for the values of a cavalier, regardless of who displayed them, stayed with him throughout his life.

In his reminiscences, Alfred Pirtle, Lytle's aide de camp in 1862 and 1863, described two incidents that exemplify the general's character. Lytle's sterling integrity and sense of honor came through in an 1862 episode on a rare occasion when he deemed it necessary to discipline the Tenth Ohio.

In this instance, men of one of the companies refused to obey Lytle's order to carry their knapsacks when they broke camp at Fayetteville to march to Huntsville. Lytle explained that he had made the order to relieve the wagons. He told the soldiers they had five minutes to retrieve their knapsacks from the wagons before he would commence shooting. He "sat like a statue" for two minutes and then began to unbuckle his pistol holsters. No sooner had his hand started to draw a pistol than the men "made a rush for the company wagons."

The other incident demonstrates Lytle's instinctive gallantry and grace in all social situations. One day when riding at the head of his staff, perhaps somewhere in Tennessee, he could not find a match in the whole party for his cigar. The men came to a humble-looking woman leaning on a fence and watching the Yankees go by. Glimpsing smoke coming from the woman's chimney, Lytle paused, raised his hat, and asked the woman if she could provide a light for his cigar. She took his cigar and disappeared into her house. When she came out she was smoking the cigar with great delight but handed it over the fence to the Union officer. "With all the style he would have used in addressing a duchess, he returned his thanks and rode off puffing a cloud in our faces." His staff, equal to the occasion, did not laugh until he gave the example![126]

Just six weeks before his death at Chickamauga, General Lytle gave an inspirational, almost poetic speech at Bridgeport, Alabama, when the officers of the Tenth Ohio presented him a jeweled Maltese cross. In accepting the tribute from his first Civil War command, Lytle said, "So long as in God's providence, my life is spared, I shall look on it, gentlemen, and be reminded of many a stirring both in your experience and mine." Lytle paid homage to the Tenth, recounting its engagements, and spoke admiringly of the First Brigade. Not knowing "whether the end [was] near or not," Lytle forecast a Union victory, for "this generation of loyal men will . . . endure its heavy cross, and until the broad daylight of peace and order and victory shall come, will stand to arms." They should "heal up the sores and scars and cover up the bloody footprints that war will leave, to bury in oblivion all animosities against your former foes and, . . . to carve the flowing epitaph that tells of Southern as well as Northern valor."[127]

Lytle's Bridgeport speech received many favorable reviews. Cincinnati newspapers printed it widely. His heroic battlefield death weeks later brought an outpouring of emotion and tributes from his fellow citizens, both Northern and Southern. This gifted man willingly gave his life for what he loved most of all, liberty and his country. From the youthful cavalier's first hastily penned letter in Mexico at Vera Cruz to those composed just weeks before his death at Chickamauga, Lytle's correspondence reveals his courageous, spirited, and sometimes quixotic personality. The letters presented here complement the official record of the military service of William Haines Lytle and help illuminate the character of the man who died a hero's death.

Notes

1. See James M. McPherson, *What They Fought For, 1861-1865* (Baton Rouge, La.: Louisiana State Univ. Press, 1994), 88.

2. For example, William H. Lytle to Elizabeth Lytle, July 11, 1856, Lytle Papers, Mss qL996P, box 33, no. 467. Writing from Philadelphia, Lytle said, "I declare this town is a miserable little two story brick stiff prim fried meat one horse & a poney at that—." Note: All letters unless otherwise cited are in the Lytle Papers (LP), Mss qL996P, Cincinnati Historical Society (CHS), Cincinnati Museum Center (CMC).

3. In *Population of the United States in 1860* (Washington: Government Printing Office, 1864) Cincinnati was the seventh largest city as Brooklyn and New York both ranked above it separately. Cincinnati had 45.71 percent foreign-born residents in 1860. See also Daniel Hurley, *Cincinnati: The Queen City* (Cincinnati: The Cincinnati Historical Society, 1982), 76.

4. In the three decades immediately preceding the Civil War, the population center of the United States moved steadily closer to Cincinnati. From nineteen miles west-southwest of Moorefield, Virginia, in 1830, the population center shifted in 1840 to sixteen miles south of Clarksburg, Virginia. By 1850 the population center was twenty-three miles southeast of Parkersburg, Virginia; in 1860 the center was twenty miles southeast of Chillicothe, Ohio, or about one hundred miles directly east of Cincinnati, Ohio. See Gorton Curruth, *The Encyclopedia of American Facts and Dates,* 8th ed. (New York: Harper & Row, 1987), 182, 212, 238, 268.

5. Daniel Aaron, *Cincinnati, Queen City of the West, 1819-1838* (Columbus: Ohio State Univ. Press, 1992), 318.

6. James M. McPherson, *Battle Cry of Freedom* (New York: Oxford Univ. Press, 1988), 293.

7. Lowell H. Harrison, *The Civil War in Kentucky* (Lexington, Ky.: Univ. Press of Kentucky, 1975), 3-10.

8. Edward Lytle to William H. Lytle, June 17, 1850, LP, box 33, no. 384.

9. Charles B. Heinemann, compiler, *First Census of Kentucky 1790* (Baltimore: Genealogical Publishing Co., 1965), 60. Glen Clift, compiler, *"Second Census" of Kentucky—1800* (Baltimore: Genealogical Publishing Co., 1966), 178. As Capt. William Lytle died in 1797, the William Lytle in the 1800 census was the grandfather of William Haines Lytle who had not yet moved to Ohio.

10. Randall Capps, *The Rowan Story: From Federal Hill to My Old Kentucky Home* (Cincinnati: The Creative Company, 1976), 4.

11. The Lytle Papers contain letters to William Lytle from John Rowan describ-

ing the construction of his house. Stephen Foster and William Haines Lytle became friends during Foster's four years in Cincinnati, 1846-50. (See Fletcher Hodges Jr., "Stephen Foster—Cincinnatian and American," *Historical and Philosophical Society of Ohio Bulletin* 8 (2): 92-93 (April 1950). Both Lytle and Foster were born in 1826, had family ties to the Rowans, and participated in Cincinnati's artistic and literary circles.

12. E.D. Mansfield, *Personal Memories: Social, Political, and Literary with Sketches of Many Noted People, 1803-1843* (Cincinnati: Robert Clarke & Co., 1879), 287.

13. Louis Leonard Tucker, "Cincinnati: Athens of the West 1830-1861," *Ohio History* 75: 11-25 (Winter 1966).

14. Eliza Stahl Lytle died in 1821. In 1822 William Lytle married new Jersey native Margaret Smith Haines (1772-1851), the widow of Capt. Job Haines (d. 1807).

15. Both Franklin Pierce and Thomas Hamer became generals in the Mexican War. Hamer, whom Ulysses S. Grant had expected to become president one day, died from disease contracted during his military service in Mexico. Thus, of the three first-term congressmen who adhered to Andrew Jackson's principles and became friends in 1833-35, only Pierce survived until the 1852 presidential election.

16. Elizabeth Lytle to Joanna Reilly, October 1, [1837], LP, box 25A, no. 192.

17. William Lytle served as surveyor general from June 1830 until his death from consumption in March 1831.

18. Elizabeth Lytle to William H. Lytle, November 17, 1847, LP, box 33, no. 446.

19. Elizabeth Lytle to Elias H. Haines, September 23, [1851], LP, box 32, no. 243.

20. Robert T. Lytle to John S. Lytle, December 8, 1827, LP, box 29, no. 31; Margaret Lytle to William Lytle, May 9, 1828, LP, box 6, no. 54.2; Elizabeth Lytle to William Lytle, May n.d., 1828, LP, box 6, no. 54.1; Robert T. Lytle to William Lytle, July 25, 1828, LP, box 25A, no. 140.

21. Virginius Cornick Hall Jr., "From Tomahawk to High Finance, the Life of General William Lytle (1770-1831)" (Cincinnati, 1957), 87-88. Typescript in the Cincinnati Historical Society Library, CMC.

22. Charles J. Livingood, "Four Lytles: A Biographical Sketch of the Lytles in Ohio Dedicated to the Memory of William Lytle Foster." Typescript dated July 1, 1932, in the collections of the Cincinnati Historical Society.

23. Margaret Lytle to Elizabeth Lytle [undated but June 1830], LP, box 29, no. 4.

24. William Lytle to Ezekial S. Haines, January 13, 1831, LP, box 6, no. 100.3.

25. Robert T. Lytle to Elias H. Haines, February 11, 1831, LP, box 29, no. 12.

26. Joanna Haines to Elias H. Haines, March 4, 1831, LP, box 27A, no. 150.1.

27. Robert T. Lytle to Elizabeth Lytle, June 27, [1832], LP, box 29, no. 63.

28. Elizabeth Lytle to Robert T. Lytle, July 26, [1834], LP, box 25A, no 197.

29. Elizabeth Lytle to Elias H. Haines, April 28, 1832, LP, box 25A, no. 169.

30. Robert T. Lytle to Elizabeth Lytle, June 27, [1832], LP, box 29, no. 63.

31. Margaret Lytle to Elizabeth Lytle, February 4, 1835, LP, box 29, no. 2; Elizabeth Lytle to Margaret Lytle, February 12, [1835], LP, box 25A, no. 187.

32. Joanna Reilly to Elias H. Haines, October 10, 1837, LP, box 27A, no. 111.

33. Margaret Lytle to Robert and Elizabeth Lytle, August 2, [undated but probably 1837], LP, box 27A, no. 121.

34. Elizabeth Lytle to Joanna Reilly, September 13, 1838, LP, box 27A, no. 99.

35. Elizabeth Lytle to Margaret Lytle [undated but probably July 1841] and William H. Lytle to Margaret Lytle [undated but probably July 1841], LP, box 25A, no. 189.

36. Elizabeth Lytle to Mary Darrah, June 19, 1841,LP, box 25A, no. 160.

37. Margaret Lytle to Elizabeth Lytle, August 21, 1840, LP, box 29, no. 102. J. Findley Harrison married a Lytle relative, Caroline (Carrie) Alston. Referred to as a cousin, Carrie Alston's exact relationship to the Lytles is not clear. Harrison had been enrolled at West Point but left in 1845 for reasons that are not clear. See letter from William H. Lytle to Elias H. Haines, May 4, 1845, LP, box 27A, no. 86.

38. William H. Lytle to Findley Harrison, [January 15, 1842], LP, box 30, no. 2. The friendship between Lytle and Harrison lasted a lifetime. Harrison was with Lytle as a volunteer aide during the battle of Chickamauga.

39. William H. Lytle to Elias H. Haines, November 5, 1842, LP, box 33, no. 551.

40. Edward Lytle to William H. Lytle, March 6, 1843, LP, box 33, no. 377.

41. Elias H. Haines to William H. Lytle, June 3, 1843, LP, box 27, no. 10.

42. William H. Lytle to Elias H. Haines, June 4, [probably 1844], LP, box 33, no. 416.

43. William H. Lytle to Elias H. Haines, May 4, 1845, LP, box 27A, no. 86.

44. Richard Bruce Winders, *Mr. Polk's Army: The American Military Experience in the Mexican War* (College Station, Tex.: Texas A & M Univ. Press, 1997), 66-87.

45. The Montgomery Guards were named after Brig. Gen. Richard Montgomery (1738-75), who was killed while leading an assault against Quebec City on December 31, 1775. Montgomery was Irish, as were most members of the Montgomery Guards. The name Montgomery Guards was used in both the Mexican and Civil Wars by predominantly Irish Ohio volunteer units recruited in Cincinnati.

46. *Official Roster of the Soldiers of the State of Ohio in the War of the Rebellion, 1861-1866, and in the War with Mexico, 1846-1848,* vol. 12 (Norwalk, Conn.: Laning Co., 1895), 479-80.

47. Josephine Lytle to Elias H. Haines, August 28, 1848, LP, box 32, no. 231. Sarah Bullock was one of Margaret Lytle's sisters.

48. Hiram Powers was born in Vermont in 1805 and moved with his family to the outskirts of Cincinnati in 1819. Early on he worked on a farm and as a collector of debts for Luman Watson, an accomplished clock and organ manufacturer. Visiting a Cincinnati museum he became intrigued with a statue of Washington made from a plaster cast. He began to develop new techniques and specialized in making busts. Powers also worked for six years making wax figures for the Western Museum. Nicholas Longworth, a Cincinnati millionaire, claimed Powers as a protégé and sent him to Italy, the world's leading center for sculpture. Powers remained in Florence from 1837 until his death in 1873. Cincinnatians took great pride in Powers, often claiming him as a native son. See Louis Leonard Tucker, "Hiram Powers and Cincinnati," *The Cincinnati Historical Society Bulletin* 25 (1): 21-49 (January 1967).

49. William H. Lytle to Hiram Powers, December 12, 1848, Powers Letters, CHS, CMC.

50. Hiram Powers to William H. Lytle, January 26, 1849, Powers Letters, CHS, CMC. Later, on December 13, 1849, Edward Lytle also requested a copy of his brother's bust (Powers Letters, CHS, CMC).

51. William H. Lytle to Hiram Powers, January 25, 1851, Powers Letters, CHS, CMC.

52. Margaret Lytle and Elizabeth Lytle to Elias H. Haines, July 22 and 23, 1850, LP, box 33, no. 436.

53. Edward H. Lytle to William H. Lytle, November 27, 1849, LP, box 33, no. 382.

54. Margaret H. Lytle to Elias H. Haines, [July 22, 1850], and Elizabeth Lytle to Elias H. Haines, July 23, 1850, LP, box 33, no. 436.

55. Joseph R. Buchanan to William H. Lytle, June 18, 1851, LP, box 31, no. 134.

56. Elizabeth Lytle to Elias H. Haines, October 19, 1851, LP, box 31, no. 59.

57. William H. Lytle to [Edward H. Lytle] October, no date, 1851, LP, box 30, no. 19.

58. William H. Lytle to Elizabeth Lytle, undated but probably March or April 1852, LP, box 33, no. 498.

59. William H. Lytle to Josephine Lytle, April 15, 1852, LP, box 30, no. 20.

60. Henry Clay died in Washington, D.C., June 29, 1852. After his remains lay in state in the rotunda of the Capital, the funeral cortege proceeded to Baltimore, Philadelphia, New York, and Cleveland. From Cleveland it went by railroad to Columbus, Xenia, and Cincinnati. At Cincinnati the remains were transferred to steamboat for transport to Louisville and then to Lexington. The Clay Guard of Cincinnati watched over while Clay's body lay in state in the study in Ashland, his Lexington home. See Robert V. Remini, *Henry Clay: Statesman for the Union* (New York: W.W. Norton & Co., 1991), 780-86. The Lytle family's relationship with Henry Clay dated back to William Lytle, who apparently attended school with Henry Clay and John Rowan. There is an indication in the Lytle Papers that Henry Clay acquired the property where he built his home Ashland from Capt. William Lytle.

61. Elizabeth Lytle to Elias H. Haines, July 11, 1852, LP, box 31, no. 114.

62. Edward H. Lytle to William H. Lytle, July 26, 1852, LP, box 33, no. 388.

63. William H. Lytle to Elizabeth Lytle, undated but probably December 1852, LP, box 33, no. 458.

64. Edward H. Lytle to William H. Lytle, December 19, 1852, LP, box 33, no. 389. Edward worried about the constitution of individuals marrying into the Lytle family, as his three brothers and one sister and both his parents died of consumption. None of Edward Lytle's four siblings reached forty years of age; his sister Eliza Lytle Macalester was only twenty-nine when she died.

65. Charlotte Haines to William H. Lytle, January 6, 1853, LP, box 32, no. 291.

66. William H. Lytle to Elias H. Haines, March 26, 1853; March 31, 1853; and April 4, 1853, LP, box 30, no. 54; box 30, no. 55; and box 30, no. 53.

67. William H. Lytle to Josephine Foster Lytle, June 28, 1853, LP, box 30, no. 24. In the letter to Josephine Foster, Lytle said he declined the Chile legation secretaryship because it would mean being separated from his family for too long after he had just spent much of the last several years away from home. Although his family strongly urged him to remain in Cincinnati, this had not stopped him before.

68. Elizabeth Lytle to Joanna Reilly, October 12, 1854. Lytle's friendship with Louisville's Pirtle family proved important for his Civil War years. Judge Pirtle's son Alfred served as Lytle's aide de camp throughout most of the strenuous campaigns of 1862 and 1863.

69. *Cincinnati Post*, January 28, 1904, 4.

70. William H. Lytle to Elizabeth Lytle, undated Wednesday but August 15, 1855, LP, box 33, no. 500.

71. Undated newspaper clipping in Lytle Scrapbook, but from 1856.

72. Eugene H. Roseboom, *The Civil War Era 1850-1870*, vol. 4, *The History of the State of Ohio*, ed. Carl Wittke (Columbus: Ohio State Archaeological and Historical Society, 1944), 327-29.

73. William H. Lytle to Ezekial S. Haines, September 30, 1857.

74. Newspaper clipping in Lytle Scrapbook dated Columbus, Thursday morning, August 27, 1857.

75. Clipping from the *Ohio Statesman* providing a letter to the editor from Upper Sandusky, September 9, 1857.

76. William H. Lytle to Samuel J. Broadwell, September 6, [1860], LP, box 33, no. 540.

77. Margaret H. Lytle to William H. Lytle, November 17, 1847, LP, box 33, no, 446A.

78. As a small child, Lytle was given alcohol in beverages. His parents, undoubtedly well intentioned, did not comprehend the possible long-range implications of their giving him brandy-laden tonics. Encouraging their youngster to drink by terming the beverage "Grandpa's grog," Elizabeth and Robert Lytle reflected the customs of their time. See Elizabeth Lytle to William Lytle, May n.d., 1828, LP, box 6, no. 54.1. Nonetheless, Will acquired a taste for spirits at an early age that stayed with him for life.

79. See letters by Lily Broadwell to William H. Lytle, March 22, 1862, and William H. Lytle to Josephine Foster, July 22 and July 29, 1863.

80. William H. Lytle to Elizabeth Lytle, July 10, 1855, LP, box 33, no. 460. Lytle commented that *The Marseillaise* was his favorite painting at the Academy of Arts in Philadelphia.

81. William H. Lytle to Elizabeth Lytle Broadwell, June 12, 1858, LP, box 33, no. 470; undated newspaper clipping in the Lytle Scrapbook.

82. Joanna Reilly to William H. Lytle, January 29, 1848, LP, box 33, no. 449.

83. William H. Lytle to Josephine Lytle, September 6, 1852, LP, box 30, no. 21.

84. William H. Lytle to Joanna Reilly, undated but probably 1855, LP, box 30, no. 56.

85. William H. Lytle to Elizabeth Lytle Broadwell, June 12, 1858, LP, box 33, no. 470.

86. William H. Lytle to Elizabeth Lytle, undated but probably March 1852, LP, box 33, no. 498. See also Edward Lytle to William H. Lytle, December 19, 1852, LP, box 33, no. 389.

87. Lily Macalester was the daughter of Robert Todd Lytle's only sister, Eliza Ann Lytle Macalester (1806-35). Charles and Eliza Macalester married at the Bardstown, Kentucky, home of her uncle Judge John Rowan on October 6, 1824. The Macalesters made their home in Philadelphia, where Lily Macalester was born on July 29, 1832.

88. Charlotte Haines to William H. Lytle, January 26, 1853, LP, box 32, no. 290; Josephine Lytle to William H. Lytle, undated but December 1852 and February or March 1853, LP, box 32, no. 267, and box 32, no. 258; and Edward H. Lytle to William H. Lytle, June 28, 1853, LP, box 32, no. 103.

89. Elizabeth Lytle to William H. Lytle, undated but late July 1855, LP, box 31, no. 103.

90. William H. Lytle to Elizabeth Lytle Broadwell, July 10, 1858, LP, box 33, no. 471.

91. Alfred Pirtle to Lily Foster Livingood, December 25, 1923, LP, box 34, no. 638. Also Ruth Carter conversation with Virginius C. Hall, great grandson of Josephine Lytle Foster, August 1995.

92. William S. Irwin in an undated newspaper clipping written for the *Sunday Republic* recalled that he and William W. Fosdick were among those visiting Lytle at his home while the poet recuperated from a severe illness. Lytle, in a melancholic mood, got up and quietly wrote "Antony and Cleopatra" then brushed it aside. Fosdick, not wanting the poem to "share the fate of many others of rare merit which the General had written only to destroy," took the manuscript with him and saw to its publication in the *Cincinnati Commercial.*

93. William H. Lytle to Elizabeth Lytle Broadwell, undated but possibly August 14, 1859, LP, box 33, no. 495.

94. William H. Lytle to Elizabeth Lytle Broadwell, June 12, 1858, LP, box 33, no. 470.

95. Elizabeth Lytle Broadwell to William H. Lytle, July 19, 1858, LP, box 31, no. 71.

96. Edward H. Lytle to William H. Lytle, July 25, 1858, LP, box 33, no. 404.

97. William H. Lytle to Joanna Reilly, April 10 [1860], LP, box 30, no. 29.

98. Elizabeth Lytle Broadwell to William H. Lytle, September 13, 1860, LP, box 31, no. 73.

99. Dr. Andrew C. Kemper, "A Paper Read before the Loyal Legion, on William Haines Lytle, . . . Burnet House, June 6, 1883." (Cincinnati: Thomson, n. d.)

100. Robert J. Wimberg, *Cincinnati and the Civil War* (Cincinnati: Ohio Book Store, 1992), 25. Wimberg says that Ohio officials telegraphed Lytle to set up Camp Harrison as a place for troops to rendezvous as opposed to him receiving orders in person in Columbus. Wimberg's sources are sometimes not cited.

101. James M. McPherson, *Battle Cry of Freedom,* 274-75.

102. Commission from Governor William Dennison to William H. Lytle, dated May 6, 1861, in Cincinnati Historical Society Collections. See also Wimberg, *Cincinnati and the Civil War,* 41, and an undated newspaper clipping in the Lytle

Scrapbook that reports Lytle's unanimous election to colonel of the Montgomery Regiment (later the Tenth Ohio). Stephen Z. Starr, "Camp Dennison, 1861-1865," *Historical and Philosophical Society of Ohio Bulletin* 19 (3): 173 (July 1961), observes that the Tenth was not exclusively an Irish regiment for it had a healthy number of Germans. On June 4, 1861, the Tenth changed its enlistment period from three months to three years. With few exceptions other than battlefield casualties, the officers stayed together until the regiment was mustered out in June 1864. Lytle and his men bonded; he and his officers became like family. Those who stayed with the Tenth for the duration included Joseph W. Burke, major (later lieutenant colonel and colonel); William W. Ward, captain of Company I (later major and lieutenant colonel); John Hudson, captain of Company C (later major); James Grover, second lieutenant and acting adjutant (later first lieutenant and adjutant); and Father William T. O'Higgins, chaplain. The Tenth's original surgeon, Dr. Charles S. Muscroft, resigned in June 1863.

103. Jacob Dolson Cox, *Military Reminiscences of the Civil War,* vol. 1 (New York: Scribner's, 1900), 36.

104. A handwritten copy of Gallagher's speech is in the Lytle Papers, Cincinnati Historical Society.

105. *Poems of William Haines Lytle,* edited, with memoir, by William H. Venable (Cincinnati: Robert Clarke Co., 1894), 16-17.

106. McPherson, *Battle Cry of Freedom,* 299-301.

107. Ibid., 83-87, 124, 130.

108. Terry Lowry, *September Blood: The Battle of Carnifex Ferry* (Charleston, W.Va.: Pictorial Histories Publishing Co., 1985), 83-88. Lowry provides a detailed description of the battle of Carnifex Ferry and the events immediately preceding it in western Virginia. He notes that Lytle's men apparently made their charge without the consent of General Benham, the commander of the First Brigade. Though Benham described Lytle's effort as "the ridiculous assault of the hare-brained Colonel," many Confederates and Union men believed Lytle nearly changed the course of the battle.

109. Newspaper clipping, November 30, 1861, in Lytle Scrapbook, CHS, CMC.

110. Undated clipping in Lytle Scrapbook, CHS, CMC.

111. A call on Sarah Childress Polk seems to have been *de regieur* for Union officers with any ties to the late President James K. Polk. John White Geary, a Pennsylvania politician turned Union officer, also paid his respects to Mrs. Polk. William Alan Blair, ed., *A Politician Goes to War: The Civil War Letters of John White Geary,* selections and introduction by Bell Irvin Wiley (University Park, Pa.: Pennsylvania State Univ. Press, 1995), xxi, 125.

112. Kenneth A. Hafendorfer, *Perryville: Battle for Kentucky* (Louisville: K.H. Press, 1991), 271-80.

113. Venable, *Poems of William Haines Lytle,* 23-25.

114. Telegram from William H. Lytle to Samuel J. Broadwell, Lytle Papers, CHS, CMC.

115. *The War of the Rebellion: A Compilation of the Official Records of the Union and Confederate Armies,* 128 vols. (Washington, D.C., 1880-1901), series 1, vol. 16, pt. 1, 72 (hereafter cited as *O.R.*). Lytle's testimony at the Buell Court of In-

quiry is reproduced in Appendix A. It includes his chronology of his division's march from Nashville to Louisville between September 7, 1862, and September 26, 1862.

116. See James M. McPherson's *What They Fought For, 1861-1865* (Baton Rouge, La.: Louisiana State Univ. Press, 1994) for an eloquent discussion of what motivated soldiers in both the Confederate and Union armies. According to McPherson's sample, 78 percent of Union offers expressed patriotism.

117. Elizabeth Lytle Broadwell to Ezekial S. Haines, October 5, 1863. Lily Broadwell shared with their uncle Ezekial S. Haines the account by Joseph Guthrie of General Lytle's last few days. Guthrie had brought Lytle's horses, saddle, sword, and chest to the general's sisters in Cincinnati.

118. Thomas J. Ford, *With the Rank and File: Incidents and Anecdotes During the War of the Rebellion, as Remembered by One of the Non-Commissioned Officers* (Milwaukee: Press of the Evening Wisconsin Co., 1898), 22.

119. Different interpretations were placed on Lytle's Chickamauga battlefield actions almost immediately. In her letter dated October 6, 1863, to Charlotte and Ezekial Smith Haines, Josephine Foster quoted some papers as describing her brother as "brave even to rashness." But both a Captain Trowbridge and Lytle's aide Grover said the statement did Lytle an injustice and "emphatically" assured "that he acted most gallantly & bravely—but *not* in the *least rashly*. . . . Capt T-says when *he* last saw him—he was 'leading his men to the charge—at a double quick—with his drawn sabre—over elevated & a braver & more chivalrous deed, he never saw.'" Captain Trowbridge was probably Capt. Charles F. Trowbridge of the Sixteenth United Sates Infantry. On October 11, 1863, Elizabeth Lytle Broadwell wrote Ezekial Haines more details of William H. Lytle's last moments gleaned from Captain Trowbridge. According to Broadwell, Trowbridge said that Lytle ordered a charge after sensing that conditions warranted an extraordinary effort. According to Trowbridge it resulted in "the most magnificent charge of the war—& equal to the 'charge of the light brigade'!" Whether rash or not, Lytle died the brave, heroic battlefield death so honored by himself and other poets.

120. Peter Cozzens, *This Terrible Sound: The Battle of Chickamauga* (Urbana, Ill.: Univ. of Illinois Press, 1992), 388-89.

121. Undated newspaper clipping in Lytle Scrapbook, CHS, CMC.

122. *O.R.,* ser. 1, vol. 30, pt. 1, 581.

123. William R. Taylor's classic *Cavalier and Yankee: The Old South and American National Character* (1961; reprint, New York: Harper & Row, 1969), notes on page 335 that the legendary southern planter with a "reputed obliviousness to money matters" contrasted in popular imagination with the northern Yankee who was perceived as acquisitive, a man on the make. Though not a plantation owner, much of Lytle's inheritance was in land; a third-generation elite, William Haines Lytle did not have the same type of drive and ambition as his grandfather William Lytle. Rather, he alternated between bursts of activity, whether in law, politics, or the military, and a tendency toward a more leisurely life in which he indulged in writing poetry and enjoying parties.

124. William H. Lytle to Josephine Lytle Foster and Elizabeth Lytle Broadwell, May 6, 1862, LP, box 33, no. 481.

125. See James A. Ramage, *Rebel Raider: The Life of General John Hunt Morgan* (Lexington, Ky.: Univ. Press of Kentucky, 1986), 306.

126. Alfred Pirtle, "Personal Reminiscences of Brigadier General W^m H. Lytle," Louisville, Ky., 1893. Handwritten manuscript in the Lytle Papers, Cincinnati Historical Society, CMC.

127. General Lytle's speech at Bridgeport, Alabama, on August 9, 1863, is reproduced in its entirety in Appendix B.

# THE MEXICAN WAR LETTERS
# 1847-1848

THE ANNEXATION OF TEXAS by the United States in 1845 was the catalyst for the outbreak of war between Mexico and its northern neighbor. From the beginning of the fighting in 1846, General-in-chief of the Army Winfield Scott believed Vera Cruz should be the approach point. When the Mexicans showed no signs of giving up, Scott took over direct command of an invasion of Vera Cruz. After a siege of two weeks, the Mexicans surrendered Vera Cruz March 27, 1847. Fighting continued over the summer of 1847 as Scott's army tried to advance toward Mexico City. The last resistance ended with Scott's victory at the battle of Chapultepec just outside Mexico City September 13, 1847. The next day General Scott triumphantly rode through the city square.

During September 1847, as General Scott began the occupation of Mexico City, William Haines Lytle joined other Cincinnatians in volunteering for the army. In the course of the war Ohio sent a total of five regiments.[1] Most Ohio troops entered early in 1846, but some units were formed in the fall of 1847, including the one Lytle joined, originally an independent company, later Company L of Ohio's Second Second Regiment. These reinforcements provided the manpower necessary to maintain the occupation of Mexico City and a few outlying areas, including Puebla under the command of Brig. Gen. Joseph Lane. The Second Ohio was assigned to Lane's command.

Youthful eagerness, a desire for glory, and his training as a gentleman characterize Lytle's Mexican War letters. They reflect his upper class assumption of privilege as well as the sense of responsibility felt by many leaders of this period. A long heritage of family connections with the rich and powerful had imbued Lytle with many social graces as witnessed by his calls on family acquaintances while in New Orleans and other American cities. Conscious of his elite class, he expected deference and courtesy as an officer. Also present are concern for his men and a desire to achieve personal recognition. Several letters show a keen observer's eye for scenery and everyday life among the people. Another theme, echoed later during the Civil War, is an intense longing for mail from friends and family.

1. Ohio contributed five regiments to the Mexican War. The regiment intended as the Fifth Ohio Volunteer Infantry was mustered in and out as the Second Second O.V.I. Perhaps the confusion arose because Lieut. Col. William Irvin of the Second Ohio Volunteer Infantry was elected colonel of the Second Second O.V.I. The regiment left Cincinnati on September 10, 1847. See *Official Roster of the Soldiers of the State of Ohio in the War of the Rebellion, 1861-1866, and in the War with Mexico, 1846-1848, vol. 12,* (Norwalk, Conn.: The Laning Co., 1895, 479). Unless another source is explicitly stated, all information about the Ohio Regiments and Company L of the Second Second O.V.I. is taken from the *Official Roster of the Soldiers of the State of Ohio.*

### To Ezekial Smith Haines

*When his family's efforts failed to stop him from joining the army, William Haines Lytle left with his unit for the river journey to New Orleans, the embarkation point for Mexico.*

Wednesday morning
Louisville [early October] 1847

Dr Uncle

We arrived here safely this morning. Gen Butler[1] is I regret to say absent from the city.

I have as yet seen none of my friends but will endeavor to do so if we have time.

Love to all—

I will write again from Baton Rouge.

Affly yrs
WH Lytle

1. Maj. Gen. William Orlando Butler of Kentucky, a volunteer officer, reported to Gen. Zachary Taylor in August 1846. Lytle hoped to win appointment to Butler's staff. Butler, the Democratic vice-presidential nominee in 1848, would have known Lytle's great uncle John Rowan from Kentucky and Lytle's grandfather William Lytle, who lived in Kentucky from 1781 to 1801. On October 17, 1847, Alice Wakefield, a daughter of John Rowan, wrote to Margaret Lytle with the information that General Butler expressed interest in learning that William Lytle's grandson would be with the Ohio troops and said he would be pleased to pay him some attention.

## To Margaret Lytle

*While waiting to hear from her grandson, Margaret Lytle, distressed over Will's depar-
ture, had written to her niece Alice Rowan Wakefield in hopes of gaining sympathy.
Although understanding the elder woman's unhappiness, Wakefield pointed out that
Will merited admiration for not resting on his family's laurels. Instead, in Wakefield's
view, the young Lytle wanted to make his own mark as had his grandfather, who at age
fourteen fought for his country when "the savage was the terror of the whole west," and
whose "courage and intrepidity were the leading features of his character." Wakefield
continued, "Were he now alive . . . William Lytle would say 'go my son and defend the
flag and honor of your glorious country.'"[1]*

Jefferson Barracks.
New Orleans
Oct. 30 1847

My dear Grandmother—

We arrived in this city last Thursday morning. I would have
written immediately but have been very busy and moreover have been
expecting very soon to start for Vera Cruz and intended to write on the
eve of our departure. We are in camp about 4 miles from the city near
the barracks. The climate is in the day time delightful though the nights
are cool. The health of the city is excellent. No cases of the fever have
occurred for some time and nothing is to be apprehended on this score.
Though the streets of Orleans are narrow and confined it is still a very
beautiful city. The public buildings are numerous and splendid—the
river is crowded with shipping and the thorough fares are thronged with
various races speaking various tongues. Vegetation is here as fresh and
exuberant as with us in July. The Camp is daily thronged with Creole
women from the neighboring plantations. The[y] bring for sale fresh
milk, butter, pecans, and willow baskets filled with lemons, bananas and
other fruits—As I write one passes with "bon suir Monsieur" carrying a
basket of oranges.

My own health has been excellent. I feel a little stiff in the joints to
day from a ride I took yesterday. I rode to the city on a splendid charger
kindly lent me by an offer of a dragoon Com^y quartered near us. He
bounded and bounded in front of the St Charles and showed off my new
uniform finely but that hardly compensates for my sore shoulders.

I called on Mrs. Brooke yesterday but unfortunately she had gone
out. I saw her husband at his waiting room who was very polite and
courteous. I mentioned in a previous letter, I think from Memphis that
Mrs. Deveille of Orleans was a traveling companion on the way down.

She expects to visit our City again in a month or two and if she does, I want our connexions to extend to her & husband their hospitalities. She was very kind on the way down—lent me books, papers and requested me if in need of any little comfort in Mexico to write to her and she would procure it. Mrs D—— is a very elegant and accomplished lady.

Her own fine qualities would I know commend her to you, beside her kindness and welcome attentions to your absent son. We will probably leave for Vera Cruz on Tuesday next. I will write you again before we start, and add a postscript to this tomorrow in the City. Give my love to my Uncles, Aunt J, Mrs E. Kiss the little girls for me and believe me my dear grandmother

Your affectionate grandson<br>W.H. Lytle

P.S. Headquarters<br>New Orleans. Sunday Oct. 31, 1847

Dear Mother and little Sisters

I have just seen Maj. Tompkins the Quartermaster and he informs me that we will start for Mexico tomorrow afternoon on the steamship General Butler. She is a fine and new vessel and I anticipate a speedy and prosperous voyage.

Let me beg of you to give yourself no uneasiness on my account but above all dear Grandma be careful of your own health. I hope in a few months to revisit the shores of my native state with honor.

I will write as soon as we arrive at Vera Cruz by the return ship and give you a full account of our sail and the city.

Give my love to all my friends—God bless you all and now for a time farewell.

*Will*

---

1. Alice D. [Rowan] Wakefield to Margaret Lytle, October 17, 1847, LP, box 29, no. 118. The daughter of John and Ann Lytle Rowan, Wakefield was a niece of William Lytle (1770-1831).

## *To Ezekial Smith Haines*

New Orleans
Oct. 31 1847

Dear Uncle[1]

I enclose a letter to Grandma which gives a more detailed account of our progress thus far than I have time to write you. We leave tomorrow for Vera Cruz on the steamship "Butler." I shall have lived just twenty one years when we slip our cables.[2] Please send Cin[ti] papers as often as practicable—they will be very acceptable.

John Taylor I believe has my commission. If Steele[3] has not left Louisville when this arrives I should like him to forward it though I presume it is not essential. I regret exceedingly that I was forced by circumstances to draw on Burke for twenty dollars. He was very polite and attentive. I will write you all from Vera Cruz till then good bye— My love to all particularly Aunt Charlotte and Mrs E——

Yours aff[ly]
Wm H Lytle

P.S. If Butler has not left I should like my chances pushed with him. I am very anxious for the app[t].

Taylor is very well, and if you see any of J. Wrights family—their young relative stands like a man and is perfectly well.[4]

1. When seeking assistance in gaining advancement or handling business affairs, Lytle relied on his uncle Ezekial Smith Haines. One of Cincinnati's prominent attorneys, Haines provided the most immediate male influence in his nephew's life after the death of Lytle's father. According to Margaret Lytle in a letter to William H. Lytle, November 17, 1847, LP, box 33, no. 446, CHS, CMC, Ezekial Smith Haines adopted his nephew and made him heir to a large portion of Haines's property. Haines and his wife, Charlotte, did not have children.

2. Lytle's birthday was November 2, 1826.

3. John Rowan Steele (known as Rowan Steele) was the grandson of Judge John Rowan and a second cousin of William Haines Lytle. After the death of Mary Jane Rowan Steele and her husband William Steele from cholera in 1833, Judge Rowan and his wife raised their grandson. William Steele was a cousin to the Rowans and Lytles, as Capt. William Lytle (1728-97) married Mary Steele (1736-1809). Her brother Richard Steele had a large family from whom William Steele was descended. The childen of Capt. William Lytle and Mary Steele Lytle included William Lytle (1770-1831) and Ann Lytle (1772-1849), who married John Rowan (1773-1843). Randall Capps's *The Rowan Story: From Federal Hill to My Old Kentucky Home* (Cincinnati: Creative Company, 1976) provides details on the Rowan family. According to Capps, Federal Hill was originally property of Capt. William Lytle. He gave it to Ann Lytle Rowan as a wedding present.

4. Lytle refers to Company L members Howland Taylor (who survived to be mustered out with the company on July 25, 1848) and John Wright, then nineteen, (who was discharged January 18, 1848, at Rio Frio due to medical disability). Wright died in a New Orleans hospital. (See Margaret Lytle to William H. Lytle, April 2, 1848.)

## To Margaret Lytle, Josephine Lytle, and Elizabeth Lytle

*The day after Lytle wrote this letter, Mexico elected Pedro María Anaya as its interim president. That same week the United States ambassador to Mexico, Nicholas P. Trist, received an order recalling him. On November 22 the Mexicans announced they had named commissioners to negotiate a peace. As the Mexican government had not received notification of Trist's recall by December 4, he decided to stay to negotiate a treaty. This meant Lytle's arrival in Mexico coincided with the initiation of peace negotiations. He became part of the army of occupation and found himself engaged in mostly garrison duty.*

Vera Cruz Wednesday Night
Nov 10 1847

My dear Grandma and sisters

We left Orleans on the 4th day of this month and have been in Mexico about a week. I hasten by the first steamer to forward you a line though I must be very brief as I have a hundred things to attend to before morning. Tomorrow we leave for the interior under command of Maj Calhoun. Our destination is not yet known but is probably Jalapa.

We escort a train and will move in strong force. Our Camp (Bereganda) is some 3 miles from the city and embodies the Georgia battalions—Jersey battalion a detachment of the 15th and other bodies of volunteers numbering in all some three or four thousand. Volunteers have for two days been pouring in under Gen Butler from Kentucky and Tennessee— In a few days there will be concentrated here some 12 or 15 thousand men— Rowan Steele has not yet arrived and unless we are detained a day or two I shall again miss him.

I met yesterday, sister Joe—Jack Heddleson a brother of Bettys— He was delighted to see me. A large train came in on Tuesday from Mexico.

The streets are thronged with officers of all ranks & grades returning to their home after the recent battles near Mexico— Among them many of my acquaintance. they will give you all the recent news.

I must postpone my dear little sisters till my return an account of all the strange things I see and hear. Vera Cruz is an old spanish city, one of the oldest on the continent. What shows very forcibly was the remarkable cleanliness of the city and people. The very street scavenger is dressed in clean white linen spotless as snow. The houses are built in old spanish style and are half barn, half palace— Barns in their lofty ceilings, dreary corridors and spacious areas and palaces in their [ . . . ] magnificence. As we entered on last tuesday morning the spacious harbor, San Juan (the castle) lay on our right with the stars & stripes waving over its grim towers while before us on the low sandy beach was spread the city surrounded by walls flanked at an angle by the fortress of Santiago at the other by Fort Conception which over the fortifications and seeming to crest the batteries and ramparts waved the green palm tree the daughter of the tropics. The climate is not so unpleasant in the "terra caliente" (the warm country Lill) as I supposed. It is as warm as with us in August but we have had during our whole stay northers blowing fresh and strong from the sea. Everything is dear here but fruit which is very abundant and the natives and citizens impose on us in every possible way. A common wool hat worth three bits at home costs six dollars, a lunch of bread and chocolate two and so on— So you see Grandma that a poor fellows pay doesn't carry him far. Fruit though as I said is in profusion— Oranges the largest and sweetest I ever saw & for a pie—plantains bananas and scores of others of whose names I am ignorant.

Well I must break off here as the night is creeping on and I have many things to do. I will write by every opportunity but if you do not hear from me you must not be uneasy as sometimes long intervals elapse in the departures of the trains & mails. Write to me often Joe, as not having yet heard from you I am getting anxious to hear from home already. Direct to Lt Wm H Lytle, care of Col Irvin, 2ᵈ Ohio Volˢ Vera Cruz Mexico—Capt Kenneallys Cyⁱ— Tell Uncle I intended writing him but am forced to conclude. Be careful very careful Grandma of your health Mother, and little girls take good care of her and Aunt Ann— Give my love to all. Aunt C. Mrs Eberle. Tell Aunty she must write me. Love to Cousin Carrie (both) Aunt Sallie and the rest—

God bless you. *Will*

The health of all is fine here
Taylor and Wright are both well.

---

1. William Kenneally, the first elected captain of Company L of the Ohio Second Volunteer Regiment, died December 21, 1847. William H. Lytle was elected captain December 24, 1847.

### To Ezekial Smith Haines

*Lytle's letter of December 8, 1847, indicates that he wrote his family about the middle of November, just prior to his company's departure from Vera Cruz to Puebla. Although Margaret Lytle's letter of December 17 refers to receipt of a letter Lytle wrote on November 16, that letter is not in the Lytle Papers.*

*It is not clear whether or not Lytle had received his grandmother's letter, written November 15, at the time he wrote to his uncle on December 8, 1847. Whenever received, her letter probably caused at least a twinge of guilt, for she urged him not to let his busy life "obliterate" from his mind the affection "justly due" his last "earthly parent." She expressed her fond but forlorn hope that Lytle would choose to excel as a lawyer rather than sacrificing the advantages of his father's "warm and many friends" and his "Uncles assistance and influence" for "that misarable degraded war."[1]*

Puebla. Wednesday Dec 8<sup>th</sup> 1847

Dear Uncle

I embrace the opportunity afforded by the departure of my friend Douglas to write you from this city. We arrived here on the 2<sup>d</sup> of the month after a very rapid march from Jalapa. Our company left Vera Cruz somewheres about the middle of last month (the precise date I have forgotten—I wrote you the night before we started). The march from Vera Cruz to Jalapa we made in less than four days, and *alone* for both of which facts we take no little credit as the distance is ninety miles and the region between the two cities is generally infested by guerrilla bands.[2]

The whole route was to me a source of interest. Every thing was new and strange. The climate the productions the scenery—All. From the Coast to Jalapa rather to Peroté there is a gradual yet very perceptible ascent. The road—the great national road of Mexico is, or has been—it is now out of repair, a splendid work. It is very wide strongly built of heavy stone—all public works in Mexico are constructed with great solidity—and covered for most of the way with a cement as hard as rock. The first day brought us to San Juan. We found there a battalion of mounted men from Georgia.

Completely worn out with the fatigue of a long march I had just thrown myself on the ground and fallen into a sound sleep when the *long roll* beat and in five minutes, though officers & men were perfectly worn out, our company was formed and the first on the ground. It was a false alarm.

Near San Juan is one of the numerous haciendas of Gen Santa Anna.[3] It was a splendid structure but was burnt by a party of Rangers and is now in ruin. I started one morning with a party of officers to visit it, but crossing a prairie we saw a drove of wild horses and all joined with a cheer in pursuit. We captured several fine mustangs but the excitement of the chase led us far away from camp and Hacienda.

The next day brought us to the far famed National Bridge. A more fairy like scene than the valley I never beheld. Amid romantic bluffs a cool clear mountain torrent rushes over and round the rocks, spanned by a magnificent bridge 800 yards in length.

On this bridge you will remember several American officers have fallen, among others young Twiggs.[4] On the left on a rocky and almost perpendicular eminence commanding the whole valley is a fort garrisoned by a company of Georgia foot. The day after our arrival in company with a friend I ascended the hill and was amply repaid for my pains. A more magnificent prospect I never saw and never expect to see. The whole country for leagues around was displayed like some gorgeous panorama. At our feet the beautiful valley the splendid bridge, the brawling stream foaming against the rocks—its voice unheard in the distance. A little further on remote from the road another Hacienda of Santa Annas whose possessions are immense. Turning from the bridge on our left upon the horizon's verge we saw dimly the ocean and the gleam of a white sail in the harbor of Vera Cruz.

In front loomed up Orisaba with his crest of snow fifty miles distant—and on the right the mountains that include the pass of Cerro Gordo. Two days march from the bridge brought us to Jalapa where we found our regiment. Jalapa is said to be a very pleasant place but we had no time to see it as the next morning under the command of Gen Cushing we started for Puebla.[5] Four days after we arrived at Peroté. This city is at a great elevation above the sea. It is surrounded by vast pampas skirted by ranges of lofty mountains. The weather here was horrible. It did not rain exactly but we were almost constantly enveloped by a cold mountain fog. At Vera Cruz the heat at mid day was intolerable at Peroté we were in the region of ice and snow. From Peroté the weather gradually moderates till you reach Puebla. Puebla is a delightful city. Next to the city of my home and birth it pleases me most. Here in December mid winter with us—the air is as soft and balmy as our Indian summer.

There are many splendid works of art of the churches—of their grandeur—their magnificence I can give you no idea The most famous is the Cathedral de los Angelos. I strolled into it the other day and was overwhelmed by the gorgeous magnificence of everything around me. The church in the interior is in form of a cross. The floor is of tesselated marble.[6] Huge pillars of stone support the roof draped from Capital to base with rich crimson velvet fringes with gold. The walls are covered with splendid paintings with images of saints and martyrs buried in velvets and jewels. Near the centre court detached from the main building is a dome reaching almost to the roof supported by marble pillars fluted with gold and surmounted by a marble statue of S[t] Peter.

A description of this alone would cover pages. The huge candelabras are all of silver. Some of the minor altars or shrines scattered round the church are of exquisite beauty. I noticed one in particular built of varigated marbles of the most brilliant and richest hues more beautiful than you can conceive. In some of the churches away up in the elaborately carved and gilded domes, and recesses of corinthian capitals fluttered and sang birds of rare tone and rich plumage. Were it not for the magnificent scale on which these churches are built the very profusion of ornament would tend to decrease the effect—as it is, there seems no square foot of space on floor or walls or sweeping arch on which the utmost skill of man has not been expended. (It is *said* (so at least I have been told by several officers in Lanes[7] command) that the General is resolved on the first hostile demonstration on the part of the citizens of Puebla to hurl the very first bomb into the Cathedral de los Angelos. This I can hardly believe).

The public gardens and promenade of Puebla are very fine. The principal one the *Alameda* excels anything of the kind I have ever seen. It is planted with long avenues of trees and adorned with beautiful fountains and statuary.

Altogether Puebla is a delightful place. I would be very well satisfied to spend some time here, but intend moving on, upon the first opportunity to rejoin my company. Col Irvin is now at *Rio Frio* with six seven companies The balance of the Regiment is here under Lt Col Latham.[8] I was a little unwell the morning they started and determined to remain here a few days and go up with Gen Butler and his train. I cant say that I regret my temporary indisposition. The 4th Ohio has treated us with much courtesy and politeness

The night of our arrival they gave us a splendid supper which passed off very handsomely. Col Brough[9] has had several brushes with the enemy, the particulars of which you will receive with this letter, in which his regiment fully sustained the reputation it won on the other line and the credit & honor of the State of Ohio.

Sunday

I have just heard that Gen Twiggs[10] and train who will carry our letters down to Vera Cruz, and Gen Butler are both entering the city. I will not have time therefore to say much more, as I have my preparations to make for leaving. The means of intercommunication are so tedious that we know here little more, if as much as you, of the general aspect of affairs.

Of the termination of the war we can predict nothing with certainty.

The Mexican Congress is said to be convening at Querétaro and it is *rumored* that Paredes is there concentrating a large force. The train has probably brought down news which I will try and give you in a postscript. There are a number of my friends here and I feel quite at home. [Warner] Spencer—Mosher, Pugh, Benham—who left a day or two since for the city with Capt Hemselmans command, Thompson of Columbus, Dr Langdon, Ned Foote—Douglas who has been acting as aide to Gen Lane and to whom I am under many obligations and many others.

I saw Butler at Vera Cruz after I wrote you, and delivered my letters. I expect nothing from him as his staff is filled up. The line suits me very well however and all I ask is *opportunity.* Col Latham is a gallant officer and perfect gentleman. I regret exceedingly that we must be separated—Col Irvin I have not seen so much of, but what I *have* seen I like.

I wish I could send you some of the delicious fruit which we are enjoying here in mid winter. Such oranges and limes and pineapples and peaches I never saw, while the streets are crowded with baskets of flowers rarity and brilliancy would drive Mrs Eberle mad.

This has been a kind of family letter which must excuse its rambling style. Send me plenty of papers for heavens sake you dont know how they are appreciated.

Tell Hilton I intended writing him—particularly with regard to the state and influence of the church here but must delay it. Give my love to all my friends about town, especially to Rives Harrison,[11] Jack Taylor and Keys Wright Neil &c. Be good enough to say to my friend Dr Eaton that his little account though [unpaid] is not forgotten. That it is not settled is the result of a mistake— I will have it attended to as soon as possible. I hope Grandma is careful not to expose herself and enjoys good health. Tell Mrs E—— that I have not yet seen Maj Galt—I hope soon to meet him in Mexico—though the lord knows how long we may be kept at Rio Frio. Rio Frio is the last of the chain of posts connecting the city of

Mexico and the coasts— It is about Midway between here and the City—about 40 miles from the latter place— I hope we may soon be pushed on. Well good bye. Give my best love to Aunt Charlotte and Mrs Eberle. I dont know when I may be able to write you again as there are long intervals between the trains—but tell all my particular friends to drop me a line when in the humor and believe me yours affly

*Wm H Lytle*

1. Margaret Lytle to William Haines Lytle, November 15, 1847, LP, box 33, no. 445.

2. Company L arrived in Mexico after the other companies of the Second Second Ohio.

3. Antonio López de Santa Anna was the dominant figure in Mexico from its independence in 1821 until 1844. After military commands made him famous, Santa Anna was elected Mexico's first president in 1833. In 1836 he led a campaign into Texas, including the storming of the Alamo. He went to Washington as Andrew Jackson's guest where he signed the treaty of Velasco, which recognized the independence of Texas. On returning to Mexico, Santa Anna was deposed. In 1841 he maneuvered his way back into Mexico's presidency and continued the Texan border war. In 1844 he was forced out of office again but returned during the Mexican War to lead the government and military until November 1847. In 1853 Santa Anna once again became president. He served until 1855 when a liberal revolt terminated his dictatorial control of Mexican affairs.

4. Maj. Levi Twiggs, USMC, fell September 13, 1847, during the fight for Mexico City when Twiggs' command attempted to reinforce Maj. Gen. Gideon Pillow. See K. Jack Bauer, *The Mexican War, 1846-1848* (New York: Macmillan Pub. Co., 1974), 316-17.

5. Brig. Gen. Caleb Cushing's brigade was transferred from Taylor's command to Scott's army in October 1847. In 1848 (April 13-22 and June 5-July 6), Cushing was a member of the Court of Inquiry investigating Winfield Scott's command.

6. Tesselated means mosaic.

7. Brig. Gen. Joseph Lane's brigade occupied Puebla in December 1847.

8. William A. Latham was promoted to lieutenant colonel from captain of the original Second Ohio, Company D, September 4, 1847. He was mustered out with the regiment on July 26, 1848.

9. Cincinnatian Charles Brough served as colonel of the Fourth Ohio volunteer regiment during the Mexican War. A lawyer, he served as prosecuting attorney of Hamilton County and later became presiding judge of the court of common pleas. He died in Cincinnati of cholera in 1849. His brother, John Brough, was elected governor of Ohio in 1863 on the Union Party ticket.

10. Brig. Gen. David E. Twiggs was honored on December 8, 1848, at a dinner given by Gen. Winfield Scott on the occasion of Twiggs's departure from Puebla to take command at Vera Cruz. John S.D. Eisenhower in *So Far From God: The U.S. War with Mexico, 1846-1848,* characterizes Twiggs as a prominent second-level figure in the Mexican War. The "big three" were President James K. Polk, Gen. Winfield Scott, and Gen. Zachary Taylor.

11. Lytle usually refers to his friends by their last names. For example, Harrison refers to Lytle's college friend, J. Findlay Harrison (Fin or Findley), a grandson of William Henry Harrison, and Rives was probably the son of Landon C. Rives a prominent Cincinnati doctor and Lytle family friend.

*To Margaret H. Lytle, Josephine Lytle, and Elizabeth Lytle*

Puebla—Mexico   Dec 12th 1847

My Dear Grandmother & Sisters

I have written Uncle a long letter to which I must refer you for an account of my travels— I hope Grandma is careful of herself and never subjects herself to the least exposure— My own health is first rate though I had a little headache the other day which has given me a chance to see the fine city of Puebla— The next time you write to Uncle Elias give him my love and say I intend writing him—

You must write me girls frequently and give me all the news.

Remember me Joe to cousin [Buk] Taylor—Give my love to Aunt Ann, Cousin Carrie Alston—both of them—Aunt Bullock and all the rest—

Good bye girls and take good care of Grandmother and Aunt Ann

Will

I saw Rowan Steele at Vera Cruz and he is not in this City. We will January 8 sup together.

Give my respect sister Joe to Harrison Rives and the rest of my cronies— Tell them to write.

Once more Good bye. God bless you.

brother Will

*To Ezekial S. Haines*

Rio Frio Mexico
January 1st 184[8]

My dear Uncle

Young Benham is on the point of starting for home. It is now late at night and I am very busy making out discharges &c.

I have just learned to my infinite mortification a report that the great mail in Marshalls train has fallen into the hands of the enemy. In this case I shall not hear a word from home for months to come— You may imagine my feelings.

I hope and believe the rumor incorrect. I send tonight home by young Benham— My health is very good—

Love to all

farewell— W.H. Lytle

*Recipient Unknown*

*A Cincinnati newspaper published the following letter excerpt.*[1]

Rio Frio Mexico
January 15, 1848

My Dear Sir— I have got so far into the country, that I hardly ever
expect to hear from home. I find it very cold here at this post,
notwithstanding it lies between the tropics. At this, however, you will
not be surprised when I inform you that the elevation above sea is nine
thousand three hundred feet. In addition to the cold, there is a want of
oxygen in the air. From all these causes you may think, and think rightly,
that this post is not a very pleasant one. A week or two since Col. Irvin
went to the City of Mexico, and while there, dined with Gen. Scott, and
tried his best to induce the General to abandon this Post with no effect.
The General has an idea that it is of importance, and that there are more
guerrillas in this neighborhood than any other part of the line.

I never was more disagreeably disappointed in my life than in the
country lying between Mexico and Vera Cruz. From the barren and
sterile soil on the other line I was wholly unprepared to meet with so rich
and fertile a country. Even this mountain top is as rich as many of our
valleys. We ought to keep it. I cannot believe that it is intended by
providence that the rule, or rather misrule, of such miserable devils
should continue much longer over such a beautiful country. I asked a
Mexican a few days since, why the good and industrious portion of them
did not endeavor to exterminate the bands of robbers, who are constantly
plundering on the road. His reply was that good men were far inferior in
numbers, and therefore dared make no demonstration.

The most magnificent sight in the world is to behold from a
distance, a Mexican city. The immense number of domes and turrets
rearing their lofty heads far above everything around them, makes the
view most striking and picturesque. To add to the beauty and splendor
of the scene, they are generally situated in valleys, whilst on all sides, the
mountains pile themselves up, in some instances with their summits
covered with snow.

Indeed, everything, as far as scenery is concerned, is full of
enchantment; but, alas! on entering one of their cities how great the
disappointment. A land like this, on which the sun ever shines, should
have happy children; but when you look into the dark, sullen, and

unintelligent faces of her people, instead of happiness, you see that it is filled with ignorance, and vice, and misery. —Cursed with a military despotism, ruled by a depraved and corrupt priesthood, a republic in name but no more freedom than enjoyed by the serfs of Russia, they are miserable indeed. The Autocrat of Russia secures the lives and property of his subjects from all but himself, while here both are—

1. This letter was published in a Cincinnati newspaper, and the original does not exist in the Lytle Papers. The 1848 *Cincinnati Commercial* and the *Cincinnati Enquirer* have been searched to determine the place of publication but without result.

### To G.H. Hilton

*An undated clipping from a Cincinnati newspaper carried an extract of a letter from William Haines Lytle written in Rio Frio, Mexico, on January 25, 1848. The column stated only that it was made available by a friend. In all probability this was Lytle's promised letter to his friend Hilton.*

January 25, 1848

I intended, the first time I wrote you, to say a few words on the present condition of the Mexican Church; this I must defer till my return, if it is written. You have often heard me admire the eminent—the pre-eminent devotion, or rather devoutness, of the Catholic people, particularly manifested in their houses of worship and during the performance of religious exercises. There was a little incident in this connection, which affected me more than even the splendor and gorgeousness of the Cathedrals of Puebla or the capital. As the advanced guard of the column was moving on toward the former city, several officers in front heard, as they at first supposed, strains of martial music in the distance. We halted. It was a bright balmy morning in October and far as the eye could reach was spread out before us the green table land. Proceeding slowly on, we discovered what we at first thought the bugles of a hostile force to be the tones of an organ, commingling with human voices in a sacred hymn. The peasantry of the vicarage had gathered in a little solitary chapel, by the wayside and were sending up their morning tribute of praise to God. As we looked through the ivy covered doorway, we saw old and young bending in supplication before the altar. Timid and rude, had they met us elsewhere, they would have fled in terror, but here they exhibited no fear, no dismay. The column passed on with its heavy tramp battalion after battalion swept along, but with all their untutored curiosity not a form raised up, not a head was turned from the holy shrine, and calmly and earnestly they worshipped on. The early beams of the morning sun seemed to smile on that little chapel by the road-side. It was a green spot on the havoc [ . . . ] of war. It was religion in the desert."

### To Elias H. Haines

Rio Frio Mexico
Jany 26th 1848

My dear Uncle[1]

I have been intending to write you especially ever since my departure, but all my epistles have been *family* letters designed for all.

My duties have been such that I have had little time for writing though I believe I have not neglected a single opportunity. The life of the soldier was entirely new—I had everything to learn, everything to *begin*, and the labor and responsibilities of the commander of a company are not a little arduous I assure you. Here is little news to communicate. We are awaiting anxiously the next dispatch from the City which it is rumored will have an important bearing upon the peace question.

Gen Lane passed through some time since on his way to Orizaba— If there is any fighting to be done Lane will do it *there*.

I visited the Halls of the Aztecs some time since a full description of which I have given in some of my other letters.

My letters and numerous friends there secured me a cordial reception among the élite of the Army. Capt Jim Irvin particularly showed me every attention. Invited me to breakfast dine sup with him and make his house my home. He is a true model of a gentleman.

Gen Butler was in the City during my visit—but I didn't honor him with a call. I thought he took my letters at Vera Cruz with a 'hauteur' which I could not brook even in a Major Gen[l]. We met also in Puebla— he knew I was in the city yet made no enquiries no allusion to me. I have now however thank God a position which elevates me above his favor or charity and he and his staff may both go to the devil.

The officers of his two Kentucky regiments treated me with great politeness. Col Reston suggested a transfer of my company to his command—an offer which I politely declined. The fact is the 2[d] Ohio is superior considering its short experience to any volunteer regiment in the field. That *it* should garrison Rio Frio while such regiments (entre nous) as those of old Kaintuck go forward is a burning shame. It is some consolation however that the advance movement appears suspended, which would seem indicative of Peace.

Rowan Steele I left in Mexico in fine health and spirits. He sends his kind regards to all. I rec'd a letter from Sister Joesie dated in New York which surprised me much. Receive my warmest thanks for the very handsome effort you have made in her behalf[2] and with love to all believe me My dear Uncle

yr affc nephew<br>Wm H. Lytle

1. Elias Henry Haines, the younger brother of Ezekial Smith Haines and Lytle's mother, Elizabeth Smith Haines Lytle, lived in Sandusky, Ohio, where he held the position of customs collector from 1837 until 1846 and operated a store and hotel. Elias Haines often spent winters in Cincinnati.

2. Elias Haines paid the tuition for Josephine Lytle's year at school in New York City.

### To Ezekial Smith Haines

*Although Lytle's existing correspondence does not mention it, he received several interesting pieces of news from his family in letters written between January 3 and March 1, 1848.[1] Returning from Mexico, Gen. Franklin Pierce took the time to stop and visit the Lytle home to inquire about the children of his intimate friends Robert and Elizabeth Lytle. Pierce expressed disappointment that Will was in Mexico because, if the young man had his father's talents, he would be much more useful to his country as a statesman. Meanwhile, Elias and Ezekial Haines and Margaret Lytle communicated their frustration that Will was not at home to take advantage of John Rowan's appointment as minister to the court of Naples.[2] On January 3, 1848, Margaret, believing that Will would make a perfect secretary of legation for his second cousin, reported she had written Rowan to that effect. Elias Haines added that if the application to John Rowan failed, President Polk should be contacted for an appointment for Will. All family members feared constantly for his safety and agreed that Lytle should return from Mexico.*

*Lytle wrote his sister Josephine on January 24, 1848, and added a postscript on February 15. That letter has not survived. In it, Lytle described the princely palaces of the wealthy landowners and talked about the rumors of peace.[3]*

*Apparently ignoring his family's entreaties to return, Lytle included in his letter dated February 21, 1848, an original sketch of Rio Frio made by a private in Lytle's company.*

Rio Frio
Feb 21ˢᵗ 1848

My dear Uncle

As I have written to nearly all my friends by this mail I have little to communicate. It was rumored some days since that the Mexican Congress at Querétaro had ratified the articles of peace negotiated by their Commissioners. This again has been contradicted. I *think* however that our recall may be predicted before many months.

Enclosed I send you a view of Rio Frio taken by a private of my company. It is remarkably exact. The view is from the hill in rear of the parade ground. The peak on the right is Popocatapetl.[4] On the left of the picture is the peak of Chalilo behind Puebla some 40 or 50 miles distant. *a* is the great road to the City. *c* the rear of the honda or public house. *B* the church. *4* the quarters of my men. The other companies are quartered in cabins hidden by the honda and Church.

Yours Affʸ
W.H.L.

1. Margaret Lytle to William Haines Lytle, January 3, 1848, LP, box 33, no. 448; Ezekial S. Haines to William Haines Lytle, January 10, 1848, LP, box 32, no. 319; Margaret Lytle to William Haines Lytle, March 1, 1848, LP, box 33, no. 443.

2. John Rowan Jr. (1807-1855) was Robert Todd Lytle's cousin.

3. Josephine Lytle to Elias H. Haines, April 8, 1848. LP. box 32, no. 229.

4. Lytle later honored the volcanic mountain in his poem "Popocatapetl."

### To Margaret Lytle

*On February 2, 1848, the United States ambassador Nicholas P. Trist, with the support of Gen. Winfield Scott, signed the unauthorized Treaty of Guadalupe Hidalgo with representatives of the Mexican government. Although Polk had issued an order recalling Trist in late November 1847, he honored the treaty and agreed to submit it to the United States Senate. Hostilities ceased while the treaty was submitted to the ratification process in both governments. While awaiting news of the treaty's ratification by both sides, Lytle and the Second Ohio's Company L remained on garrison duty near Rio Frio.*

Feb 29th 1848

My Beloved Grandmother

I had the unexpressable pleasure of receiving yesterday three letters from home two from my uncles and one from yourself and little Bess. There is a train just starting for Vera Cruz and I have only time to drop you a line. The train is just coming in and I presume Gen Scott is with it on his way to Puebla to attend a Court Martial.[1] I have just heard a rumor that an armistice of two months has been declared for the purpose of negotiating a peace. If this is the case I shall very probably return either on furlough or by resignation. A life of inaction I cordially loathe. Tell dear little Bess that I have read her letters a dozen times already.

My love to all. Particularly Aunt Joan—Martha & Sally.

Howland Taylor is still with me in fine health & spirits. I expect to visit Mexico in a day or two for the purpose of drawing my mens pay.

farewell

yr affec^te Grandson

*Will*

1. Eisenhower describes General Scott's orders to attend the court of inquiry convened in late February in which he was both a defendant and an accuser. When the court suspended in late April 1848, Scott left for home, refusing all ceremonies and honors. See also John S.D. Eisenhower, *Agent of Destiny: The Life and Times of General Winfield Scott* (New York: Free Press, 1997) 315-20.

### To Ezekial Smith Haines

Rio Frio Mexico
April 7th 1848

My dear Uncle

Enclosed is a draft for $80 drawn by Capt Grayson City of Mexico on the Ass^t Com^y of Subsistence New York in my favor. The money was raised by my Comp and designed as a present for Mrs Kenneally. I ought also to mention that Co. *I* came forward and subscribed a portion of the amount. There is a balance not yet collected which I will forward as soon as possible—some 30—or 40 dolls. You will be kind enough to hand over the money to Mrs Kenneally herself or *Bickham* the *Coal Merchant.*

The amount is not large but hearing that the widow of Capt Kenneally was in destitute circumstances the boys at my suggestion made up the purse. I have received by all the late mails a number of letters & papers from you for which both I and the Regiment return you many thanks. I regret however to learn from Sister Joe that one or two of my own epistles have got into *print.* My letters are written in the hurry of the camp and are neither designed nor intended for the public eye. *Letter writers* beside are just now rather below par in the army.

We are looking with anxiety for news from Querétaro. The Congress is now sitting and I understand yesterday from the Prussian Consul who passed down, with a very fair prospect of bringing matters to an amicable conclusion.

Such at least is the opinion in the City. Maj Churchill[1] who spent a day with me on his way to Puebla informs me that all arrangements for *evacuation* are *made.* The troops pass down in bodies of 7000 men. Should it be sickly at Vera Cruz they march from Jalapa to *Alvarado* and there embark. The whole naval force of Gov[t] on the Gulf is to be brought in requisition. Should it be sickly at Orleans we are to pass on and disembark at Baton Rouge. So you see the powers that be, are confident of a speedy termination to hostilities.[2]

Rives has not yet got up nor was he a week since at Puebla. He must have been delayed somewhere on the route longer than he expected. Now I think of it O Sullivan my second L[t] has resigned. He went home some month or so ago and I want to put my friends on their guard against him. He is a miserable dog and left in disgrace. Had he not resigned he would have been court martialed.[3] There is no news here of any importance. I am writing to you from my cabin which my boys have built for me.

It is a regular *Tippecanoe* and Tyler too—affair. Counted one of the most elegant buildings in the village as it boasts of a *mat carpet* and a 9 by 10 *glass* window. The rainy season has set in but I do not find it very disagreeable For about half the day it *pours* then the sun comes out warm and brilliant and the balance of the day is delicious. I wrote home by every Mail and hope you have rec'd my letters.

My love to Aunt Charlotte Mrs E et al. I will finish this on the arrival of the diligence[4] from Mexico hoping to send you some news—

April 8th

The diligence was delayed yesterday till near night by being robbed. Nothing new—We just learn from the City papers of [S . . . ] appointment. The congress is said to be disposed to Pierce. The health of the regiment is good—our post is the healthiest in the country. The duplicate of the Bill I have forwarded to the Com$^y$ at N. York.

I hope you will have no trouble in the matter. Some time since I wrote to Bickham that I had forwarded the $80 to *him* by Cheever, the Serg$^t$ Major of the Regt—for you to hand the money to Bickham and let him pay it over. I did not send the money by Cheever for reasons known to myself.

I learned last night from an officer from Jalapa that Shovers battery[5] was at Vera Cruz and there was some doubt as to whether it would come up.

Give my love to all my friends. Tell Hilton that young Lufferty passed up a few weeks since in fine health. I delivered his letters.

farewell
Yours affly
*W.H. Lytle*

1. Lytle may be referring to Col. Sylvester Churchill.
2. The Mexicans ratified the Treaty of Gaudalupe Hidalgo on May 30, 1848 (see Bauer, *Mexican War,* 387). The Second 2d Ohio reached New Orleans on July 4, 1848.
3. William Sullivan, mustered in at age twenty-six in September 1847, resigned on April 7, 1848.
4. *The Random House Dictionary of the English Language,* 2d ed. unabridged (New York: Random House, 1987), defines *diligence* as: "a public stagecoach, esp. as formerly used in France (1735-45; short for F *Carosse de diligence* speed coach.)"
5. Capt. William H. Shover commanded the Third Artillery.

## To Elizabeth Lytle

Rio Frio—April 8th 1848

My dear little Sister[1]

Brother has time to write you only a very few lines as the mail closes in a short time. I have received two letters from you since I have been here which gave me a great deal of pleasure. I hope you take good care of Grandma and Aunt Ann and continue to be a hard student.

You must tell Carrie Taylor that Howland is very well and in fine spirits. Say also to Cousin Ann Buchanan[2] that I left Rowan Steele two weeks since in the City of Mexico in good health. Say to Grandma that I do not think it will be very long before the Army will leave Mexico and I shall see once more my friends and dear little sisters. You must write on to Sister Joe that you have heard from me and that I am very well. Tell her that I have got several letters from her lately and will write her a long letter by the next opportunity.

Give my love to Grandma and all at home. Remember me also to aunty B—— M—— Cousin Sallie Miller—cousin Carrie Alston[3] and all the rest. Good bye Bessie— I have got a beautiful present for you but will not let you know what it is till I return.

Brother Will

1. Lytle's sister Josephine spent the winter and spring of 1847-1848 attending school in New York. His youngest sister, Elizabeth (known as Lily or Bess), remained in Cincinnati with their grandmother.
2. Ann Buchanan (1812-1876), the daughter of Judge John Rowan and Ann Lytle Rowan, was married to Dr. Joseph Rhodes Buchanan, a prominent scientist and physician.
3. The exact relationship of Sallie Miller and Carrie Alston to the Lytles is unclear. Alston later married Lytle's friend J. Findlay Harrison.

## To Ezekial Smith Haines

*Company L of the Ohio Second 2d Volunteer Regiment did not return to Cincinnati until July 1848. Though Lytle's last extant letter written from Mexico is dated May 8, 1848, his family continued to write to him there as late as May 27. Throughout May soldiers arrived back in Cincinnati daily and the newspapers were filled with talk of an armistice.*

Rio Frio May 8th 48

My dear Uncle

I have been so much engaged for two or three weeks by the settings of a military commission for the trial of several very important cases that I have had no time to write you a long letter.

In fact there is very little news to communicate.

It is expected that our Com[rs] leave to day for Querétaro— There is at last a quorum in the Congress and the general opinion is that the treaty will be ratified. The city papers of yesterday stated that of the 90 or 93 senators & deputies but 14 or 15 were *war* men. I am obliged to visit Mexico in a day or two and if the armistice is prolonged shall resign. Mr Clifford[1] assured me however that he would make short work of it.

If our Com[rs] are still in the city when I get up I shall apply to Clifford for leave to accompany him out to Querétaro in the capacity of Sec[ty].

All well here. This post is very healthy. The climate at this time of year is much like yours at home—though with less rain. Morgan[2] passed through a few days since, as well as Rives—all in fine health. Love to all.

Affly yours

W.H.L.

1. President Polk sent Attorney General Nathan Clifford and Senator Ambrose Severier to Mexico with the Treaty of Guadalupe Hidalgo after its ratification on March 10. The Mexican Senate ratified the treaty on May 25. (See Eisenhower, *So Far From God*, 366-68.)

2. Lytle probably refers to Col. George W. Morgan of the Second Ohio. His regiment was mustered out June 22, 1847, but Morgan was not discharged until August 7, 1848. On March 15, 1848, Lytle's friend G.H. Hilton wrote that he was sending his letter by Colonel Morgan.

*On May 30, 1848, three weeks after Lytle's last letter from Mexico, American diplomats met with Mexican officials at Querétaro and exchanged official ratifications to end the war. Evacuation of the sick and wounded had begun in anticipation of the peace treaty's ratification as early as May 19. Withdrawal of the primary body of troops started May 27. The last American troops, Brig. Gen. William J. Worth's division, left Mexico City on June 12. Vera Cruz served as point of departure for the American troops to either New Orleans or Pass Christian, Mississippi.[1] Once on their native shores, units soon made their ways to their points of origin.*

*Firing canons and ringing bells announced the arrival in Cincinnati of Captain Lytle and the men of Company L, along with three other companies of Colonel Irwin's Second Ohio Regiment Mexican War veterans, on Saturday, July 15, 1848.[2] Additional units arrived July 16 and 17. On July 19 grateful Cincinnatians hosted an elaborate dinner to welcome the volunteers home.*

*The celebration included a march from Fourth Street through the city's center to the Merchant's Amphitheatre on Ninth Street, the site of the dinner. The march was led by the military of the city and surrounding country, in uniform. Officers and men of the Fourth and Second Regiments of Ohio volunteers, discharged volunteers with service in Mexico, officers and soldiers of the war of 1812, and officers of the army and navy of the United States currently in the city followed. City officials including the mayor and city council mem-*

*bers, judges, the sheriff, the press, the committee of arrangements, and those who collected money for the occasion completed the procession.*[3]

*The volunteers enjoyed a dinner in the circle of the ampitheater, where seven tables were surrounded by flowers and evergreens. R.M. Corwine, on behalf of the city, welcomed the volunteers home with a "neat" speech. Colonels Morgan, Brough, and Irwin responded. The entire event was very pleasant with total harmony existing.*[4] *Amid martial music, patriotic speeches, and adulation, the veterans stored up happy memories of a glorious time. William Haines Lytle was home and ready to practice law, but his military experiences were never far from his consciousness. During the thirteen years between his return from Mexico and the outbreak of the Civil War, Lytle expressed his martial spirit through his poetry and by joining the Ohio Militia. His service in the Mexican War was a critical part of turning Lytle the youth into Lytle the man, a man who became a brigadier general during the Civil War.*

1. Bauer, *The Mexican War*, 387-88.
2. *Cincinnati Enquirer*, July 16, 1848.
3. *Cincinnati Enquirer*, July 19, 1848.
4. *Cincinnati Enquirer*, July 20, 1848.

# THE CIVIL WAR LETTERS

DURING THE CIVIL WAR William Haines Lytle wrote family and friends ninety letters that have survived. Herein they are grouped by year: 1861, 1862, and 1863. Each fall Lytle participated in a battle that brought an end to his active duty for the remainder of that year, in the third case permanently.

The seventeen notes and letters from 1861 vividly exemplify his personal traits and his activities as colonel of the Tenth Ohio Volunteer Infantry. Lytle's earliest undated notes probably were written in May or early June from Camp Harrison and were followed by one from Camp Dennison. After his arrival at Grafton, Virginia, on June 24, his war-zone letters trace the movements of the Tenth Ohio from Grafton to Clarksburg, Buckhannon, Walkersville, French Creek, and Sutton. They reveal his frustration with the difficult terrain and the lack or poor quality of equipment and supplies. Lytle wrote his last 1861 letter on September 7, three days before his first battle experience. Disappointed after missing the July 12 battle of Rich Mountain by a few hours, Lytle and his regiment received their eagerly awaited opportunity to fight on September 10 at Carnifex Ferry in the Kanawha Valley. True to his cavalier's nature, Lytle acted daringly under fire in order to inspire his men.

His severe leg wound from the Carnifex Ferry battle kept Lytle in Cincinnati at the residence of his sister Lily Broadwell for almost four months. Overall, the engagement at Carnifex Ferry was a small part of the series of moves and countermoves by the Union and Confederate forces vying for the loyalty and control of the area that became West Virginia. Despite losing time and experience through his enforced convalescence in the first year of the conflict, Lytle gained valuable seasoning and the devotion of his men.

There are forty-three extant letters written by Lytle in 1862. He wrote many others, both to relatives and friends, but a number were captured or not saved. In addition to these letters, the Lytle Papers at the Cincinnati

Historical Society contain approximately a dozen 1862 letters to Lytle from his sister Lily Broadwell and aunt Joanna Reilly.

Whereas Lytle's 1861 letters expressed distress with what seemed senseless marching back and forth and a lack of clear direction on the part of Union commanders, the early 1862 letters contain few complaints. His frustration surfaced again on the agonizing march from Alabama to Kentucky in September 1862, and by the following year he was criticizing inept maneuvers even more freely. Throughout the three years, however, the need to maintain the Union was a constant theme in Lytle's correspondence. As displayed by his second battlefield injury, received in October 1862 at Perryville, Lytle typified the officer ideal of his time, when brigadier generals led from the front even though it put them at great risk.[1]

As 1863 dawned, William Haines Lytle fretted at home in Cincinnati, awaiting exchange to permit him to return to active duty. Meanwhile, his old regiment, the Tenth Ohio, participated in the ferocious battle at Stones River near Murfreesboro, Tennessee. Lytle's eagerly sought exchange finally arrived February 4, 1863, and within days he left for Murfreesboro. General Rosecrans, commanding the Army of the Cumberland, greeted his returning officer cordially but did not immediately assign him a command because confirmation of his promotion to brigadier general had not arrived. For some reason, probably the continuing investigations into the command of General Buell, Lytle returned briefly to Cincinnati in mid-March 1863. Monday, March 23, he left home for the last time.

Thirty surviving letters written by Lytle during 1863 are included here. These letters shed light on Lytle's interactions with Generals Rosecrans and Sheridan as well as his activities upon his return to active duty in mid-February. They chronicle the Army of the Cumberland's slow pursuit of the Confederates through Tennessee and Alabama. Lytle's patriotism, intellectual interests, and love of family and friends shine through letters often filled with details of military procedures and events including outpost duty, skirmishes with the rebels, and other day-to-day activities. On more than one occasion Lytle voiced his compassionate approach to treatment of the rebels once the war ended. Though he foresaw a Union victory, he believed the way to make the Union strong after the conflict was to bring the rebel states back into the fold without reprisals. Published copies of his August 9, 1863, speech circulated widely and gained considerable attention during the last few weeks of his life.

September 1, 1863, the day after Lytle wrote his last known letter home, he completed his bridge-building assignment. After his death, a letter from his sister Lily Broadwell, dated September 2, 1863, was found in his pocket. Though he longed for adventure, action, and glory, the need to maintain close contact with family was a constant for William Haines Lytle. Frequently written when he was tired or pressed for time, his letters often reveal his personal side. They also describe his actions and concerns in western Virginia in 1861; Bardstown, Tennessee, Huntsville, Alabama, and the march to Kentucky that culminated in Perryville in 1862; and his final bittersweet campaigns in 1863 that led to the fateful battle of Chickamauga.

1. McPherson, *Battle Cry of Freedom,* 330.

# 1861

*To Elizabeth Lytle Broadwell*

*Lytle's first hastily dashed off notes from camp are not dated. The sequence of the first two notes is not clear. They were, however, written from either Camp Harrison or Camp Dennison. The following letter was written on stationery imprinted "Head-Quarters Montgomery Regiment."*

Monday 2. P.M [May?] 1861

Dᴿ Sister

Thank Sam for his very acceptable present.

It is just the thing.

My face is better.

Hope to be down in a day or two.

Mrs Jonas has just left.

Love to all.

In great haste
Will

*To Elizabeth Lytle Broadwell*

[May?] 1861
Monday Evening

Dear Lil

Tom Gaylord very kindly offers to carry you this.

I am overwhelmed with cares as you may suppose— have hardly slept for 4 nights—

My love to dear Aunt Joe Nannie Sam and Doctor.

Am pretty well—considering.

Don't know when I will be in— Hope soon.

Good Bye
Will

## To Elizabeth Lytle Broadwell

*The stationery Lytle used for this short note had a picture of a woman holding the United States flag and the words "Liberty and Union, Now and Forever" printed on it. As per custom, the Tenth expected to receive its colors (flag) in a public ceremony. In a rare reprimand, Colonel Lytle instructed his sister Lily not to take it on herself to make arrangements for delivery of his unit's colors. Ultimately, patriotic women provided the flag with the stand of colors on June 3. Lytle received a black horse, which his Irish troops named Faugh-a-Ballaugh, meaning "clear the way." The next day, June 4, 1861, Lytle received commission as colonel from Gov. William Dennison.*

[Monday, late May or June 1861]

Dear Lil:

I heard you thought of inviting Dr Thompson[1] to deliver our colors—
It *wont do* Lil—It will *never* do.

No one respects the Doctor more than myself but we must not mix up the church in the matter—Dont select any one till you see me.

I am much better than when I left but *working* hard all the time. Cant be down for several days.

Will

1. Dr. Reverend Matthew La Rue P. Thompson was the pastor of the Second Presbyterian Church in Cincinnati in 1861. See *Williams Cincinnati Directory, City Guide and Business Mirror for the Year Commencing June 1, 1861.*

## To Josephine Lytle Foster and Elizabeth Lytle Broadwell

*Amid much fanfare Colonel Lytle and the Tenth Ohio left Camp Dennison for western Virginia on June 24, 1861. Lytle, riding his handsome black horse, shouted "Faugh-a-Ballaugh" and the Tenth was on its way. Fighting in western Virginia in 1861 was a struggle to control four major transportation routes in the region: the James River and Kanawha Turnpike, the Parkersburg and Staunton Turnpike, the Northwestern Pike, and the Baltimore and Ohio Railroad.[1]*

Grafton
Wednesday June 26th

Dr Girls

We got here at daylight this morning—two nights without sleep—
We will from here be hurried on this morning— God bless you dear girls— Love to Aunt Ann Uncle Dr Sam little Nan John— Good bye—
Remember me also to Aunt Charlotte.[2]

Most Affly
*Will*

1. Stan Cohen, *The Civil War in West Virginia* (Charleston, W.Va.: Pictorial Histories Publishing Co., 1976), 13.

2. Lytle explicitly remembered all of his immediate family in this, his first letter after arriving in western Virginia.

## To Joanna Reilly

Camp Lytle June 26th 1861
Wednesday night

My beloved Aunt

We did not advance as I expected when I telegraphed Sam this morning but were ordered to take post at this point—about a mile from Grafton—and await orders. It is a little village called *Fetterman.* My men have dubbed it Camp Lytle. We are waiting I suppose for our tents and wagons, and expect in a couple of days to be sent on.

I am comfortably lodged in a little room with Dr Muscroft & Wilson[1] who is by my side reading I *suppose* his bible. My orderly sleeps by my door. Tattoo has just beat— The patrol is going the rounds & this commences our first night in Virginia. I will write you whenever I can & hope the girls will write often. For the present I suppose if you direct my letters to Grafton they will be forwarded, though I fear the mails may be interrupted.

I was very glad indeed we were sent here as I was wearied out & did not like the idea of sleeping without tents tonight on the wet ground. The labor of reshipping the regiment & stores at Benwood was immense, and last night coming over the road was a sleepless one for me.

It is rumored that a battle is imminent but I know nothing definite.

Please ask Mr Broadwell to call on Miss Elizabeth Hughes on Western Row & tell her I was so busy before leaving I had no time to call on her. Sam understands the matter. I will try & send her what I owe the first money I get.

God bless you dear Aunt. My sincerest love to the dear girls & all the family & I hope to meet you all again in peace & happiness.

Good night and may God have us all in his keeping.

Yr affc nephew

1. Charles S. Muscroft, the surgeon for the Tenth Ohio, served until his resignation on June 6, 1863. After the war Muscroft became one of the founders of St. Mary's Hospital in Cincinnati. John Wilson, an African-American, was Lytle's personal servant. He was described as "weeping uncontrollably" at Lytle's funeral.

## To Josephine Lytle Foster and Elizabeth Lytle Broadwell

*The Tenth Ohio was poorly supplied when ordered to western Virginia. Lytle was not unique in his complaints during the early months of military action in 1861 about sending forward units before they were properly supplied and trained.*

[Late June 1861]
Friday Evening

Dr Sisters

While practicing my men to day at target shooting Mr Ch Fosdick unexpectedly stepped off the train & I seize the chance to forward you a line.

We are all well—no sickness in the Regiment— My own health is good enough. Last night an order came suddenly from M'Clelland at Grafton to send three of my best companies & a field officer to him. I forwarded them under Maj Burke[1] & learn to night they are posted ten miles from Grafton on the Parkersburgh Road. My men have behaved very well here & have elicited (at this moment the boys stroke up a beautiful serenade at my door—a song of home) great praise for their orderly conduct *among* the citizens— I fear however there is a strong *deep seated bitter* antipathy to us all even here in Western V[a]— We are *surrounded* by *spies*. I can *trust none of them* & constantly impress on men & officers the necessity of sleepless vigilance.

I am waiting here for the balance of my equipments—tents canteens &c being unwilling to hurry men forward before they are ready— It is shameful that we were sent forward as we are—

The villainous imbecility of our state officials is beneath contempt

—Since the above was penned I have had a talk with Father O'Higgins[2] *who has sources of information which I have not.*

I tell you it is tight papers here. I hope a merciful Providence will protect my men & myself. The boys are hungry for a fight & they will probably soon be gratified—

My best love to dear Aunt, Uncle Smith whose kindness to me from boyhood up I can never forget Aunt Charlotte the Doctor (to whom I will write soon if I can) Sam and Johnnie—*everybody* not forgetting poor Margaret my old chambermaid the Rev Briscoe & all— Good night—it is ten o'clock nearly.

Yr affc brother
*Will*

1. James W. Burke, twenty-six, was the Tenth Ohio's major. (Also cited in the *Roster of Ohio Soldiers, 1861-1866* as Joseph W. Burke.) Burke was mustered out of service with the regiment on June 17, 1864.

2. William T.O. Higgins served as chaplain for the Tenth Ohio. He was mustered out with the regiment on May 23, 1864.

## To Ezekial Smith Haines

Clarksburgh July 4th 1861

Dr Uncle

We arrived here Monday night & pitched our tents in the midst of a drenching rain. The regiment is receiving its wagons & trains to day. This pretty much completes our equipment *at last,* as we got our canteens yesterday. We will probably in a day or two *march* to Buckhanon & some 28 or 30 miles in advance, in charge of a large convoy.

The boys are celebrating the day on their own hook— I expect this evening to parade the regiment through Clarksburgh—about a quarter of a mile distant. The regiment is in fine health. I wish General you or Broadwell would see my friend Miss Hughes on Western Row & Lin & make some arrangement with her about my debt of a $100. If there is anything coming to me in any way I want her to have it. I want also some arrangement made for Marietta. Wilson is a devoted servant, but feels uneasy about his wife. I write in great haste & in the midst of constant interruptions.

This *is a big contract* General & no mistake. It keeps me constantly at work, night and day and a man carries his life in his hand. Gen McClellan promised me at Grafton last week "that he would not forget the truth." A collision is daily expected. My horse is well, and has got along finely. I will try & write whenever I have leisure. My sincerest love to dear Aunt Charlotte and *all*— Good bye.

Affly *Will*

## To Josephine Lytle Foster and Elizabeth Lytle Broadwell

*By the time Will wrote to his sisters July 5, he may have received Lily's letter dated June 28, 1861.*[1] *Lily had written that she was "almost heart-broken" since her brother's departure. While Josephine and her children expected to leave for Yellow Springs, Ohio, within a week, Lily was too depressed over Will's service to travel. Meanwhile, General McClellan, writing July 5 from Buckhannon, revealed that Lytle's regiment while en route from Clarksburg to Buckhannon had signaled its advance into the countryside by breaking into and robbing a grocery store in Webster.*[2]

July 5th
Clarksburgh V[a]

My beloved Sisters

I have just time to scrawl a line. I expect to move by daylight
tomorrow for Buckhannon, in charge of a large convoy. I *hope* if we can
get an early start to reach there tomorrow night or Sunday.

From my tent I now see the long line of wagons (100 or 150)
forming on the road in the valley below.

My men are well & my own health quite as good as usual—My
labors are incessant.

Lillie Swayne sent me at Columbus a beautiful handkerchief with
my initials embroidered on the corners—I never got it until a day or two
since, the basket in which it was being mislaid. I paraded the regt
yesterday through Clarksburgh in honor of the day— What a change in
a year! You remember last 4th of July I made the oration at Madisonville.
*Then* all peace & a glorious Union, now *war* with all its attendant
horrors.

After the parade I called on Judge Moore a prominent Union man
of the town & was agreeably surprised to find in his wife an old friend of
Joe's—Jennie Adams a daughter of Jennifer & sister of Charlie.

She appeared very glad to see me and sent her love to you—

My kindest regards to the Doctor & Sam. I hope I shall be able to
stand up under the march— My love to the children Aunt Ann & all.

In great haste
Yr affc brother
Will

1. Elizabeth Lytle Broadwell to William H. Lytle, June 28, 1861, LP, box 31, no. 77.
2. Stephen W. Sears, ed., *The Civil War Papers of George B. McClellan: Selected Correspondence, 1860-1865* (New York: Da Capo Press, 1989), 46.

### To Josephine Lytle Foster and Elizabeth Lytle Broadwell

July 8th (Sunday night)
10 o'clock

My beloved sisters

We left Clarksburgh yesterday morning and arrived here about
three hours ago—a march to this camp of about 32 miles—having
conducted safely a convoy of 125 wagons. We entered town with drums

beating & colors flying. The men are much wearied as the sun today was intensely hot. But we can have no rest as I have just rec'd orders to have my regiment ready at 7 o'clock *tomorrow.* It is pretty hard on us. Gen McClellan goes along. A battle is expected very soon.[1] Your letter Lil enclosing Sed's and Sam's is just rec'd to my great delight.

It will be impossible for me to write again for some time.

May the Almighty watch over us all my dear Sisters. Remember me affly to Sed Doremus. Tell Uncle to try and arrange in some way my note to Miss Hughes.

In case of any accident I want Todd & Wm Fosdick[2] to look over my papers in my Secretary & burn any not worth preserving. I write to you both girls as I have no time for separate letters.

God bless you children. My love to Auntie Uncle Sam the Doctor and everybody. I have no time for more, as I expect to be busy nearly all night nearly & must be up at 3 or 4.

Adios "et au revoir"

Will

1. Lytle's regiment missed action in the battle of Rich Mountain, July 11, 1861, by a few hours.
2. Lytle refers to his law partner Alan Todd and his friend William F. Fosdick, a poet.

### To Josephine Lytle Foster and Elizabeth Lytle Broadwell

*Lily Broadwell wrote to her brother July 10 that the family was happy to receive his letter written on the eve of marching for Buckhannon but that they lived in constant dread that he was fighting. Already her anxiety had translated into losing twenty pounds in two months. His sisters enclosed their pictures for Lytle to wear in his breast pocket. Along with providing news of aunts and cousins, Broadwell complained that the local newspaper devoted too much attention to Col. Robert L. McCook and the German regiments from Cincinnati and not enough to him. Her letter ended with a reminder to Lytle to pray.[1] Meanwhile, Lytle and the Tenth marched toward but missed by a few hours the battle of Rich Mountain on July 11. The victory by Federal troops there helped sway public opinion toward the formation of a new state in western Virginia. It also set the stage for McClellan's call to Washington to assume command in the East following the Union troops' defeat at Bull Run on July 21.*

Buckhannon
July 16th 1861

My dear Sisters

I brought the rear guard of my regiment into town last night after a hard march yesterday of 25 miles. It is eight days since we left for

Westville. I sent Korff back from that Post with four companies and marched with five companies myself across the country to Buckhannon via Bulltown a little village on the head waters of the Monongehela expecting to come up with the enemy in force. We had no engagement however the rebels falling back as I advanced. It was a great disappointment to me to miss the action at Rich Mountain. It is not likely we would have taken much part in the action but at least we could have *seen* the fight. We would not probably have done much fighting because only Rosecran's command had a chance.

Our march was a very laborious one. Rain—drenching pouring rains that wet a man to the skin *every* day. From Glenville to Bulltown our route lay through a deep mountain gorge which the enemy had filled with great trees to impede our advance. We had literally to *cut our way through,* having often 40 or 50 men at work at once with axes; with scouts, flankers & skirmishers out in every direction. I expected an attack every moment & proceeded with great caution. About midway 25 or 30 shots were fixed on us from the rocks doing however no serious injury. Gen M<sup>c</sup>Clellan sent me two dispatches to join him as soon as practicable. I marched yesterday 25 miles, but missed Rich mountain after all. The truth is I think the enemys force at Glenville was much exaggerated.

My orders being to join the Gen as soon as my regiment is no longer needed at Glenville. I expect to march tomorrow towards Beverly unless I receive counter orders. My health continues very *good* thank God, notwithstanding the fatigue & exposure.

Tell Uncle not to let the black cooks bother him. It is none of his business or *mine.* Our own cook got here safely. I found here to my great delight your photographs which I think are *admirable,* as also your two last letters. I think none of your letters have miscarried. My horse is a little lame but I trust nothing serious.

It would be a great loss to me were he to become crippled as he is thoroughly broken. Our scouts took a number of prisoners on the march, horses rifles &c &c. God bless you my dear children. I suppose Joe is at the Springs Lil; you must forward this as I have only time to write a family letter. The charge of a regiment is a great responsibility. I think more arduous than even a general command as you have to go into the smallest details.

My love to dear Aunt, little Nannie & John. They must not forget Uncle.

Dont forget my kind regards to the Doctor & Sam, whose kind letter I received to day, as also Todds.

My love also to Uncle & Aunt Charlotte. In great haste good bye.

Affly Will

My letters are only for the family

1. Elizabeth Lytle Broadwell to William H. Lytle, July 10, 1861, LP, box 31, no. 76. Robert L. McCook was an Ohio-born lawyer who came from the family of McCooks that sent seventeen soldiers and sailors to Union forces. His initial assignment was colonel, Ninth Ohio. He had brigade commands with the Army of Occupation-West Virginia during 1861 and in March 1862 received promotion to brigadier general. McCook was killed near Decherd, Tennessee, on August 5, 1862.

### To Josephine Lytle Foster and Elizabeth Lytle Broadwell

*When Lily Broadwell wrote to her brother from her sick bed on July 19, 1861, she had just read reports in the Times of his marches for the past nine days in drenching rain. She admonished him for wearing himself out by relieving soldiers of their rifles and knapsacks. Broadwell confessed that she worried even more about the hardships Lytle had to endure than the bullets. And she bluntly stated that she wanted him to get his share of the glory along with the hardships. Their brother-in-law, Dr. Nathaniel Foster, enclosed a box of cigars plus some tobacco. Foster also had told Broadwell that her sickness was merely nervous prostration. Broadwell closed her letter the following day with the note that Lytle's room was rented out and that she would give Wilson's wife Marietta some funds from the rent money.*[1]

Weston— Va
August 2ᵈ 1861

Dear Sisters

I march tomorrow with 4—companies for Bull Town on the Sutton Pike.

It is 3 o'clock at night. I am tired—

My best regards to the Doctor & Sam.

Good bye
Will

My love Lily to dear Aunt Ann. Tell her I *know* that God in his infinite wisdom has so spared me heretofore & that she & I will meet again—

Your brother
Will

Take care of Marietta.

(Having been in command here for a week & overwhelmed with care—I *must* sleep.)

Poor Euslachi—one of my german officers was buried to day—
Grover went home yesterday very ill— *Both* camp dysentery. Tell
[Horter] *I am very well.*

1. Elizabeth Lytle Broadwell to William H. Lytle, LP, box 31, no. 96.

### *To Ezekial S. Haines*

*On July 21, 1861, the day the Confederates won a tactical victory over Federal soldiers
at the first battle of Bull Run, Edward Lytle wrote his nephew a noteworthy letter. In it
the elder Lytle queried Will regarding his relationship with McClellan, stating that the
old friendships of the two families would probably induce friendly feelings toward Lytle
on McClellan's part despite Governor Dennison's influence.*[1]

August 2d 1861

My dear Uncle

It is nearly 2 o'clock in the morning. I march tomorrow to occupy
Bull Town. My health continues good (thank God).

Uncle, tell my dear Aunt that I hope I shall return to hear her talk
to me and have her hand in mine— She has been a sister to me all my life.

God bless her & tell her not to forget *Will.*

My candle is nearly out—I have but *one.*

My horse is *all right.*

I have a long story to tell but must close—

Good bye dear Uncle— I have been commanding here for a week
& leave tomorrow.

God bless you & yours.

Will

1. Edward Lytle to William H. Lytle, July 21, 1861, LP, box 33, no. 410. Edward
Lytle's letter suggests that Ohio's Republican governor William Dennison did not like William Haines Lytle. George Brinton McClellan was born in Philadelphia and attended the
University of Pennsylvania before entering West Point, where he graduated second in the
class of 1846. When war broke out McClellan resided in Cincinnati at Third and Pike, just
one block from the Lytle mansion at Third and Lawrence. He was the president of the Ohio
and Mississippi Railroad. Governor Dennison appointed McClellan major general of the
Ohio Volunteers with command of all Ohio forces, militia and volunteer, on April 23,
1861. On May 13, 1861, McClellan received appointment as major general in the regular
army with command of the Department of Ohio. It included Ohio, Indiana, and Illinois
troops. He commanded the battle of Rich Mountain on July 11, 1861. McClellan's success
at Rich Mountain just days before the Federal loss at Bull Run led to his appointment as
commander of the Division of the Potomac. The Lytles would have known McClellan and
his family through several venues, including social and business connections in both Cincinnati and Philadelphia.

*To Ezekial S. Haines*

Buckhannon

Aug 9th 1861

Dear Uncle— I arrived here yesterday after a most fatiguing march of 35 miles from Bulltown. We had just arrived at Bulltown, and had barely had time to put our camp in order—clear away several tons of stones that covered the hill side, cut away the brush and make our temporary home somewhat comfortable when we were again ordered to move. The courier arrived at 4 AM. The order was peremptory to make a rapid march. I was in a dilemma. My Quartermaster had gone to Weston with my whole train, but after great exertion I managed to collect enough transportation to move us. We started about 10 am and marching night reached here yesterday —It was a very hard march as the road was mountainous & the sun intensely hot. I forgot to tell you that I came very near shooting off my toes some weeks since. When riding very fast one of my pistols exploded in the holster. My foot was of course thrown forward and the ball must have grazed my boot by a hairs breadth.

Night before last I had a still luckier escape. I was riding fast to get in advance. The night was very dark, and my horse stumbled over a large tree lying on one side the road. Horse and rider both went down. somehow I partially managed to withdraw myself from under, but as it was the horse fell partly on my leg. It was a miracle almost that I was not killed—neither horse nor rider however received a scratch. It was a mountain road & Faugh a Ballagh came near rolling down a steep precipice.

The horse is in fine health. Looks as well as ever, and has since recovered from his lameness.

He has great endurance has splendid bottom—only one fault a little tender in the feet.

I am in command here—four companies of my regiment. Korff[1] will join me with three tomorrow. Burke leaves with two tomorrow for a point about 9 miles off.

The 5th Regt Col Dunning is here—I was very glad to meet them. I owe some bills in Cin which I will pay when I get money. $100 to Miss Hughes—132 to John Beesely & about 35 or 40 to M'Kee & Roth— Please say I will pay them as soon as I can—

I have not yet drawn a dollar from the Govt. Have you had my rolls cashed yet?

The probabilities are there will soon be hard fighting in Western

V[a]—Wilson showed me a letter from Marietta to day in which she complains she is starving[2]— I hope the poor thing will be taken care of. Do tell the girls & the family to write me when they can— I have not rec'd a letter for *two weeks*. Our Band has not yet reached us. I fear it never will. I think King a knave. Tell Todd I would have written him long since but positively have no time.

My duties are extremely arduous. My Adjt is at home sick my quartermaster a *yeoman* & new in his office, and now in addition I am really *civil* & *military* Governor of Buckhannon.

My health continues as good as usual— I forgot to say that when my horse fell the other night one of the repeaters you gave me fell from the holsters. I did not discover it was gone till daylight and near Buckhannon.

Of course I gave it up. But to my great delight my private Secy Greene to day handed it to me— He was marching ten miles in the rear & picked it up on the road—

Give my love to the girls; my Aunts—Broadwell Foster and all. Do not forget Aunt Sallie & Aunt Martha.[3] I trust sincerely I may find them in good health on my return—if I ever do.

Remember me kindly to John Dolan— Tell him Guthrie & the horse are both *bricks.*

Good bye General. I hope your health continues good.

Most Affly
*Will*

1. Herman J. Korff, a Cincinnati German, was lieutenant colonel in the mostly Irish Tenth Ohio Volunteer Infantry. Korff was discharged December 12, 1861.

2. Unfortunately, the Civil War letters referred to here between Wilson and his wife, Marietta, no longer exist.

3. Sarah (Sallie) Bullock and Martha Brown were sisters of Lytle's grandmother, Margaret Smith Haines Lytle.

### To Joanna Reilly

Buckhannon
Aug 9th 1861

My beloved Aunt
One of my officers being about to go home on furlough I seize the opportunity to send you a line. I send Uncle a long letter which you can read.

Can you not send me three or four pair muslin drawers. I need them badly. I am now in command here with 4 companies of the 10th & Dunning's Regt from Cin^ati the 5^th. I have just received a courier from Col Korff that on the march from Glenville to join me, he was fired into between Glenville & Bulltown. One of our men was killed & five wounded, the enemy fled among the mountains with it is supposed considerable loss.

The attacking force was a guerilla party—My health dear Aunt continues pretty good, considering the great exposure, *very good.* My love to the girls—thank Foster for his most acceptable presents of cigars & tobacco.

Ask little Nan & John if they remember Uncle. Tell the girls write whenever they can.

tell Aunt Sallie & Aunt Martha not to forget me.

My kind regards to Dr & Mrs Ritter—I trust dear Aunt your health is still improving.

Most Affly<br>
Will

Take care of poor Marietta—Wilson is a most invaluable servant & really seems to be devotedly attached to me.

My kind remembrance to Old Arthur.[1]

1. An African-American servant, Arthur had been with the Lytle family for at least three decades. He is mentioned in family correspondence in the early 1830s.

### To Josephine Lytle Foster and Elizabeth Lytle Broadwell

*Lytle wrote this letter after receiving letters from his sisters, then in Yellow Springs, Ohio. Broadwell noted on August 3 that McClellan's wife was expected to arrive at the springs that day, joining other Cincinnati area residents, including William Henry Harrison's widow, who frequented the popular summer resort. Broadwell observed that the war was the only subject of thought or talk.[1]*

August 20th 1861<br>
Walkersville

My beloved Sisters

I was ordered to this point 25 miles from Buckhannon on Sunday, in order "to meet a regiment of southern troops said to be advancing from the head of Elk towards Sutton." We were ordered to march with three days cooked rations, and without tents. It was the hardest march we have yet had.

I slept on Sunday night on the wet ground in a drenching rain.

*Yesterday* we had on the march a rain such as I never saw before. It rained all day *terrifically.* Our way as usual lay across the mountains. Hundréds of torrents came bursting down the precipices. Rills became rivers— rivers lakes. Even *on the road* in the hollows the water in many places was *breast deep.* Our poor boys went through it all gaily, singing and cheering, but we all suffered very much. I am heartily tired of this infernal western Virginia. We have been up here now *three times* & I should not be at all surprised if just as we get to camp we are ordered back again.

Our marches are arduous in the extreme, and we are marched & countermarched around the country in what *I* think (privately) an absurd manner. Last night I rec'd an order to go back again towards Buckannon & camp about ten miles from there at the French Fork— there I left Burke with 3 Com^s. I have 5 with me— One at Buckhannon & one at Glenville— I do not like it *at all* that my regiment is thus split up.

I should write you oftener my dear Sisters but am *constantly* occupied. My health has been pretty good though I have perhaps taken on myself too much labor. Your photographs came *near* being ruined yesterday as the rain ran down my neck under my water proof coat. Fortunately the likenesses are not at all hurt only the case.

Uncle sent me a slip from the Com^l, which no doubt emanated from Capt [Sedam].[2] [Sedam] is a poor devil—despised by his own men and by every officer in the reg^t—

Lt Col Korff is at Buckannon under arrest.

You may rest assured there is no end to the perplexity & annoyance connected with the command of a regiment—unless your officers are all gentlemen & soldiers. *Still* my own personal relations have been agreeable with all.

The *men really* seem to be attached to me & are so fine a body of men as I ever saw. Darr I miss a good deal but I have a very efficient man in his place—at least very active & energetic—Lt Frederick—a german.[3]

I am quite anxious to see Grover who has not yet returned— Neither has my Band arrived which I much regret. It is very unfortunate we cannot get one & that the scoundrel *King* behaved so badly. How I would love to see you all! I got your letters from the Springs which interested me very much— Write often I beg of you. Good bye dear girls— My warm love to all the family.

I will have to carry this down myself tomorrow to French Creek & there forward it by courier to Buckhannon.

I see with dismay that my large *riding boots* are beginning to give way. They have been invaluable. *Wilson* the "Professor" is known by all the army.

He is *devoted to me* & is certainly the most extraordinary character I ever saw. He knows a *good deal* of *everything* and knows it *well*. He showed me the other day a *terrible letter* from his wife. Marietta does not seem to ap,°rove of his connection with the service & demands his recall. I do not think however the Prof will *go*—unless his health should fail. Good by once more. Tell Uncle Smith the Paymaster has not been here yet. We are all poor as rats—

Tell Uncle also I have seen no better horse than mine in the state. He is the pet of all the boys & the horse seems to know them all. With love to Aunt Ann Uncle & Aunt C—— the old ladies Doctor Sam *All*. Good bye.

Most Aff[ly]

Will

1. Elizabeth Lytle Broadwell to William H. Lytle, LP, box 31, no. 78.

2. Lytle probably refers to James P. Sedam, who entered service April 25, 1861. Sedam accepted appointment as captain, Company G, Tenth Ohio, on June 3, 1861.

3. Francis Darr was promoted from first sergeant, Company B, to second lieutenant and acting quartermaster, Tenth Ohio, on June 3, 1861. He resigned on August 1, 1861.

*To Ezekial S. Haines*

Aug 24th 1861

Camp Charlotte

French Creek V[a]

Dr Uncle— Robinson is going home & I have just time to drop you a line. Ferguson is in Cin[ti] so I got my own draft on you cashed yesterday for $200 & bought a very fine steel grey mare. Guthrie thinks highly of her. She has a neck like a stud horse & is finely limbed, though a little too heavy for the saddle. Guthrie thinks she would bring $250 in Cin. I paid $115 for her. The Govt will owe me 6th of next month four months pay $872—Let me know what amt I must send home. Good bye.

In great haste

Affly

### To Josephine Lytle Foster and Elizabeth Lytle Broadwell

*By the time Lytle wrote to his sisters on September 7, 1861, he knew a battle was imminent. Based on Lily Broadwell's letter dated September 1, the family had learned of plans to confront the enemy through a visit from the Tenth Ohio's major, Joseph Burke. Broadwell wrote that although she tried to be realistic about the greater dangers her brother faced from hardship than in battle, it was difficult for a woman with her idol in the midst of combat.[1]*

*Despite the lack of a clear victor at Carnifex Ferry, the battle helped secure West Virginia statehood along with the Federal army's realization that West Virginia's terrain was too mountainous to permit effective military procedures. This battle brought the bloodshed of war to painful reality for Ohioans, when the Twelfth Ohio's Col. John Williamson Lowe became the state's first field grade officer casualty.[2]*

Camp Alice— Sutton V$^a$

Sep 7th 1861

My beloved Sisters

It is very late at night but I could not sleep without writing to you. An engagement is expected very soon—probably tomorrow. I am not at liberty to give particulars—except that I *heard* tonight unofficially that my regiment would have the advance. Tell Uncle that the Govt owes me four months pay today, and that I have a claim against the State of $100 or $200 for my services at Camp Harrison— I owe Miss Hughes a $100, [Bessely] $125 or thereabouts & McKee & Roth $40 or $50— My regiment was today reunited for the first time in seven weeks. I hope we will give a good account of ourselves.

Good bye my darling sisters. I hope a merciful God may re-unite us in this world, but if otherwise ordered let us hope to meet in a better. To dear Aunt Ann & Uncle Smith Aunt Charlotte, Foster, Sam, the old ladies & all my friends remember me most affly.

Tell Uncle Smith that I drew on him for $200 as he requested to buy another horse. I fear he is too liberal & will remit him the whole or a portion of the money when I am paid off.

I bought a beautiful [rose] grey mare which *Guthrie* says is worth $400. The boys have christened her *Grenouaille* (ask the Doctor if that is correctly spelt)—after a beautiful Irish queen— I hope to ride her yet in Cin$^{ati.}$

My kind regards to Jno *Dolan* & *Arthur.*

And do not forget little *Nan* & *Johnnie*— Pardon me for putting them after the servants but I write in haste. Remember me most affy to my dear old friend Fosdick from whom I rec'd a beautiful letter— Tell

Judge Storer & Tom Gallagher that they have warm places in my heart. Good night my children. I must sleep a little tonight.

Should any accident befal me remember that I am only discharging my duty to God, my country and [ . . . ] now tarnished with dishonor— Do not either forget I beg of you to write immediately to Uncle Edward and tell him that I hope to write him very soon.

Again dear girls

Good night

*Will*

1. Elizabeth Lytle Broadwell to William H. Lytle, September 1, 1861, LP, box 31, no. 79.

2. Lowry, *September Blood*, vi-vii.

*A serious leg wound sustained during the fighting at Carnifex Ferry did not stop Lytle from filing his battle report the following day to Brig. Gen. Henry W. Benham, U.S.A., Commanding First Brigade.[1]*

### HDQRS. MONTGOMERY REGIMENT, TENTH O.V.
*Camp Scott, Carnifix Ferry, September 11, 1861.*

SIR: I have the honor to report that, agreeably to your orders, I proceeded with my command on yesterday, September 10, at 3 o'clock to reconnoiter the position of the enemy, supposed to be in force in the neighborhood of Gauley River, yourself accompanying and directing the advance with me. Our road led uphill through a densely-timbered forest, and as I advanced I then sent out flanking parties to the right and left and skirmishers in advance of my column. After passing through the woods for half a mile our skirmishers were suddenly engaged in front, and I pushed on to their relief until I reached a cleared space on the summit of the hill, where for the first time the enemy came in view, posted in force behind an extensive earthwork, with twelve guns in position, sweeping the road for over a mile. A ravine separated the hill by which we approached from the right of the breastworks of the enemy, which were composed of logs and fence rails and extended for over a mile to the right and left of their intrenchment affording secure protection to their infantry and riflemen.

When the head of my column reached a point opposite the

right center of their earthworks their entire battery opened on us with grape and canister with almost paralyzing effect, my men falling around me in great numbers. I ordered the colors to the front for the purpose of making an assault on their battery, perceiving which, the entire fires of the enemy was directed towards us. The men rallied gallantly on the hill-side under withering volleys of grape and canister with small-arms, and a part of three companies, A, E, and D, actually moved up within pistol-shot of the intrenchments, and for some time maintained a most unequal contest. Both my color-bearers were struck down. The bearer of the State color, Sergeant Fitzgibbons, had the staff shot away and his hand shattered, and in a few moments afterwards was shattered in both thighs while waving his colors on the broken staff. The bearer of the national color, Sergeant O'Connor, at the same time was struck down by some missile, but recovered himself in a short time, and kept waving his color in front of the enemy's lines.

About this time I received a wound in the leg, the ball passing through and killing my horse. Perceiving the fearful odds against us, I directed the men to place themselves under cover. A portion rallied behind the log houses in front of the battery and kept up a spirited fire for at least one hour before any other regiment came into action, and the remaining portion of the right wing, under command of Lieutenant-Colonel Korff, resumed in good order its position under cover of a corn field in front of the right of the battery, from which position, having been soon after supported by artillery, a steady fire was maintained against the enemy until night, after which Companies G, H, I, and K, and a great portion of D and E, by order of General Rosecrans, remained on the ground during the night, throwing out their pickets, under command of Lieutenant-Colonel Korff.

While the right wing of the regiment under my command engaged the enemy on their center, a portion of the left wing, consisting of Companies I, F, K, and C, under command of Major Burke, pushed through the woods on the left of the road and assailed the stockages of the enemy's infantry, a deep ravine intervening. This portion of the command held its position, in face of a terrific fire, until every round of ammunition was expended and the companies relieved by artillery, when it rejoined the right wing, already in position in front of the enemy's battery, the men dragging our guns through the woods in their progress and helping to place them in position.

For men for the first time under fire the conduct of the regiment was highly creditable. Having been disabled in the early part of the action I was necessarily separated from a greater portion of the command, but among those who came under my own notice I would especially mention Capt. S.J. McGroarty, commanding the color company; Lieut. Jno. S. Mulroy, Company D; Lieutenant Fanning, Company A. Both Lieutenant Fanning and Captain McGroarty were severely wounded, the latter while rallying his men around his colors and the former in leading his men to the attack. Captains Steele and Tiernon are also worthy of special mention for their gallantry. I would also mention the name of Corporal Sullivan, Company E, who in the midst of a galling fire went across the front of the enemy's batteries and returned with water for the wounded.

Of the portion of the regiment under Major Burke that officer makes highly honorable mention of the names of Captain Ward, Company I; Captain Robinson, Company K; Captain Hudson and Lieutenant Hickey, Company C; Captain Moore, Company D; Sergeant-Major Knox, for their gallantry and intrepidity under a most destructive fire, and also of the chaplain, Rev. W. T. O'Higgins, who remained on the field during the action in performance of his sacred duties.

I beg leave to inclose a list of killed and wounded of the command.[2]

All of which is respectfully submitted.

WM. H. LYTLE
*Colonel Tenth Ohio Regiment, U.S.V.I.*

1. *O.R.,* ser. 1., vol. 5, 136-37.
2. Included in Report No. 14, *O.R.,* ser. 1., vol. 5, 146.

# 1862

## To Isabel Carlisle

*Colonel Lytle wrote this letter in Cincinnati just prior to leaving home to return to active duty following nearly four months of recuperation from the leg wound he sustained at Carnifex Ferry.*

> Cin Jany 1st 1862
> Mrs Isabel Carlisle
> Secy of the West Sixth St
> Ladies Aid Society

Madam

I am just in receipt of a note from you informing me that your society has forwarded to my Regt 540 prs mittens, 250 shirts, 53 towels, 11 prs socks, 20 prs drawers, 8 gowns & 6 doz hdkfs.

You tell me also that this shipment has been made "in compliment to the gallant and fearless behavior of my regiment at Carnifex Ferry."

On behalf of my command I beg leave to tender your society our heartfelt thanks for this most acceptable donation.

I know I can say to you that my men if necessary would discharge their duty as soldiers even if unsupplied with the articles your patriotism has so kindly furnished.

But on the march or in the fight it will lend them additional nerve & courage to remember that their fair country women do not forget them.

In the affair at Carnifex to which you have thought proper to allude in so complimentary a manner the Regiment introduced itself to the acquaintance of a rebel army and did its best.[1]

In battles yet to come no soldier of the 10th will hesitate for a moment to offer up his life if need be under the sacred flag of the Union and those of us who survive will tell how the beautiful women of 1861 & 1862 were as brave & patriotic as the heroines of our Revolutionary era.

During all the hardships & privations of a winless campaign, the sentry on his beat, the chilled picket, the sick man in the hospital, all of us on the march or in battle, or in tedious garrison will endure every thing without a murmur when thus cheered by your sympathy & approving smiles.

In the hope and firm faith that the God of our fathers will lead up our people from these present troubles to Peace and a Union stronger and more glorious than before & with the sincerest thanks of us all, officers and men to your noble association, I remain madam

Most Resly

Yr obt Serv

Wm H Lytle

1. This letter is from Lytle's draft, which he kept for his copy. In his draft the phrase "acquaintance of a rebel army" originally read "acquaintance of our misguided yet beloved brethren of the south."

## [To Elizabeth Lytle Broadwell]

Louisville Hotel

Sunday Jan 6th 1862

My dear Sister

You will be surprised to learn that I am here again—So *am I.* On my arrival yesterday at Bacon Creek (which I reached at 12.No) I repaired immediately to the quarters of Gen Mitchell where I found an order from Gen Buell[1] for me to report "immediately to Louisville to take temporary command of the Barracks at this point." And here I am after a fatiguing trip. I reported immediately to Capt. Fry, Chief of Staff,[2] who informed me that it was not *intended* I should rejoin my regiment immediately & that they supposed I was in Cin[ati] & the order had been sent there. I was vexed that they had not communicated the order on Friday, as I reported to H[d] Q[rs] and not only that, but left a card for the Gen at the Galt House[3]—being thus put to an expense of $16. for nothing, besides the trouble & fatigue of the trip. I *infer* that Gen Buell means kindly & thinks I am not yet strong enough for duty— which is true enough.

My duties will certainly not be *arduous* as the Barracks are *not built*—though you need not mention this out of the family.

My men were delighted to see me & seemed totally *mistified* & dumb-founded by my sudden departure.

My regiment has a splendid camp—neat as wax—and look *well*.

Please read this to Uncle Smith & the rest.

In haste & hoping to hear from, or *see* some of you.

Affly<br>Will

In case I am ordered away suddenly I will telegraph you.

*Pirtle* was right—& the staff probably thought I had rec'd the order before leaving.

1. Lytle refers to fellow Cincinnatian Ormsby MacKnight Mitchel, who commanded the Third Division, Army of the Ohio, from December 2, 1861, through July 2, 1862. In January 1862 Brig. Gen. Don Carlos Buell commanded the Department of Ohio.

2. James B. Fry, a West Point graduate (1847) and Mexican War veteran, served as chief of staff to General McDowell during the first Bull Run campaign. Later he served as chief of staff to General Buell and saw action at Shiloh, Corinth, and Perryville. In 1863 Fry became the army's first provost marshall general. He was a native of Illinois.

3. The Galt House was a hotel in Louisville, Kentucky.

### To Elizabeth Lytle Broadwell

*Lily Broadwell's letters to which Lytle refers are not in the Lytle Papers. It is probable Broadwell asked her brother to stay away from alcohol, as she had a continuing concern in this regard.*

Louisville Hotel<br>Friday 11th Jan 1862

I was delighted my dear Sister to receive your letter yesterday evening—also two short ones from Uncle.

I had begun to feel quite anxious to hear from home. I have rec'd no further orders and am quietly awaiting them. My presence here I can explain in no other way than that referred to in my first letter. A week or two here would be of great service to me as I have my wounds dressed twice a day and am perfectly regular in my habits. My horses I brought back preferring to have them with me, but unless the Quartermaster makes a liberal *commutation for my board & forage, will send them back to camp, as my expenses here for board & forage are about $4.60 a day.*

I am entitled you know to board & forage & fuel from Govt but not for enough I suppose to cover my bills.

*The Steeles are very kind & I have the best room in the house—that formerly occupied by Gen Anderson[1] —Rather too much style* for a bachelor but devilish comfortable.

Please forward as soon as possible, my *camp chair, odd slipper* & a doz. daguerres for my friends here.

I met Miss Watts here last night. Mrs. Steele introduced me to her in the ladies parlour—Her son is with her—a *Sergeant—not a captain!* He is a big lubberly boy—in baggy breeches. I was really charmed with the old lady, who seemed much gratified that I solicited an introduction.

I called yesterday afternoon on Mrs Pettis who was very cordial. There I met your friend Mrs Shreve who spoke of you most kindly & invited me to her house.

Last evening I called on my old friend Eliza Thompson & had a very pleasant visit— She was far more cordial than I deserved as you know I never went to see her in Cin^ati. Dr Johnson called yesterday & seemed much annoyed at Mary's remark about not calling. Of course— she meant nothing.

My dear Lil, if it *will contribute any to your happiness I most cheerfully give you the promise you ask.* So put your *mind at rest.* I owe this to my dear Sisters for their love and devotion. I will write often & telegraph should I be suddenly ordered away.

I shall write Uncle as soon as I can get the inside track of some recent events here. Tell him my friends should press my claims on *Todd* & the War Dept. Groesbeck has I hope written— Love to all. Remember me to Miss Charley.[2]

Affly
Will

1. The Steeles were relatives of the Lytles and the Rowans. See the discussion in connection with John Rowan Steele and the Mexican War. General Anderson refers to Robert Anderson, a native Kentuckian, who commanded Fort Sumter when it surrendered. Anderson commanded the Department of Kentucky (May 28-August 15, 1861), which merged into the Department of the Cumberland, which he also commanded (August 15-October 8, 1861).

2. Charlotte Pendleton was one of Lytle's many female friends. She commemorated Lytle's bravery and quest for fame in her poem, "The Last Ride of the Good Steed Faughaballa." Pendleton's poems were collected in *Songs of the Year and Other Poems,* published under the pseudonym "Charlton" by Robert Clarke & Co., 1875.

### To Josephine Lytle Foster

Louisville
Tuesday
Jan 14th 1862

My dear Sister

I rec'd only *one* of yr letters, which went first to Bacon Creek. Dear Lily's arrived yesterday—I *do hope* you are *both* well by this time. [Ella Watts] from Lil's letter is a poorer concern than I even supposed *before*. She is not perhaps entirely sound in her upper story.

Gen Mitchel[1] ran up last night from Bacon Creek—Buell telegraphed for him. Young *Fred* his son & aid spent the evening until 9 o'clock in my room. I then called on Mitchel at the Galt. After waiting an hour he finally got through his talk with Buell & I had a few words with him.

He seemed glad to see me—Says no doubt I was ordered here as a sort of *amends* on the part of Buell—*to make* all *things right* &c & that I will no doubt be sent to the Regt in case of an advance.

Ella Pirtle & Eliza Thompson spent the day here yesterday. I dined with them & the Steeles & had a most agreeable time.

How I do wish you or Lil or Uncle or *somebody* could run down again before I leave.

I ride out every day & look fifty pr cent better than when I left you— Take care of dear Aunt—I hope she is good health.

Good bye—It is nearly dark.

Affly,
Will

kindest regards to Foster—cant he run down? Higbee has left.

1. Lytle knew Ormsby Mitchel as a contemporary of his father's in Cincinnati society and from Cincinnati College, where Mitchel was a professor when Lytle was a student.

### To Elizabeth Lytle Broadwell

*His leg injury not fully healed, Lytle received orders to take command of Camp Morton at Bardstown, Kentucky. There his duties included recruiting and training.*

[January 16, 1862]
Louisville Hotel
Thursday 11 P.M.

My dear Sister

*Both* of Joe's letters were finally rec'd—having first gone to Bacon Creek.

As I despatched you tonight I leave tomorrow at three P.M for Bardstown in compliance with the order of which this is a copy—
"Spec. Order
No. 12
Col Wm H. Lytle 10th Ohio Vols will repair without delay to Bardstown Ky and relieve Brig Gen Wood[1] in the command of the camp & troops at that point."

There is a large body of troops there. *How many* I dont yet know.

This *is* or *seems* to be a big *contract*. I feel much embarassed by the want of a staff, which I shall have to detail from among strangers—also by the absence of my body servant. I will try & make arrangements to have Wilson shipped down after me.

The order is certainly complimentary & I shall trust to good luck to put me through.

I *hope* soon to be restored to my Regiment or *some command* of which *it is a part.*

Of one thing you may rest assured dear Sister & that is of my firm adherence to my resolve alluded to in my last.

I suppose this command is temporary, but of course *know* nothing.

The Steeles have been very kind. Try & show Mary some attention.

I will write from B—— as soon as I *can*. Love to all.

I must close, as I need sleep. I hope you are entirely recovered. As for myself you have no idea how my rest here has benefitted me. Good night & good bye dear Sister.

—Will

1. Brig. Gen. Thomas John Wood commanded the Fifth Brigade, Second Division of Ohio, from December 2, 1861, until January 8, 1862, after which he commanded the Sixth Division, Army of the Ohio (February 11-September 29, 1862). He served in the Tullahoma campaign and fought at Chickamauga and later Missionary Ridge, the Atlanta campaign, and the battle of Franklin.

*[To Elizabeth Lytle Broadwell]*

[January 19, 1862]
Bardstown Sunday night

My dear Sister— we arrived here safely on Friday night, horses & all. The Professor[1] came to hand last night in good condition. I will remit you the $10 by the first safe opportunity— I am a little afraid to send it from here by mail—will probably *express* it.

Gen Wood turns over the command tomorrow. There are 2500 men here now—3 Regts—one In^a, one Michigan & one Regt of Ky Cavalry— Two more—1^st & 2^d Kentucky are expected in a day or two. I shall have my hands full!

I have not yet called on the Rowans—

Young Jno Rowan the second son—a young man of 21 called on me today—having accidentally heard I was here—

He is quite a handsome gentlemanly fellow & seemed delighted to meet me—I shall call the first leisure time I have & *report*.

The Rowans & Wickliffes are about the only two old families left here. The glories of Bardstown have pretty much departed.

I had a real good time in Louisville— When they got to know me the people at the Hotel were all very polite.

Miss Speed & I got quite thick— She is a real little lady. I had asked her in joke for *her colors* to wear on my flags. The day I left she sent me to my utter surprise (accompanied by a very pretty note) a beautiful *knot* or *cockade* of blue ribbons with long ribbon streamers to it—each ribbon has on it a motto in gilt letters on one "none but the brave deserve the fair" another "Lytle & the 10th"—the whole thing very pretty & tasteful.

Please send my daguerreotypes to Miss Eliza Thompson & Rosa Speed care Louisville Hotel—that is all— I have asked for *Grover* to be sent here— Am much bothered about my Staff. Have not heard from home since your letter by Wilson— Hope to hear tomorrow.

I send this to Louisville by private conveyance & must wind up— Send any newspaper articles that name me—either complimentary or *not*— Write often.

Love to all.

In haste
Affly
Will

1. Lytle refers to his personal servant, John Wilson, an African-American.

*To Joanna Reilly*

Bardstown Jany 23$^{d}$ 1862
Thursday night

My dear Aunt

I embrace the first leisure moment today to drop you a line. I assumed command here last Monday relieving Gen Wood.[1] There are now here six Regts and two more expected tomorrow. The regts here are the 1$^{st}$ & 2$^{d}$ K$^{y}$, 24$^{th}$ Ky 11$^{th}$ Michigan 35$^{th}$ In$^{a}$ & 4$^{th}$ Ky Cavalry— We have besides 400 men here in Hospital—occupying for that purpose two large buildings—St Josephs College & a female Academy. The command you see is a very important one. My Staff is organized as follows

1$^{st}$ Lt Frank Cunningham 33$^{rd}$ In$^{a}$ Ast Adj Gen

1$^{st}$ Lt Jos W Miller 2$^{d}$ Ky—Aid de Camp

Capt Brinkerhoff Asst Quar$^{r}$ U.S.A.

Capt Alexander Asst Com$^{r}$ U.S.A

D$^{r}$ Chambers—Medical Director

I occupy an entire house for myself & staff office &c. In case of a forward movement however I am most anxious to be relieved, especially as the duties here are so onerous.

I have called twice on the Rowans. Old Federal Hill reminds me much of *our* old Homestead,[2] though by no means in as *good repair.*

It is indeed, in a sorry condition. The paper half off the parlour walls—the doors creaking on their hinges and the whole building presenting an air of decayed splendor—

And yet it is an imposing looking old place. Mrs. Rowan[3] is apparently a woman of about 55. Her dark hair much sprinkled with gray. Not so tall as I expected—with very soft & elegant manners, a beautiful brow & other traces of great personal attractiveness. Her *portrait* taken when young is exquisitely beautiful. It reminds me something of Therese Chalfant. She has *nine* children living. John the second son is a fine looking fellow of 21 or 2— William is in the Southern Army. *Lytle* Rowan I have not seen— He is about 18 & said to be very handsome.

Cousin Josephine is quite handsome. Cousin Rebecca who has just left the Academy at Nazereth is not so fine looking as her sister, but is quite attractive & apparently highly educated and intelligent— Some of the little children are *perfectly beautiful*—especially a pair of twins— Mary & Maude—about 8 or 9 years old Mary a brunette with dark eyes

& black ringlets & Maude a blonde with the most beautiful head of
wavy golden hair you ever saw

They gave me a warm reception. Archbishop Parsell & Bishop
Spaulding of L——e[4] called on me yesterday.

We have just heard of Zollicoffer's defeat[5]— I am most anxious to
rejoin my regiment, as my responsibilities here are very great & I fear
there is little glory— Besides I prefer my own boys to any I have seen—
many of our regiments are badly disciplined.

*Today to my infinite pain a very wealthy & respectable old man & a
known man at that, was assassinated—shot dead—by a ruffian soldier. I
hope to get hold of the murderer & shall put him through—Such is War!*

Give my love to Aunt Sally & Aunt Martha Brown—& all at the
old House. Tell Uncle my sorrel horse is greatly admired & I do not care
to part with him.

Wilson has been sick or at least *grunting* ever since he arrived—
Unless he does better I shall *ship him. Seybert* was a smart fellow, &
capital servant but had some faults—I *may* take him back. He is now
with Col Engart in Camp. The poor devil was much cut down when I
discharged him— My kind regards to Foster[6]— I believe he knows D^r
Chambers— White & Mendies are both here. My health continues
good. My leg is nearly well—though still troublesome to some extent.

I wish Joe would send me three or four daguerreotypes. My love to
my dear sisters—not forgetting my little pet Nannie & the *boy John.* I
asked by the way a young nigger this morning "who was the first man"?
His answer was *"Jesus"* "And who was the first woman"? *"Jesus' wife"*— A
few hours after he corrected himself by saying that it was not Jesus who
was the first man but "Our Saviour."! I write this to give you an idea of
the *very* mixed theological notions of the darkies.

I cant find the daguerres of my sisters— If I left them behind tell
Lil to express them to me, or send them *somehow.* Good night.

Most affly
Will

1. Lytle commanded Fort Morton, a camp for rendezvous and instruction, which averaged ten thousand troops.

2. The Lytle mansion was the first brick house built in Cincinnati. The city tore it down
in 1906.

3. Rebecca Carnes Rowan (1813-1897) was the widow of John Rowan Jr. (1812-1855).

4. Louisville.

5. Felix Kirk Zollicoffer commanded the First Brigade of the District of East Tennessee at the battle of Mill Springs (also known as Logan Cross Roads) in Kentucky on January 18, 1862. Federals shot and killed Zollicoffer during a lull in the action.

6. Lytle refers to his brother-in-law Dr. Nathaniel Foster.

### To Elizabeth Lytle Broadwell

[January 27, 1862]
Head Quarters U.S. forces
Bardstown, Ky 1 o'clock
Monday night

My dear Sister— Your letter of thursday was rec'd this evening to my great delight & I cant go to bed even at this late hour without writing you—especially as tomorrow I may have no time—

*Burke* & I have just had a famous talk. Yes! the *Major*— To my great surprise I saw his yellow head at the Tavern tonight at supper. Our cook had misunderstood my order & having no supper at home I went over to the Hotel for a cup of coffee. *There* to be sure was the Lt Col who had meditated a *surprise.* He reports the Regt in fine health & in high state of drill. I was delighted to see him, as I was most anxious to hear from the boys.

Everything here goes on well. My staff & I have a house to ourselves— We breakfast from 8-9 *did* dine at *6,* but have altered the hour today to *3,* as we all got very *hungry* yesterday— We have a negro woman for cook & a first rate one she is. I took tea yesterday with the Rowans—we had a nice Kentucky supper & Mrs R—— is certainly a most lady like woman— we talk very freely yet very pleasantly about political matters.

Cousin Joe[1] remarked last evening that "Beauregard had put his army to work & built a railroad 40 miles long in two days." Yes, I told her, we always thought he would be good at *"making tracks"*— Guthrie[2] acts as one of my orderlies. I have besides 4 mounted orderlies from the Cavalry.

Guthrie is an elegant rider & we make quite a stylish appearance— My little sorrel on parade is a perfect beauty— In fact tell Uncle, both my horses are much admired here. Night before last I took tea by invitation at Mr Bukhams—He is a son in law of Gov Wickliffe. Mrs Bukham, a sister you know of Aunt Charlotte's friend Mrs Merrick, is a *very* handsome woman. I passed a most agreeable evening. Mrs B—— had often heard of Aunt & was exceedingly polite. I quite fell in love with her—She told me Josie Rowan was engaged to a Mr Reed of New Orleans & that her marriage was prevented by the war. Reed is a *Secesher* & cant get across the lines. Josie had even bought her bridal trousseau— Poor Joe, no wonder she is a little blue. Guthrie & Wilson seem to homologate very well now—The Professor is in his element, as we have quite a lot of niggers about the kitchen who seem to regard him as a nigger Solomon. There are now, Col Bruce having come up—*seven* regiments here and 400 men in hospital—I have a Provost marshal & 200 men in town. The camps are in the vicinity, within a radius of 5 miles. I wish Sam or Foster could run down—You can leave Cin^ati in the early train & be here at night—Leaving Louisville at 3 P.M. My pistols have been duly admired—they are the handsomest I have seen. Give my love to Sharley Pendleton—Tell her to write frequently. And do *you* write often for possibly I may be soon ordered where mail facilities are not so good. Tell dear Joe *all* of her letters have I believe come up. Well—I must go to bed—I hope Burke will spend tomorrow with me.

With love to Uncle Smith Aunt Ann Sam everybody.

Most Affly
Will

If you find your daguerreotypes send them on by express.

1. Lytle refers to his second cousin Josephine Rowan, daughter of Rebecca Rowan and the late John Rowan Jr. Lytle could not resist a humorous retort to her reports of General Beauregard's accomplishment in railroad building.
2. Joseph Guthrie may have been a son of James Guthrie, who studied law with Judge John Rowan.

## To Elizabeth Lytle Broadwell

Bardstown Feb 3^d 1862

My dear Sister

Your very welcome letter came to night. Did you receive the $10 I sent? You say nothing of it.

I have sent Wilson up stairs to see if I have any citizens clothes. I got also tonight Uncle's letter & his latter Telegraph. Jim Graham arrived here this evening & left the office a little while since. What a puppy he must be!

I am *very* weary to night dear Sister having visited this afternoon my *camps*—through the mud & rain. They *look well.* The main camp is

4½ miles from here. (Wilson reports *no* citizens clothes—I *had* an elegant black frock coat, made by M'Kee & Roth—I think it must be somewhere about)—There are nine Regts here—there will be another in a day or two.

Pirtle I see by the Com¹ has been com^d as 2^d Lt¹—I am glad of it—though I applied for a 1^st Lt^s in his behalf. He was here to see me a day or two ago—You do not know how delighted I am to get your daguerres again. I do not know how I came to leave them.

My health continues good— I wish Nat Foster & Sam could run down & see me.

Tell Foster I should like him to inspect the Hospitals.

Capt Greene of Buells' Staff was here a day or two since—He is a very agreeable fellow. I took a great fancy to him—

I have again sent for Grover, though I hate to part with young Cunningham—the *Rowans* I have not seen for a week—

Tell Miss Pendleton that if *she* had been at Bardstown *I* should not have stopped at Louisville.

My love to dear Josie Aunt Joan the old ladies & Uncle.

Tell Uncle my horses are very much admired & I think will suit me admirably—We shall have the telegraph extended here in a day or two & in operation in my office.

Good night

Aff^y
Will

1. Alfred Pirtle was the son of Judge Henry Pirtle of Louisville. Henry Pirtle and Robert Todd Lytle studied law together with Judge John Rowan. Pirtle served as Lytle's aide during 1862 and 1863 and was close to Lytle when he was killed at the battle of Chickamauga. The Com¹ refers to the *Cincinnati Daily Commercial.*

### To Josephine Lytle Foster

Bardstown Friday night
Feb 7^th 1862

Dr Joe—

I rec'd your last letter yesterday. Everything here goes on smoothly though the labor is very great. I forward you a letter from Miss Foster¹— Is it not beautifully written.

It will be three weeks tomorrow I believe since I came here— though I dont know what they think at H^d Quarters. The inference from my remaining here this long would indicate favorably. I send you an account of Calhouns execution which appeared in the Journal today. Everything went off smoothly to my great satisfaction—We only got the order the night before & it took me nearly all night to make the arrangements. Some of the regiments had to move six or 8 miles, but everything was *sharp* on *time*. I have now a telegraph line *from my office* to Louisville. *Grover* paid me a visit yesterday & is very anxious to join me. Lt Lacey is said to be here to night though he has not yet called—

Have you seen the *song* in which my name figures? Grover says it is set to music & is a fine thing. Let me know what my bill is for Photographs—

You have never sent me any. My horses are in fine condition & beat anything in the command.

Tell Aunt Ann my pistols are the envy of my whole staff.

Good bye dear Joe—Write often—With love to dear Lil Auntie & all. Believe me, In haste

Yr affc Bro<br>*Will*

Kiss the children for me.

1. Lytle had received a letter from his five-year-old niece, Anna Haines Foster.

### To Josephine Lytle Foster

Bardstown Feb 11th 1862

My dear Joe—

I have this moment rec'd your letter—or rather *just* read it—as my office has been crowded all the evening. I was truly glad to hear from dear Aunt & hope when the wars are over to meet her in renewed health & spirits.

Charley Engart & Caleb Bates arrived this evening. The illustrious Graham is here also—as I returned from the Penn^a camp today I stopped at the Rowans & to my surpise found *John* very ill—so low that he is not expected to live. I heard tonight from Maj Buford Qua. General that Mitchels Division had been ordered to Green River—If this is so I shall probably ask to be relieved, as my Regt must not get into a fight without me. The *ball* seems about to open. Mrs Pirtle has just written me a note which I enclose. The Penn^a Cavalry today expressed a desire through their Col to constitute a part of my Brigade—if I *was to get* one. The 1^st & 2^d Ky are strongly my friends and the officers wanted to get up a memorial—but I would not let them. Everything here thus far goes on smoothly. Grover has not yet been ordered here that I know of. Tell Uncle Smith that I will write him soon & that my horse is not very sick—

Please send me some *Pomade* for the hair.

Why dont Lil write? I went to church *twice* yesterday—once tell Aunt Sallie to the Pres^en & once to the Methodist church. Tell her that next Sunday I shall patronize the Catholics, unless she objects.

Good bye dear Sister, Love to All.

Affly
Brother Will

## To Elizabeth Lytle Broadwell

*On February 25, the day before Lytle wrote this letter, Gen. Albert S. Johnston evacuated Nashville, Tennessee, after unsuccessfully trying to hold the town for the Confederates following his retreat from Kentucky. Union forces moved into Nashville that day and held it for the remainder of the war.*

Bardstown Feb 26th 1862
Wednesday Evening

My dear Sister Lillie—

Your hastily written note—in pencil came to hand this evening—My time is so constantly engrossed—that it seems almost impossible to write you—though my thoughts are with you continually. I have been detailed on the Military Board of Examiners at this point in addition to all my other duties—the duties are very laborious as I am not a *Cavalry* officer & have to make myself acquainted with the drill of that arm of the service, in addition to my own. I shall make a strong appeal tonight to H^d Quarters to be relieved from this additional duty—which is to me *exceedingly* distasteful.

There is something inquisitorial about it. My colleagues are Col Duffield of the 9^th Mich—one of the most gifted gentlemen I ever met and Col Harris of the Regulars—a Cavalry officer of distinction. You do not know how anxiously & with what eagerness I await the mail each evening & how bitterly disappointed I am when I hear nothing from the family—which has been the case for several nights past. My excellent Uncle is the best correspondent I have among you all. Dont wait for me to answer your letters, but write when you have time. The people here seem disposed to be very kind to me. I have declined a number of invitations out & visit little. By the way Mr Bukhams family have been very kind and I want *Sam* to send me *right off* for Mr Bukham a dozen of wine. I want a dozen of *Bogen's* sparkling Catawba—If not Bogens Longworths— I should prefer on second thought a ½ doz of the native Isabella—the *red wine*—ladies wine and a ½ doz of the other— If he cant get Bogens send Longworths[1]—and right away—for fear I may be ordered off—by Express *with the bill.* They have been so *very* polite that I really must tax my pocket though my funds run low. I have broken up my *mess* since the staff left. I sleep and keep my office here but board at a private boarding house, where there is a much better table at a *much* less cost— In fact I only pay for *myself* $2 per week. The house is kept by a widow lady & I find the change very much for the better in every way. Doctor Chambers & wife, Capt Brinkerhoff & wife & several other very pleasant people board there also. My black horse tell Uncle is very badly hurt & I fear will be unserviceable for many weeks. If ordered off I shall leave him with Bukham till he gets well. My Adjt Gen is now, Capt Chadwick of the Michigan Regt and I now run the machine with him & a single clerk. [Hunter] Brooke's regiment passed through a few days since & he spent some time with me. He has been acting as a sort of aid for McCook. I should like to have kept him & he wanted to stay but as the poor fellow is only a *private* it could not be done regularly as an *aid* must be a commissioned officer. I felt sorry for poor Brooke & hope he may be promoted.

I yesterday departed from my usual rule & accepted an invitation to dinner—at a Mr Browns—an old gentleman rich with elegant grounds house conservatory &c some 15 or 20 were there Brinkerhoff & wife, Capt Alexander of the Commissanat Mr & Mrs Bukham Mr & Mrs Hillay, Miss Brown a very beautiful young lady & several whose names escape me. The dinner was very handsome indeed. The girls here are very pretty—very ladylike & very Secesh—though quite willing to be flirted with by federal officers— Miss Brown & I became romantically attached & I promised to call & see her often which is probably *all* of it. I think I made rather a favourable impression as I was in good spirits and looked as proud as a hog going to battle. I begin to feel most anxious to meet my boys & hope soon to be relieved though this is by all odds one of the pleasantest posts in Ky—I did not go into this fight however to live at pleasant posts but to lead men into the fight. If I am ordered off I will at once advise you by telegram. And now dear Sister "good night." Give my best love to dear Joe, Aunt J. the old ladies & the whole family. I send you a slip from the "Bardstown Gazette"—a paper rather *Secesh* as you may divine. I hope before going South to be able to run up to Louisville. In fact I *must* go I suppose to get a pay account cashed— my kind regards to Sam—

Most affly<br>Will

I have written in *great* haste & beg you not to criticize.
My *best regards* to Miss Sharley Pendleton. Tell her not to forget her friends.

1. Nicholas Longworth planted vineyards on the hillsides of Mt. Adams in Cincinnati. His Catawba and Isabella wines won prizes during the 1840s. In the 1850s, however, the wines were attacked by a fungus. By 1862 when Lytle asked for Longworth's, its wine production was minimal. Shortly afterward it ceased entirely. See Linda Walker Stevens, "Old Nick: Cincinnati Winemaker," *Timeline* 13 (2): 24-35 (March/April 1996).

### *To Joanna Reilly*

Bardstown Feb 28th 1862

Dr Aunt

This is the last day of winter—and a beautiful day it is. This afternoon—as it is the day for Inspection—I review the Mich Regt and having a few moments of leisure this morning I concluded to drop you a line.

In case I am ordered off from here—I shall send home my new military overcoat by Express—retaining the *cape* & my old one. The weather will be getting warm and I shall not need it. My black horse will not be well for at least several weeks & if suddenly relieved I shall have to leave him behind. I am *very* sorry, but must do the best I can.

My leg still troubles me but I can get along— My general health I am glad to say continues good.

I am very sorry to hear of Aunt Martha's illness and hope most sincerely that this may find her in improved health.

My best regards to her & Aunt Sallie Bullock. Remember me also to Dr & Mrs Ritter. If I remain here any time I intend to send you a photograph of my quarters.

Why dont the girls send me a few of my own photographs. I have promised several & want them forward also my *Bill.* I was in great hopes the Doctor would have run down to see me. The hospitals here might have interested him.

They are thinning out the troops here very fast, and I suppose eventually will leave only a small force here.

In front of my quarters is a large square, in the centre of which stands the old Court House. Every evening at *Retreat* (Sunset) the Post Band comes out and plays four or five airs.

This has become quite a *feature* under my administration. In fine weather a great many ladies generally congregate to hear the music. This *was* a strong secession town—very much under Southern influence, but I think we are becoming rather favorites. It is *possible* that I may have to run up to Louisville soon for a few hours to see the *Paymaster*. I wish I knew *when* as I was in *hopes* some of the family might meet me there. How are the little ones?

How I should like to see them and dear Joe. It looks *a little* as if the war might soon be terminated but not without I suspect more bloody battles. The loss of her son was a terrible blow to poor Mrs Rowan. He was her favorite son and I *found* him here full of life and animation. He had more business talent decidedly than either of the other boys—one of whom is off in the secession army.

"The Professor" is in pretty good health, though I think, a little home sick.[1] Remember me to everybody who does not forget me & Believe me dr Aunt

Most Affly
William H Lytle

1. Lytle refers again to his personal servant, John Wilson.

### To Josephine Lytle Foster and Elizabeth Lytle Broadwell

*Lytle often supplemented mail with telegrams, especially when he arrived at new locations or received orders to depart. Although his leg remained troublesome, he had received orders to join the Tenth Ohio near Nashville.*

[March 1, 1862]
Louisville Saturday
4 P.M

My dear Sisters

I am much disappointed that none of the family are here to meet me as I telegraphed on Thursday—the message I suppose miscarried. My orders are to regain my Regt without delay. I expect to leave on a Nashville boat to night though she *may* not get off until tomorrow.

Everything passed off well at Bardstown and H^dQuarters to day were very polite.

The Boat will I hope be pleasanter than the cars. In fact I could not get over the R.Road with my horse & did not wish to be separated from it. My *black* I had to leave with Mr Bukham.

My leg has been *very painful* for two or three days & I have sent for D^r Colescott whom I expect every minute.

Joe's pomades never arrived. unless my leg gets better I dont know what I shall do. I will write to you as soon as I get to Nashville.

Love to All

In much haste

Most Aff^ly
Will
Louisville
March
En route for Nashville

## To Josephine Lytle Foster

[March 6, 1862]
Louisville Thursday Evening

My beloved Sister

Uncle & Aunt Charlotte got here this morning. They have driven out to the Artesian Well & have not yet returned. I was truly glad to see them. My leg I think is better, and I hope to get off about Tuesday. I shall have two days & a half on the River for nursing. My desire to get down is very great as my orders are to move on "without delay" & I fear my stay here may be unfortunate. Of course however I shall not report unless unable to do duty.

Mrs Steele has been kind as possible & last evening I was honored by a visit from Mr & Mrs Pettit, Eliza Thompson & Lettie Thurston. Uncle & Aunt will give you all the news on yr return. I see by the paper that *two* more *Brigadiers* have been approved from Ohio. One of them Sander Pratt a man whose Reg entered V^a, as I left it. If *politics* are to control promotion the Army will be rapidly thinned out.

Of course my dear Sister being shut up in my room I have little of interest to communicate— Poor Fosdick! I was much affected by his death & feel as if he had left a vacancy in my circle of friends which can never be filled.[1]

He was a true friend of mine. I hope you are all well. Kiss Auntie & the children for me. Tell Nannie I am going to see "the brave Montgomeries."

Hoping to hear again from you dear Joe before my departure—as I know how inconvenient it will be for you to leave home—believe me with kind regards to the Doctor.

Yr Aff<sup>e</sup> Brother<br>
Will

1. Lytle's circle of close friends included William W. Fosdick, a poet, playwright, novelist, and lawyer, who was born in Cincinnati on January 28, 1825. Fosdick's mother, Julia Drake, had been a famous actress; his father was a banker and merchant. Fosdick initially attended Cincinnati College, but graduated from Transylvania University in Lexington, Kentucky, before studying law with Garret Duncan and Judge Pryor of Louisville. He practiced law in Covington, Kentucky, until 1851 when he went to New York. In the late 1850s he returned to Cincinnati and his beloved West. Fosdick is credited with recognizing the merits of Lytle's poem "Antony and Cleopatra" and arranging for its publication in 1858. Fosdick died after a brief illness—disease of the heart combined with paralysis. See *Cincinnati Daily Gazette*, March 10, 1862, and William T. Coggeshall, *Poets and Poetry of the West, with Biographical and Critical Notices* (New York: Follett, Foster & Co., 1864), 471-76.

### To Elizabeth Lytle Broadwell

[Undated but probably March 11, 1862]<br>
Tuesday night<br>
11 P.M.

My beloved Sister

Your letter & Uncle's were sent up about an hour since to my great delight. I shall not go home to Cin<sup>ati</sup> unless it becomes *absolutely necessary* to have my *leave* extended. If my limb continues to improve I expect to leave for Nashville about next Monday or Tuesday. Everything however depends on *that*. I am very much averse to asking for more time and was sadly disappointed that I could not go right on though happy also that I will see some of you. I *should* have gone on lame as I was, had it not been for the positive opinions not only of the Med Director D<sup>r</sup> Pe[rrin], but also of D<sup>r</sup> Goldsmith, D<sup>r</sup> Hines and D<sup>r</sup> Flynt, *all* of whom were consulted before I would *cave*. For what purpose Providence has *halted* me here I know not, but doutless it is *all well*.

Had it been possible for me to have done any *good* at Nashville I would have proceeded in the teeth of all the Doctors in Louisville but common sense forbade me to fling myself as a dead weight on the advancing columns.

The very moment I can do duty I shall leave, though if I get off by Monday or Tuesday it will be doing well.

My love to dear Jodie Auntie the dear little pets and my good friend & brother in law the Doctor. Sam I shall see here. I trust sincerely the Dr⁵ family are recuperating.

Do not forget my warmest regards to Dr Thompson. I hope if I survive these wars he will always be my fast friend & counsellor.

If you run down on Friday or Saturday (or before then) can you not bring some one of my young lady friends with you— The trip is a pleasant one & there are some handsome officers at the Hotel— Besides it would be far more agreeable for *you*. My regards to Miss Sharley Pendleton.

Good night dear Bessie. Hoping to see you soon and feeling that in *that* anticipation as always in this world the bitterness of delay here is mingled with the sweet.

Believe me
Yr affec Brother
*WmHLytle*

### To Anna Haines Foster

Louisville March 16th 1862

Dear Little Nannie¹

Uncle Will was charmed with your letter. It *was* very foolish in Seybest to run from a little boy like Johnnie, but then if Johnnie had a gun, he might have shot a very big man with it, just as David killed old Goliath with a sling.

Uncle is going to Nashville today to help fight the rebels and he will not see his little niece for a long while.

She must take good care of Mamma & brother & Auntie & Papa. When Uncle comes back from the war he expects Nannie will be able to read & write and will bring her a beautiful present.

Good bye
Uncle Will

1. Anna Haines Foster (Nannie) was five years old when Lytle wrote his niece this touching letter. The eldest of Josephine Lytle Foster's three children to reach adulthood, Nannie was the only one who knew her famous uncle. Her brother John Moorehead Foster, referred to in this letter, was three at the time. He died in August 1872 from a heart condition.

## To Joanna Reilly

*At this point Lytle had received unofficial word that he would command the Seventeenth Brigade, Third Division, Army of the Ohio. Brig. Gen. Ormsby Mitchel, a professor at Cincinnati College when Lytle was a student there, commanded the Third Division. The Seventeenth Brigade consisted of the Forty-second Indiana, the Fifteenth Kentucky, and the Third Ohio, along with the Tenth Ohio.*

Nashville Sunday<br>March 23<sup>d</sup> 1862

My dear Aunt

I have only time to drop you a line. We arrived here this morning having had a very delightful trip. My leg is better though not yet well. We had several very pleasant ladies on board. Among others Mrs Gen Crittenden who was placed in my charge.

Gen Mitchels Div——— is 40 miles from here at Murfreesborough. I shall leave as soon as I can find an escort—*possibly* in a few hours. Gen Dumont is here.[1] I am assigned, Capt Fry tells me to the command of the Brigade. If my wound becomes no worse hope all will go well— With love to the dear girls Uncle Foster Sam & all.

In great haste

Most affly<br>Will

1. Ebenezer Dumont (1814-1871) was a native of Indiana, a lawyer, and a state legislator. He commanded the Seventeenth Brigade, Third Division, Army of the Ohio, from December 22, 1861, through March 21, 1862.

## To Josephine Lytle Foster and Elizabeth Lytle Broadwell

*On March 22, 1862, after returning from a trip to Louisville to see Lytle, Broadwell wrote her brother a long letter. She indicated they had calculated that he had reached Nashville on March 21. Though she said to burn the letter, Lytle carefully preserved it. Broadwell reported on the naming of several brigadier generals and seemingly attributed his lack of inclusion to her brother's propensity for drink. Saying "It cannot pain you half as much to read this my brother as it does me to write it." She noted that she had his welfare more at heart than he did himself. "But when you know that promotions—respect & everything you are ambitious of awaits your abstaining from the vile poison it is incomprehesible to me why you have not moral courage to abandon it forever."[1]*

H<sup>d</sup> Quarters 17th Brigade
Camp Van Buren
Murfreesborough Tenn
Saturday night March 29th 1862

My dear Sisters

I wrote Aunt a hurried note from Nashville & also telegraphed. As Lt. Lacy expects to leave for home tomorrow I determined to send a letter by him. I left Nashville last Wednesday with an escort of 25 men from the 7<sup>th</sup> Penn<sup>a</sup> and arrived at this point about five o'clock in the evening. I came on, in an ambulance—Guthrie driving as I wished to save my leg as much as possible. The distance from Nashville is about 40 miles. As I approached the camp I saw the regiment advancing to meet me—It was a beautiful day. They halted, faced to the front and as I rode down the line (having taken the precaution to mount my horse a few miles out—my reception was *terrific* I assure you. *Such cheering* I have not heard for a long time.[2] I am now in command of the 17th Brigade & am just comfortably established in quarters.

Last night was my first under canvass for a long time & I slept soundly—for the first time in a week. Feather beds dont agree with me. My first two nights I slept at the house of Mr Bell—a son of the Hon John Bell[3]—who was exceedingly polite. There is a great deal of wealth here—in fact the whole country thus far between here & Nashville is *beautiful.*

Gen Mitchell & Staff Burke & I took supper last evening at Mr *Lytle's.* He is one of the wealthiest men in Tenn<sup>ee</sup>. Has a splendid house, any quantity of negroes, a *third* wife, 3000 acres of land worth a $100 per acre and *sixteen* children. In fact the Lytle's are scattered all round town and fine plantations in every direction.

I went out today to select a drill ground some three miles from camp. Saw a fine meadow & on enquiring of an old negro whose it was, was informed it was young Master *Bob Lytles."* "And whose is *that"* "Young Master *William Lytle's"*—I began to feel at home.

Old David Lytle the "paterfamiliae" gave me a warm reception. Says he met my father in Nashville many years ago—that they compared notes & that we are *kin* beyond a doubt. He is connected with the Foster family of Nashville. In fact old Ephraim Foster the old U.S. Senator married his sister. You know the Rowans always said Ephraim Foster was kin.

The family seems to be one of great wealth & influence & connected with the first families in Tenn. The supper last night was *really elegant.* To my utter surprise the old man seemed perfectly posted about *you* &

knew to whom you were *married!*— And who do you think was his informant. Why no less a personage than Capt Wm Lytle Blanchard of Gen Crittendens staff[3]—who together with the general was quartered with him a few weeks since! I got last night to my great surprise just as I was starting to his house a letter from "Lt Frank H Lytle 18 Tenn Regt" now a prisoner of war at Camp Chase Columbus Ohio. The lieutenant (adjutant I believe of the Regt) claims kin & wants me to help him secure a liberation on *parole.* I have any quantity of news to tell you but am so wearied by a hard days work that I must go to bed as it is very late. I have received both your letters written since Lilys return to Cin[ati]. I will number my letters so that you may know if any miscarry. Do write often dear girls & write *cheerful* letters if you *can*— I have been interrupted & it is now after midnight— Give my love to dear Aunt Ann. Tell Uncle I will write him next. I do not know how long we will be here.

If I had time I could write much interesting matter as to the tone of the people &c but must close. Josie's *pomade* I found *here* all safe. I forgot to tell you that my command is composed of the 10th, 3[d] Ohio Col Beatty (Marrow's old Regt)[5]—15th Ky Col Pope & 42 In[a] Col Jones formerly Atty Gen of In[a]. Grover is A. A. A. G. Capt Clark of Louisville the old Pres[t] of Union Club Brig. Com[g], Muscroft Brig Surgeon. His aides not yet appointed. I have besides as boot orderlies Guthrie & Robb—two clerks from the 10th & 16 mounted orderlies from Kennetts Cavalry— Good bye.

Will

1. Elizabeth Lytle Broadwell to William H. Lytle, March 22, 1862, LP, box 31, no. 92.

2. Ella Pirtle shared with Lily Broadwell her brother Alfred's description of Colonel Lytle's return to the Tenth. Lytle gave a "beautiful speech," and "In one tremendous shout the boys gave utterance to their love and admiration for their gallant leader, following it by cheer upon cheer . . . company after company paid their tribute to a leader they are perfectly devoted to." Ella Pirtle to Elizabeth Lytle Broadwell, April 7, 1862, LP, box 34, no. 745.

3. John Bell (1797-1869), a lawyer and politician from Tennessee, was the candidate for president on the Constitutional Union Party ticket in 1860.

4. Gen. George Bibb Crittenden, a Kentucky native, commanded the Confederate District of East Tennessee from December 8, 1861, until February 23, 1862, and the Second Division, Army of Central Kentucky, Department #2, from February 23 until April 1, 1862. Blanchard is mentioned later as serving on General Johnston's staff, so he was a member of the Confederate Army.

5. Isaac H. Marrow entered military service in April 1861 as captain, Company A, Third Ohio. He accepted appointment as colonel, Third Ohio, Volunteer Infantry, on June 12, 1861. On that same day John Beatty was appointed lieutenant colonel, Third Ohio Volunteer Infantry.

*To Elizabeth Lytle Broadwell*

[Undated but probably written in
Murfreesboro, Tennessee,
about March 30, 1862]

Lil— tell Miss Sharley Pendleton that I want her photograph—
Ask Uncle to write my friend Mr Bukham at Bardstown care Capt
Alexander U.S.A & enquire about his black horse— I am most anxious
to get him up before we move on. He can readily reach me *here*—ship
him by water to Nashville by a safe man who can ride him down. I *hope*
he may be well by this time. Horses here are scarce & very expensive— If
anything can be done for Lt Lytle at Columbus conveniently—why *do it.*

*To Josephine Lytle Foster*

(Private) No. 3
Murfreesborough
April 2ᵈ 1862

My dear Josie— I rec'd your very welcome letter last night and one this
evening from Uncle. Gen Mitchel just sent for me to know *how soon the
Brigade could move.* We shall probably leave *tomorrow for Shelbyville.*
    I have only time for a hurried line as it is now 10 o'clock. Tell
Uncle Smith my sorrel is the handsomest horse in the Division & holds
out gallantly. I enclose two letters, one from a *cousin* & one from Secy
Chase. My letter to the latter was marked *private.* He ought not to have
shown it but *let her slide.* I read it to Sam who will tell you its contents. I
have got along thus far very smoothly. My review the other day was
*Superb.* I *do* wish you & Lily could have seen it here 3500 men were on
line, the weather is delightful as warm as our June, and the whole
country in bloom. You can imagine my beloved Sister that I have a
thousand things to do tonight & have no time to devote to the dear
friends at home. As I know you are anxious as to my health I am happy
to say that it is improving daily— My leg has come out wonderfully
though I have been constantly in the saddle. I trust it will soon be
entirely well— Do not repeat what I write the family of army movements.
    Good bye my dear Sister. Kiss all for me.

Most affly
Will

### To Elizabeth Lytle Broadwell

*Lytle wrote this hastily scribbled note just hours before the Tenth Ohio left Murfreesboro for Shelbyville.*

April 3d

Guthrie tore up my letters last night & threw them out—which accounts for their appearance— You will have to tack them together the best way you can— we move in a few hours— Good bye.

### To Josephine Lytle Foster and Elizabeth Lytle Broadwell

H$^d$ Q$^{rs}$ 17$^{th}$ Brigade
Camp Harrison
Shelbyville April 6th 1862

My dear Sisters. *The mail* has just arrived at my quarters, and amongst the letters—was *one* for *me* from dear Jodie— If you only *knew* how joyfully a letter is received I am sure you would not fail to remember me in that way, as often as possible.—

It is Sunday night. Grover & my aid *St John* (3$^d$ Ohio)[1] are both busy writing home. The band of the 10th has just retired from the front of my tent where they gave me an elegant serenade just before tattoo. They played the "Anvil Chorus" and an air from "Lucia 'di' Lammermoor" exquisitely.

The day has been delightful. At least a hundred ladies & gentlemen came out to see our dress parades. They were delighted. In fact our reception here has been *most cordial.* I have no time for visiting but have received to day, at least a dozen invitations to dinner. Our troops have conducted themselves with the greatest propriety and are winning golden opinions from even the Seceshs. Before this reaches you I think you will have heard of a great battle on Mississippi.[2] What our chances for a fight are I hardly know. The people here had all read the accounts of the Carnifex fight, and, gave me today a hearty reception. They thought I was killed. I told them "not *permanently* and that I had brought down my own remains." My tent today was thronged with people, ladies and gentlemen. You can hardly imagine how delighted the union people are to see *us.* They have been under a reign of terror and many of them have behaved *nobly.* A most intelligent people they are too. An exceedingly well bred & highly educated population with few provincialisms. A people of whom our country may be proud.

I do not think we will be here long. I rec'd the letter with poor Fosdicks photograph. How life like it is!

My camp is perfectly beautiful and the whole command in excellent health and spirits. The loss of my horse is a great misfortune to me, though the sorrel holds out admirably.

*Robb* is with me again as *clerk*. Guthrie & Reardon are my orderlies. I have a mounted escort of 16 men a sergeant corporal & lieutenant com^g from Kennetts[3] Cavalry. These with Grover Fanning Clark Muscroft & St John compose my military family. Give my love to dear Aunt Ann. I shall feel greatly worried about Bessie until I hear from home again.

Do what you can for Lt Lytle of the Tenn^ee Regiment. His fathers present & third wife is a very lady like little woman—a Marylander & (tell Aunt) a niece of Miss Romamia Dashiell—whom I can just remember. The Lytles in Tenn seem to be a family of large means & very well connected. Remember me to Sharley Pendleton who has yet to—well never mind, but give her my compliments.

Remember me *particularly* to Gallagher, Dr Thompson the Archbishop— Tell the old ladies I dont forget them and if I ever get home will spin them long yarns about Dixie.

My limb is almost entirely well & gives me little trouble. When I got to Murfreesborough Muscroft applied on decoction[4] of *white oak bark* which had a magical effect produced I suppose by the *tannin*. I spent two nights at Murfreesborough at the house of Mr. Bell—a son of Hon John Bell's— He was a courteous and a most agreeable gentleman. He did me the honor to say that my appointment as military Gov of Tennessee would give far greater satisfaction to the people than Andy Johnstons! He is a very conservative man—differs with his father & we became really attached to each other. I could not see him to say good bye but was told that when the 10th moved he almost shed tears.

The regiment had guarded his house & been very polite to him. Everybody almost styles me *General* and I have got along very smoothly & pleasantly thus far. What is the Govt going to do? However—if I discharge my duty to "God & the Country" the rank is a secondary matter. I *wanted* to go to church today but *could* not. Rest assured my dear sisters that I try to live up to the golden rule to love God & my neighbor as myself and that if I either hate or fear any man, I do not know it—

With kindest regards to all believe me my dear girls

Most devotedly
Yr affec^e Bro
William H. Lytle

1. Lytle probably refers to James St. John, first lieutenant in Company I, Third Ohio.

2. Lytle refers to the battle of Shiloh, which was beginning when he wrote on April 6, 1862.

3. Lytle refers to Col. John Kennett, commander of the Fourth Ohio Cavalry. At one point in the conflict, C.S.A. general John Hunt Morgan assumed the identity of Colonel Kennett for the purposes of crossing Union lines. See James A. Ramage, *Rebel Raider: The Life of John Hunt Morgan* (Lexington, Ky.: Univ. Press of Kentucky, 1986), 48.

4. *The Random House Dictionary of the English Language,* 2d unabridged ed. (New York, 1987), defines *decoction* as: "a. an extract obtained by decocting. b. water in which a crude vegetable drug has been boiled and which therefore contains the constituents or principles of the substance soluble in boiling water."

### To Josephine Lytle Foster

*Lytle received orders to move to Huntsville, Alabama, to help secure that town, a strategic transportation center close to the Tennessee River at Decatur, Alabama, where the Memphis and Charleston Railroad met the Nashville and Decatur Railroad. In a short note dated April 13, Lytle wrote Josephine Foster that to his "great disgust" his own letter had come back to him the previous evening, along with one from her. He also noted that a small portion of his brigade fought and repulsed the enemy on April 11.*

Fayetteville Ap 14th 62

Dear Sister.

We march to day at 3 for Huntsville— Good bye! I do not know when I can write again— I recd your letters *two last night—Ail* I think.

Good bye my dear sister— Kiss dear Lily who I *hope* is better.

Hoping we all may meet again in health & happiness—with kind regards to Uncle Todd (whose letter also came to hand ) with love to Aunt Reilly.

Most Affly<br>WHLytle

### To Josephine Lytle Foster and Elizabeth Lytle Broadwell

*Although Lytle arrived in Huntsville about April 14, he had no time to write immediately. On May 1 and 2 he was involved in operations near Athens, Mooresville, Limestone Bridge, and Elk River, Alabama, where Mitchel's division sought to control the Athens and Decatur road. To facilitate opening up the cotton trade, Mitchel planned to post brigades at Stevenson, Huntsville, and Athens.[1] Lytle, who had been in command at Bridgeport, received orders to occupy Huntsville.*

*In the meantime, Lytle received several letters from family members. On April 10, Broadwell reported that Sharley Pendleton had refused to send her photograph as she had made a rule not to give it to "any" gentleman. However, Pendleton had sent a new march for the band, called "Wollenhaupts Grande Marche de Concert." Broadwell also expressed dismay that Lytle had written to Pendleton from Bardstown. In Lily Broadwell's opinion, Pendleton lacked respect in town and Will compromised his dignity by corresponding with her.² It is clear from his letters that Lytle enjoyed Pendleton's friendship whether his sister approved or not.*

*April letters from home also reported that Lytle's sisters sent him two boxes of one hundred collars each, the latest Harper & Leslie, and current newspapers. They expressed their gratitude that Lytle was not involved in the battle at Pittsburgh Landing, part of the Shiloh campaign. Broadwell's letter dated April 14 indicates that her husband, Sam, learned from a telegraph operator that Lytle had captured Huntsville on April 12. Meanwhile, Smith Haines continued to search for another horse for his nephew because Mr. Bukham said Lytle's black horse would "never be fit for service again." Haines also worried about how he would be able to ship a horse to Lytle now that he had left Shelbyville.*

May
Huntsville Tuesday 6ᵗʰ 1862

My beloved Sisters. As near as I can remember I arrived in this town about the 14th of last month. Since that time my life has been one of constant activity and *incessant unremitting* toil. My command has been *oscillating* from Decatur to Bridgeport. Never in my life have I done so much hard *work* nor have I ever seen in Mexico or Western Vᵃ such laborious campaigning. As it is quite possible this letter may fall into the hands of our friends on the *other side* you must not expect a resumé of military movements. What we have been about in the last fortnight may probably leak out into the newspapers. I arrived here on Friday night last from Bridgeport after a most fatiguing march. *There* I commanded the reserves. The enemy made no fight but retreated precipitably across the river, destroying one of the bridges. We captured two pieces of artillery a secesh flag (which I have in my trunk) a considerable quantity of stores a rebel mail 40 or 50 prisoners from a Georgia Regt &c &c.

The Gen put me in command here immediately on my arrival. His own Hᵈ Quarters are near mine. My camp to night looks as picturesque (under the May moon silvering the magnificent grove that shadows it) as some garden scene in "Maude."

*Huntsville* is one of the most beautiful towns in America. It reminds me somewhat of Jalapa. There is a great deal of wealth here. The private residences very elegant & embowered in shrubbery & surrounded with fine gardens. The air is so laden with perfume they *called* it I am told the "Happy Valley."

Alas! It is no Happy Valley now. The desolating footstep of the war has gone over it and it will tell with pallid lips in years to come the bloody history of this accursed rebellion.

Brig. Gen. William Haines Lytle. (Courtesy of the Cincinnati Historical Society)

*Above left,* William Lytle (1770-1831), grandfather of William Haines Lytle.
*Above right,* Eliza Stahl Lytle (1779-1821), grandmother of William Haines Lytle.
*Left,* Margaret Smith Haines Lytle (1772-1851), grandmother of William Haines Lytle.
(All courtesy of the Cincinnati Historical Society)

Gen. Don Carlos Buell.
(Courtesy of Photo
Antiquities)

Gen. Lovell H. Rousseau.
(Courtesy of Photo
Antiquities)

Gen. Ormsby
Macknight Mitchel.
(Courtesy of the
Cincinnati Historical
Society)

Gen. William S. Rosecrans.
(Courtesy of Photo Antiquities)

Gen. Philip H. Sheridan.
(Courtesy of Photo
Antiquities)

*Above*, Spaulding Hall in Bardstown, Kentucky, was one of the St. Joseph's College buildings occupied by Lytle's forces. (Photograph by the author) *Right*, William Haines Lytle Monument in Spring Grove Cemetery, Cincinnati, Ohio. (Courtesy of the Cincinnati Historical Society) *Below*, Chickamauga Battlefield Memorial to William Haines Lytle. (Courtesy of John L. Carter)

I hear that *Blanchard*[3] distinguished himself at Corinth. I think they told me he was acting on Gen Sidney Johnstons staff that day.

Fred Mitchel called on me to day. He was captured you know at Pulaski by Col Jno Morgan. He speaks in the highest terms of the courtesy with which the Col treated him. Morgan is certainly a gallant gentleman—A man quite after my own heart.[4]

My dear Sisters I have not heard from you for nearly three weeks— It seems an age. Some of your letters have no doubt been captured, as I know of two mails we have lost within a week. I telegraphed Uncle several days since & hope he got the despatch. It was simply "all well." If you do not hear from me do not be alarmed.

The Govt I think treats me badly but I make no complaint and shall attempt to discharge my whole duty to God and the country without swerving either to the right or left—leaving in case I fall the people my beloved countrymen to do justice to me.

As yet in this great gloom I see no light in the skies but relying implicitly on the infinte wisdom of God, submit the vexed problem to *Him* knowing all *will be well.* To my friends at home to Aunt Ann & Uncle & Aunt Charlotte & the old ladies remember me most affly. My health is good enough though I am much *worn* by hardship & exposure & *look* I fear a little haggard & used up. The occupation of the line with our small force is a herculean task & the neglect to send re-inforcements seems to me a *crime.* But by the grace of God we will hold our own or if we die, *die* in our tracks with *harness on.*

Hoping however that our erring and misguided but brave & glorious countrymen of the South may soon weary of their unnatural war & return to their old flag once more.

Believe me dear sisters yr devoted Bro

*Will Lytle*

1. *O.R.,* ser. 1, vol. 10, pt. 1, 876-78, Report of Maj. Gen. Ormsby M. Mitchel to Maj. Gen. D.C. Buell, May 2, 1862.

2. Elizabeth Lytle Broadwell to William H. Lytle, April 10, [1862], LP, box 31, no. 93.

3. Lytle refers to events in early April 1862 when Gen. Albert Sidney Johnston was killed leading an attack on Union forces at Shiloh, Tennessee. After the Confederates were driven back, they withdrew to Corinth, Mississippi.

4. Lytle was a romantic and admired the equally romantic and daring John Hunt Morgan. Morgan lived in Lexington, Kentucky, between the Mexican and Civil Wars. In 1857 he raised the Lexington Rifles, a militia group. He was known for his daring raids in Kentucky and Tennessee. In September 1862 Morgan's Raiders threatened Cincinnati.

*To Josephine Lytle Foster and Elizabeth Lytle Broadwell*

Head Quarters U S forces
Huntsville Ala May 28th 1862

My beloved Sisters

*When* I wrote you last I do not remember for the past four or five weeks—in truth since I rejoined the regiment & assumed command of the Brigade I have been working harder than a darkey on a cotton plantation. I cant attempt in the few leisure moments I have to day to give you any history of my campaign. Gen Mitchel is now absent and I am commanding in his place & write you today from his tent. I am suffering a little from overwork & exertion, but otherwise feel pretty well.

No wonder I feel a little wearied, as *four* most fatiguing expeditions have followed rapidly on each other. First the expedition to Decatur of which I read a published account in the Gazzette just received from you—then *away*, the other end of the line to Bridgeport with a night march of ten miles *on foot* with my game leg, over the cross ties of the railroad—then an expedition which I commanded through Athens toward Elk River acting in conjunction with Negleys column from Pulaski and last & most exhausting of all the expedition to Stevenson from which I returned last Saturday night.[1]

I had hoped on my return to have a little rest but suddenly find myself in command of the Division with its immense responsibilities.

My dear girls I have not written you often because really I have had no time. My thoughts are with you constantly. A large number of your letters have no doubt been captured.

All of Josies between no. 4 & no. 13 are missing! I have recd very few of Lillie's. In fact I have heard if I remember correctly but twice from you in the past month.

Dear Uncle's affliction I hear of today for the *first time*. I am profoundly grieved. Do keep me advised constantly as to his condition. I trust it may be a slight attack which will soon pass over. Poor *Rives!* Poor Landon! I loved him very much with all his faults. I hear of his death for the first time today through your letters by Ferguson. And dear Aunt & the old ladies & Aunt Charlotte & the Doctor & Sam! how are they all? How gladly would I hail the return of peace—honorable peace—once more which would enable us all to meet again.

For our military operations I must refer you to the papers. Dr

Malone was absent from Athens when I passed through & *I* was away at Winchester last week when *he* was here. His family is a *very influential & respectable* one. Always treat Malone well girls. I found he had spoken of me in the handsomest terms at Athens & made a special request of his family that if any chance ever threw me in Athens in his absence—to treat me with every courtesy. To my great disgust I found that his two sisters had been *plundered* of every thing they had in his house by some of Turchin's brutal soldiery[2]— *Say nothing of this* however—it can do no good now & might do harm.

The days here are very hot—but you will hardly believe that the nights are so cold I still sleep under a blanket & my buffalo robe!

Between the people & the officers in a *social* way—there is no intercourse whatever— the women are *venomous.*

I have seen the *inside* of but one gentlemans house since I came here & he a Kentuckian. I met a couple of weeks ago Mrs Judge—I forget her name now— She *was* Laura Chenoweth. I was riding by her house—recognized her, stopped & shook hands— She told me she did not intend to revisit Cin[ati] until she could go back "independent"—did not ask me to call again. We hear rumors of a clash on every hand—our communications as you know have been interfered with. the whole division is overworked.

I am looking anxiously for news from Corinth. God bless you dear children—remember me to the little ones Nannie & John. Tell Miss Charlotte Pendleton I have a flag for her in my trunk and that her music (is it not *too bad*) never arrived—Probably captured en route. Do not be discouraged that your letters failed to reach me. Write often—It is all the comfort I have. With love to dear Aunt Ann Uncle Smith Aunt Charlotte & the whole family.

Most Affly—Brother Will

1. Ormsby Mitchel's report dated May 15, 1862, said he placed Lytle in command of a force to move from Athens and engage the enemy's attention at the mouth of the Elk River. Lytle's expedition, intended as a feint, was successful because it allowed troops commanded by General Negley to make a surprise attack on the rebels. On May 18 Mitchel sent three hundred men from the Ninth Brigade under Lytle's command toward Winchester. When they arrived there the morning of May 24, rebels troops were dispersed following a skirmish. Lytle returned to Huntsville on May 24. (See *O.R.,* ser. 1, vol. 10, pt. 1, 891-94.)

2. Lytle refers to then Col. John Basil Turchin who, while occupying Athens, Alabama, had let his troops run wild after they were fired upon by civilians when advancing.

*To Ezekial S. Haines*

H^d Quarters U S forces June 1^st 1862
Huntsville Ala

My dear Uncle. It is only within a day or two that I heard of your illness.[1] I am delighted to learn from a letter of Sister Joe's received yesterday that your health is improving. In truth her letter of yesterday gave me the first intelligible history of your attack. Before this reaches you I trust you may be about again and soon restored to your usual health and spirits. I shall feel anxious however to hear of you & hope the family will keep me constantly advised until you can again write yourself. I think now our line of communications will be safer & that we shall lose fewer mails.

We have rumors today that the enemy has fallen back from Corinth and are awaiting the particulars with great anxiety.

All the regiments of my Brigade are now here and the command having been uniformed recently looks magnificently.

Our duty however is *very* arduous. I hope the country gives the Division credit. It deserves it. A week ago today I returned from a forced march to Winchester. My force was about 650 infy—detachments from the 17th & 9th Brigades 4 pieces of artillery—two Parrots guns—& about 80 horse. With this force I drove the enemy estimated at 1600 strong (cavalry) to the mountains with a loss on their side of 30 or 40 killed & wounded. The expedition was successful, but terribly fatiguing, as I marched the first day *50* odd miles in 24 hours. My men were mounted in wagons and we went like a blue streak!

*Twice* also during that time we were formed in order of battle.

Wise and paternal treatment can I think bring this people back to their allegiance. It is a splendid people. We cannot afford to lose them from the Union. The great trouble of the South is its utter misconception of the true sentiments of the northern masses on the subject of slavery.

I fear there have been greivous mistakes made on our side but pray God that all may yet come right. Gen Mc is temporarily absent and I am in command. The days are very hot—but although the sun's rays are oppressive there is generally a fine breeze & the nights are cool.

My little sorrel holds out wonderfully. I should not advise a horse being sent me at present. The sorrel smelt gunpowder for the first time at Winchester & at Bridgeport & Decatur I was dismounted but stood in the midst of the artillery like a veteran.

Our camps here are very beautiful and I know of no locality in the south more desirable than Huntsville for a summer's Headquarters.

Gen Mitchel recommended Sill Turchin & myself a month ago for promotion but as yet the Govt makes no sign.[2] Still suffering to some extent from wound and discharging as I have ever since I left home the duties of Brigade & Division Commander it seems very unjust, that I should have such additional labors & great responsibilities without the rank.

If my life is spared though—and my health—I shall be "in at the death" as I was at the birth of this rebellion and retire to peaceful life, *and rest* which I ardently crave—with the approbation of my own conscience & I hope that of my beloved friends and countrymen.

My time being much occupied today I must close—

Remember me especially to my good friends Todd Dr Thompson— Tom Gallagher Judge Storer the Archbishop father Collins & the family generally.

Hoping my dear Uncle to see you again—both you and Aunt Charlotte to whom give my love—in good health and assuring you of my sincere appreciation of your kindness & affection for me manifested in a hundred ways from boyhood up.

I remain
Yr affc nephew
*Wm H Lytle*

1. Ezekial Haines looked on William Haines Lytle as a son. The bond between the two men, professional and personal, ran deep. The exact nature of Haines' illness is not known, but he never recovered fully prior to his death in April 1865.

2. Lytle was named brigadier general, USV, March 17, 1863, with rank to November 29, 1862. John Basil Turchin was promoted to brigadier general, USV, August 6, 1862 (with rank to July 17, 1862). Sill refers to Joshua Woodrow Sill who commanded the Ninth Brigade, Third Division, Army of the Ohio, from December 2, 1861, until August 10, 1862.

## To Governor David Tod

*Commanders often wrote government leaders requesting promotions for their subordinates or to support requests for promotion initiated by others. Here is an example of Lytle's support for two officers in the Third Ohio.[1]*

Head Quarters 17th Brigade
Camp Taylor Huntsville, Ala
June 4th 1862

Governor Tod
Sir

I am informed that the friends of Col JW Keifer and Capt Jno G Mitchell of the 3d Ohio are presenting the names of those gentlemen for appointments in the new regiments now organizing or about to be organized in Ohio. The 3ᵈ Ohio at present constitutes a portion of my command, and I know no men in the service worthier of promotion than the above named officers. Though I should regret personally their transfer from the Brigade and feel it to be a loss to my command I know at the same time that they both have earned advancement and that the general interests of the service would be promoted by giving to each a wider scope of authority and usefulness.

I beg you to believe Sir that I am somewhat chary of my recommendations just now and when I say that Lt Col Keifer and Capt Mitchell are active, energetic, and accomplished soldiers and gentlemen who in any position they occupy will reflect honor on the service the State & themselves—I mean it.

I am Sir
Yrs Resly
WH Lytle
Col

1. This letter is in the Dreer Collection at the Historical Society of Pennsylvania.

*To Josephine Lytle Foster*

Head Quarters 17th Brigade
Camp Taylor Huntsville Ala
June 5th 1862

My dear Josie— A couple of nights ago an old mail that has been floating all round the country at *last* came into *port,* and I had the extreme satisfaction of receiving nearly a *half dozen* of letters from you alone—among them your copies of the Archbishops & Col Swayne's letters, two or three from Uncle & last not least Miss Charley Pendletons music for the Band. My *stack* of letters was enormous and I was quite the envy of the staff. Since my Winchester expedition my command has had comparative rest—that is we have been *here* all the time. I always have my hands full however. Today I took an engine & special train & ran down to the Junction, that is the junction of *this* with the Athens road to visit my pickets & guards along the railway, for all that portion of the road is under my special care. The General told me the other that he had written to his daughter to come down here & wanted Lily to come also— I said nothing to *him* but *between ourselves dont think* of such a

thing *for a moment*. If I thought that you or Lily meditated such a long
& perilous trip I *should* not have a *moments rest*. We seem for aught that
yet appears as far from peace as ever— We are surrounded by enemies—
the opposite bank of the Tenn—only ten miles distant swarms with rebel
cavalry and for *ladies* to undertake a trip here when at any moment we
may be attacked is madness— If Mrs ———— mentions her fathers
invitation to you *back out* as politely and handsomely as possible. It will
*never do*—at least not until we can see *our way clear*. There is no social
intercourse here. The ladies seem handsome & elegantly dressed & there
is no rudeness of manner but at the same time no approaches towards
hospitality—I do not wonder. Besides they are *afraid*. I received a
beautiful note from a lady the other day to whose sick mother I sent
some rice—a note full of gratitude, but no invitation to *call*. I got a note
from *Malone* yesterday. He said he would be here again this week. I hope
to meet him. I acknowledged Miss Charleys music yesterday & hope she
will get my reply. It was addressed simply "Miss Charlotte Pendleton."

    I rec'd the communication from the lady president of our "10th
Aid Society" but unfortunately have mislaid the letter which was long
delayed on the route and have forgotten her name. Please say to her that
the Regt is under boundless obligations, but at present they are well clad
and I fear it will be very difficult to get the clothing through. We may
besides get marching orders or be driven out and it is impossible to tell
to what point to send them. Should we be permanently encamped here
for the summer they would be very acceptable, but under all the
circumstances perhaps the articles had best be disposed of at home.

    I hope Uncle is entirely recovered by this time. I wrote him a long
letter the other day. Give my best love to dear Aunt Ann. I am glad to
hear she is so much brighter. And so the Garrisons are in the old house. I
never knew it until day before yesterday. For how long do they take the
house—and what has become of the poor old *Ritters*? My best love to the
old ladies Aunts Sallie & Martha. I hope they will both live to see this
mad bad war die out forever & the country settle down to peace &
happiness. My Brigade is beautifully encamped here—from my own H$^d$
Qu$^{rs}$ surrounded by magnificent oaks. I have a view of the town. Loomis
battery is just by my side. Immediately below me is the camp of the old
10th. In sight is another of my regiments the 42—The 3d is near by also
and the 15$^{th}$ though two miles off is on the same (southern) side of town.
The band of the 10th is really *magnificent*. It ought to be as it costs the
officers $10,000 a year—*extra* pay. I believe you know my *family*

arrangements. Grover A.A.A Gen. Lt St John (3d Ohio) (a tip top fellow) A.D.C Capt Clarke 15th Ky Brigade Qu$^r$ Capt Fanning Brig [Com$^g$] D$^r$ Muscroft Brig Surg— It is likely I shall appoint another aide—young Wolfe of Louisville—if Col Pope can spare him. I have besides two clerks—*Robb* & Hogan. Two foot orderlies Guthrie & Reardon & 12 mounted orderlies with a Sergt. We have a capital negro cook from L——e and live at *Huntsville* quite well. Guthrie Robb Reardon & Hogan are all *excellent* fellows and seem to be very well satisfied. Joe Guthrie is *invaluable.* I have great confidence in him.

Remember me most kindly to the Doctor. Tell him my leg is nearly as good as new. In fact considering my hard riding, bivouacking &c it has got along wonderfully well. Tell dear Bessie that I recd yesterday her last letter written in pencil and that my next letter shall be to *her.* The Band by the way has brought out "Col Lytle's Quickstep" and played it last night before my quarters for the first time. It was arranged by Band Master Walters & is beautiful.[1] How I should like to march my Brigade through Cin$^{ati}$. The regiments in their new clothes really look superb. Dear little Nan & John! Kiss them for me. Uncle would give a months pay to see them.

Well dear Sister I have written you a *long* letter, for a wonder, I have not been interrupted. I suppose this sultry afternoon all are asleep.

Send my kind love to Uncle Ed$^d$ & family. Our *flag* has not yet made its appearance—where is it?

Do the people ever talk of me at home? How are all the pretty girls? Good bye dear Joe. Tell the Doctor & Sam to remember me to Gallagher & all other friends not forgetting especially D$^r$ Thompson & Judge Storer.[2]

Most Affly
Will

1. John N. Walter, age thirty-nine on entering the service September 7, 1861, held rank as a principal musician in the Tenth Ohio. Walter and the other musicians of the Tenth Ohio were mustered out at Nashville, Tennessee, on September 10, 1862, by order of the War Department.

2. Judge Bellamy Storer defeated Robert Lytle for Congress in 1834. Although on opposite sides politically, the Lytles and Storers had good personal relations.

### To Elizabeth Lytle Broadwell

*At the time Lytle wrote this letter he commanded the Seventeenth Brigade, Third Division, Department of Ohio. Ormsby Mitchel commanded the division, with Col. John*

*Turchin commanding the Eighth Brigade, Col. Joshua Sill commanding the Ninth Brigade, and Col. John Kennett commanding the cavalry unit, the Fourth Ohio.*[1]

Huntsville Hotel Thursday
June 19th 1862

My dear Bessie

I am just in receipt of a letter from you (the one announcing uncles illness) dated *May 4th* also of one from June dated June 13th. I have been here sick since last Sunday. In fact for ten days past I had been quite indisposed, but on Sunday had *to cave* & go to bed. Dr Muscroft *insisted* on Monday that I should go home on leave, but this I declined to do. I have picked up wonderfully & today feel quite free from disease— though very weak. I shall be able to return to duty in a day or two. I had a fever with a number of disagreeable concomitants.

Mrs [Torvall] the proprietors wife has been a second Mrs Steele. She has been exceedingly kind—making all sorts of nice things for me and amongst others present sending me yesterday a delicious silver goblet full of catawba sangaree—the last & only bottle of wine she had in the world. Col White's family too have been very kind. Mrs White sent me two large bowls of straw & raspberries & a pitcher of cream & little Miss White a beautiful bouquet

Tell Josie not to worry about my clothing as there is now plenty here. Several establishments have been opened where officers can get complete suits both uniform & underclothing at prices not much, if any, above those at home. You remember the little felt hat I bought at Dudds when last home— my regulation felt hat was so heavy & ugly that I had the feathers & trimmings taken off it. I then hunted up a tailor in the 10th who trimmed with them the citizens hat. It was very much admired. It is very light & comfortable quite picturesque & altogether the prettiest military hat I ever saw. You would be amused to see how the fashion spread—nearly every officer in the command now wears one.

Alfred Pirtle is well & has been very devoted to me during my illness. He is extremely popular with everybody—officers & men—is one of the most thorough soldiers I know anywhere & a splendid fellow in every way. Give my love to Cousin Ella who I am delighted to hear is with you. I believe I will send her a kiss—if not I shall certainly *bring* her one when we all get home. As to Major Millikin's matter I dont know anything about it—was not present when he was examined & have no recollection of signing any report regarding him. So *Sharley* has left you! I am very sorry & feel as if I had lost a friend. We are awaiting with intense interest for the news from Richmond. I no longer sleep under my buffalo at night. The weather has been intensely hot, though still, I think the nights cooler than with you. The Mitchel girls—all three—arrived here since I was taken sick & of course I have not yet seen them. The General has taken a little cottage & furnished it for them.

How long they will stay I do not know. I am rejoiced to hear that Uncle is getting so much better and hope before long to have a letter from him. Give my warmest love to Mrs Judge Hall. You do not know how glad I am to hear that my friends remember me. I have added to my staff as *aide* young Wolffe of L——e[2] a gentlemanly handsome little fellow. Does Miss Ella know him?

Doctor Malone has been here on a visit as I believe I wrote Jodie. He expects to visit Cin^ati soon and I trust you will be polite to him as he is a most excellent gentleman—evidently very much respected here in northern Ala.

It is rumored that the enemy is concentrating a strong force at Chattanooga. Negleys expedition down there between ourselves strictly—was a *fiasco* & did more harm than good—*be very careful* though not to *repeat this*.[3]

My most affectionate love to Aunt Ann. Tell her D^r M'Means of Sandusky is surgeon in the 3^d Ohio & has not left my room. He is an old friend of mine & a capital physician—

By the way if D^r Muscroft now acting Brigade Surgeon visits Cin^ati in a few days on Leave—I shall request him to call & give you the history of the campaign. He has been with me all the time & everywhere. He is a devoted friend & I beg you to be polite to him.

I would also suggest that you call on Mrs D^r Shumard. Her husband you know is medical Director of the Div. She is staying at Glendale I believe. Any attentions you *can* show her would be very gratifying to me.

Well dear Bessie I must wind up, as I am suffering since I commenced to write with an intense headache.

With love to Sam

Most Affly
Will

Gen [Lewis] Clemens has just called. Did not hear of my illness till last night. Called to take me to his house, but I declined as I am so nearly well.[4]

1. John Basil Turchin (1822-1901) graduated from the Imperial Military School in St. Petersburg. General Buell had Turchin court-martialed in July 1862, in part because he disobeyed orders and had his wife with the command in the field. At Mrs. Turchin's persuasion, Lincoln restored her husband to duty and promoted him to brigadier general.

2. L——e was Lytle's shorthand for Louisville, home of the Pirtles.

3. In June 1862 James Scott Negley commanded the Seventh Independent Brigade, Army of the Ohio.

4. Lytle's handwriting is not clear. He may refer to a General Lewis Clemens or to former U.S. Senator from Alabama Jeremiah Clemens. The former Senator lived in Huntsville.

## *To Josephine Lytle Foster and Elizabeth Lytle Broadwell*

PRIVATE
H$^d$ Q$^{rs}$ 17th Brigade
Huntsville Al$^a$ June 30$^{th}$ 1862

Dear Sisters

Lily's letter & Aunt C's by Col Kennett have just been received. I am sorry to learn Josie has been an invalid & hope *this* may find you all well. I feel quite depressed this morning & the letters were a *great* treat. As I wrote to Uncle yesterday I am weak & feeble and find it hard to regain my strength. In case of a sudden order to march I fear I could not stand it at present. Gen Buell is here, and we may move at any moment though all is yet uncertain. I met Brig Gen (formerly Col S—— of the 13) this morning. He said nothing to me of it but a friend whispered in my ear that he *heard* Smith was ordered to report to Gen Mitchel for orders. It seems that during his absence on sick leave van Cleaf was assigned to *his* Brigade so that he is now without a command.[1]

The trouble of my position is dear girls that I am liable to be thus outranked by any Brigadier who comes along. If *Smith should* be assigned by Gen Buell to the command of the 17th Brigade, I shall not go back to my regiment. I will resign. I have endured *enough*—as much as my sense of personal dignity—of what is due to *myself* permits. The nomination of Turchin causes much talk—

*Repeat* however *nothing* I say to *anyone*. Gen M'Cook did me the honor yesterday to pay me the first visit. I never saw him before. Col Ed M'Cook & Cousin Sam Davis of Dayton were with him.[2] The Gen says he was at Lily's "come out" party and enquired after, and sent his complts to you both. I like him *much*. Frank Dawson on Gen Buells staff also paid me a long visit last evening.

He is a warm friend. I enclose a couple of little notes from a Mrs Goodman here to show you the kind of people there are in Huntsville.

When we first arrived I sent her mother who is an invalid some *rice*. Mrs G—— wrote me a note saying none could be procured here & that it was her mothers only food & asking as a *great* favor that I should if possible send her a little. I immediately got a nice clean sack and filled it & sent Guthrie down with it and really it seems as if their gratitude had no bounds.

I have never seen her *here* but D\ Malone says she was at the party given by Mrs Gregory to the Delegates to the National Convention in 56—that he escorted her—that she was a Miss Corrinne *Acklin* a great belle & very handsome. I think he told me that he introduced you to her. I do not remember her, though she recollected my name & asked if it was the same *Capt* Lytle.[3]

Her husband is an officer of rank in the rebel service—they seem people of wealth as they keep a carriage & have a very pretty place. She is evidently a *lady—thoroughbred*—& happening to hear of my illness sent the enclosed cards with blance mange &c. You see our enemies are human beings & christians after all & that even the women are not *all* fiends. In fact *I* must say that wherever I have come in personal contact with the people I have invariably been treated like a gentleman.

Kiss my little cousin for me. Tell her Alfred comes up to see me & we have many long talks nearly every evening. I am very anxious to see him promoted— He richly deserves it.

You will allow me I hope to bestow a fatherly kiss on the young ladies as I begin to feel quite an old gentleman. This war has sown not a few gray hairs in the brown locks which you & I dear Lily used to *match* before the mirror. Poor young Haines.[4] I read Seddy's account of his death with great interest. Please convey to his father my sincere sympathy— Peace to the brave! My camp dear girls is really *very* handsome. How I wish you could see it. The men keep the ground around it as neat as wax. They have my cot covered with a blue [grease] musquito bar (to keep off the flies—which bite like rattlesnakes). The *bar* is quite ingeneously arranged over two barrel stoves, *bent* at the head & foot of the cot—*this fashion*

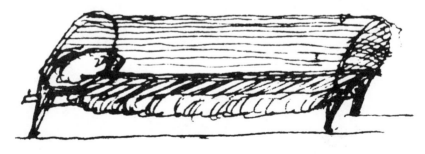

then I have in my large front office with tables, books, newspapers &c (we get newspapers now by the way three days from L——e & four from Cin^(ati)). What with my staff & mounted & foot orderlies, servants &c we have quite a little village up here on the hill— I shall leave our pleasant quarters here with real regret.

Well my dear children good bye. I have read the little life of Havelock you gave me with great interest. I should try to do what is *right & just* & trust that *our* father whose shield has so wonderfully protected me heretofore will direct my steps & give me strength to endure everything. I often sigh for a life of calm & quiet, but perhaps my bodily weakness & lassitude have an effect on my spirits just now. Remember me most aff^(ly) to all & tell Aunt Charlotte that I will write her & Uncle when I have any news. Sam's letter was received & I shall write him soon.

Most Affly<br>Will

1. Lytle refers to Brig. Gen. William Sooy Smith who from December 2, 1861-July 2, 1862, commanded the Fifteenth Brigade, Fifth Division, Army of the Ohio, and Brig. Gen. Horatio Phillips Van Cleve who commanded that same brigade from July 2-September 29, 1862.

2. Edward Moody McCook, then 29, was one of seventeen fighting McCooks of Ohio. Samuel Davis [Davies] must have been the son or grandson of Samuel Davies (1776-1843) who married first Mary Stall, the sister of Eliza Stall, William Lytle's first wife. Davies served as mayor of Cincinnati from 1833 until his death in 1843. He was responsible for the first development of Cincinnati's waterworks.

3. The Democrats held their National Convention in Cincinnati in 1856 where they nominated James Buchanan for president June 2.

4. Lytle refers to a son of Daniel Haines, former governor of New Jersey and an associate justice of the state's supreme court. Daniel Haines was a first cousin of Lytle's mother, Elizabeth Smith Haines Lytle. See *Dictionary of American Biography*, vol. 8 (1937) 92-93.

### To Josephine Lytle Foster

*Immediately after the pleasant Fourth of July celebration Lytle describes, Gen. Ormsby Mitchel was ordered to Washington. Meanwhile, word reached the Union forces at Huntsville that things looked bad for McClellan's army in the East. In fact, the Peninsula Campaign had ended with McClellan holding at Malvern Hill on July 1 and the Confederates withdrawing toward Richmond.*

H^d Q^(rs) 17 Brigade<br>Huntsville July 4th 1862

My dear little Sister

Well dear Joe here I am after a *long* ride—to Monte Sano—the mountain near Huntsville. My first visit & my first long ride since I got out of bed. We have been celebrating the 4th, and a delightful afternoon we have had. Mrs. Slocum when she gets home will tell you all about it. Our party consisted of the three Mitchel girls, Mrs Slocum, Mrs Clemens (wife of the ex Senator, *Jere) Miss Lane, Capt Bankhead, Capt Michler Lt Fitzhugh & Capt somebody else, all of Gen Buells staff Col Burke & Capt Ward of the 10th Col Lytle & Lt Wolfe of his staff & one or two others with escort &c.*[1] *We had a perfectly delightful* time. The view from "Monte Sano" is I suppose unsurpassed in the United States.

We had a tip top lunch at a most romantic spring on the top of the mountain. The star spangled banner, bold [sojer] boy, Benny Haven's Oh! by Col Burke & Lt Fitzhugh, winding up with "Old Lang Syne" by the whole company.

You have no idea of the magnificence of the scenery—nor can I paint it for you—favored as we were on descending the mountain on our way home with a *Sunset* gotten up in natures happiest mood. It has been indeed a day long to be held in remembrance—and no doubt my illness gave me a keener appreciation of the holiday. Well! Of course you know by this time that Gen Mitchel was suddenly ordered to Washington by order of the War Dept. He left on an hours notice. Sent for me—read me the dispatch, left some parting words for the Division & *was off.* I know the *whole story* but cant *write it.* Am too tired to *begin* with. The girls his daughters leave in a few days.

What is to become of us all—I dont know.

Hope to hear from the Gen[l] on Monday. He has much influence at Washington—*deservedly.* He wants his Division with him if he *remains East.* Especially I *think* does he want Loomis' Battery & *my Brigade.*

We will see.

I called yesterday on Gen Buell & saw him for the *first* time. He & his staff were very polite. My Brigade is the only one here. M'Cook's Division is 6 miles out of town.[2] He has the advance of Buells Army. Nelson Crittenden & Wood & the rest are scattered along from here *west.* M'Cook called on me, though I did not know him—a very marked compliment as you will readily understand. Gen Smith also called—he is now com[er] the Div—— temporarily. He has been very polite.

I *have much to tell you* but *have no time to write.* It *would not surpise* me if before *ten days* I was on my way to *the Potomac* with my Brigade. The news from Richmond looks *bad.* I fear M'Clellan has been defeated. Of course before this reaches you the *tale will be told.*

Tell Miss Nan I have bought a poney for her. If I come north she must have him to learn to ride on. I captured him at Winchester from the Texan Rangers—He is a regular mustang. Racks, *lopes* & runs like a deer. I bought him off the Quartermaster (to whom all captured property is turned in) for $20!—and *Joe* was offered today $75 for his bargain. Tell Nannie he is not very pretty to look at, but is a good [un] to *go*—has a long mane & tail & is quite gentle—will follow her like a dog. Good night dear Sis. It is very late. Love to Uncle Smith Aunts Ann & Charlotte the Doctor of course—dear Lily Sam—*Everybody* who remembers me— not forgetting *Johnny*—Good night. Dont fear for my health. I have regained my appetite & am doing grandly. Hoping that on the next *4th* we have may have a big time at home.

Most affly
*Will*

Always remember me to Aunt Sallie & Aunt Martha— they must have their daguerreotypes taken for me— I shall value them highly if I get thro the wars. *I insist on it.* Where is old Briscoe? Lt Col Langdon called on me this morning & we had a long talk.
Good night again, dear Sis.

Lytle probably refers to Jeremiah Clemens (b. Huntsville, Alabama, December 28, 1814), who initially held office under the Confederacy but who became a strong Union supporter. Clemens studied law at Transylvania University in Lexington, Kentucky, and served as a U.S. Senator from Alabama from 1849 until 1853. (See *Biographcial Directory of the United States Congress, 1774-1989*, bicentennial edition [Washington, D.C.: GPO, 1989], 791.)

2. Lytle is referring to Brig. Gen. Robert Latimer McCook who followed the advance of General Buell along the Memphis and Charleston Railroad in the summer of 1862.

### *To Elizabeth Lytle Broadwell*

H<sup>d</sup> Quarters Huntsville Ala
July 12th 1862

Your letter dear Bessie written on the 4th came safely to hand & I can assure you that I was *very* happy to think that even on the *4th* my little sisters did not forget me.

How *my* 4th was spent I wrote you. Since then the ladies with Gen Mitchels daughters & Mrs Slocum have honored *my* H<sup>d</sup> Q<sup>rs</sup> with a visit. They took supper with us the other night and really seemed delighted— as it was their first meal in Camp. The gentlemen consisted of my staff Mr Hook & Adjt Pirtle. The night was glorious. We could say with the poet

"The red moon, like a golden grape
Hangs slowly ripening in the sky
And oe'r the helmets of the hills
Like plumes the summer lightnings fly"

Our "kitchen cabinet" had been foraging all day, among the neighboring farms & sutlers and we gave the ladies *I* think a tip top supper—which they *pitched into* by the way at a regular "pas de charge"—the *spread* was an extemprovised table in the open air—a *real* bona fide, clean white table cloth had been borrowed for the occasion and during supper the Band of the 10th gave us a few gems of Opera. Afterwards we had cigars & several very pretty songs from the ladies. How I wished dear girls you could have been with us! (Poor M'Clure's death—Captain 15th Ky—is just announced a gallant officer—taken sick where I was & died at Hotel.)

Last night there was *war* in the old 10th—I tell you. It seems that night before last several sutlers wagons & a cotton train on the Fayetteville Road, sixteen miles from Hunstville were surrounded by the rebel cavalry. The cotton was burned & the sutlers stores carried off—but *worst of all—in one of the waggons of the Sutler was reported to be the splendid stand of colors presented to the 10th by the City of Cin^ati*. The news was immediately telegraphed in all directions, cavalry has been dispatched to every point of the compass. The whole line from here to Winchester is on the look out for the bold marauders. Every mountain road is scouted and every ford & ferry across the Tenn for fifty miles guarded. The 10th itself resembled a nest of angry hornets. A hundred & fifty picked men of the regiment under the gallant Captain Hudson were mounted in wagons & started hot pursuit at midnight. More men could not be spared as the Regiment is doing Provost Guard duty.

I still *hope* however that the *flag is* safe and for this reason—Last evening the pickets brought in a negro who was *with the train. He* says the flag was in an oil cloth cover—now *Spencer* who has been here several days says the colors were in a *long box—Ask Shillito*. Col Burke it seems had ordered some *guidans*—little flags for the guides—and *I* for one *have* strong hopes that the enemy got *them* only & not *our flag* after all.

How Spencer came to be separated from his trust I do not know. I have not seen him. Perhaps he is not to blame. But the *proper way would have been* for *the City Council* to have sent a com^ee who at Nashville should have secured a *strong escort*.

The enemy party who made this brilliant & daring dash were regular rebel Cavalry splendidly mounted & equipped. There was no body with the train but sutlers *clerks* & *teamsters*—not *a musket.* If the colors *were* forwarded in that way it was *perfectly shameful.* I do not mean to blame Spencer however as he perhaps was not in fault & is said to be a first rate fellow. There was it seems on board the train a large quantity of choice Champaigne & other wines. I have strong hopes the rebels all got *tight*—& are near the road still— *Lord have mercy on their souls if they meet John Hudson.*

(You may tell Sam to publish this about the flag if he deems it *expedient*— Perhaps nothing had better be said about Spencer who is editor of the Times— I have not seen him & am told he is much worried. Let Sam write it out & recast it.) Nothing yet as to our final destination— I am anxiously awaiting despatches from Mitchel. Lt Fitzhugh of Buell's staff paid me a long visit last night. I *am told* on good authority that Buell & his staff are strongly prepossessed in my favour. I *hear* also that the officers of the Brigade are preparing a strong paper in my behalf which they intend signing & sending to the President! *Should* this be done it would be an unprecedented honor—more grateful to me than promotion or the commission itself—but I will wait till I see it—for few men can be disciplinarians and please *all.*

My kindest regards to D^r Thompson Judge Storer, Alex Todd & Gallagher. Let us remember the beautiful saying "that true glory like the Eurydice of the poet follows him who does not look backwards" and let me tell *you* dearest Bessie that more than a general's star I value the wonderful & cherished affection of my little sisters. Remember me most aff^ly to Aunt Ann to whom I would write oftener did I not know she sees all my letters. With kind regards to all not forgetting Miss Ella[1] if she is still with you.

Most Affly
*WH Lytle*

If you think it best to say anything publicly about the colors dont connect my name with it in *print.* "Extract from private letter"— something that way.
I heard late last night that Gen Smith[2] was ordered to Nashville—as Mil Supt of R. Roads.

1. Ella Pirtle, sister of Alfred Pirtle, Lytle's aide, visited Lytle's sisters in Cincinnati.
2. Gen. William Sooy Smith commanded the Seventeenth Brigade, Third Division, Army of the Ohio, August 19-23, 1862.

## To Samuel J. Broadwell

*After agonizing all summer about who would be promoted to brigadier general, Lytle found out Joshua Sill recieved that rank July 16, 1862. Though five years younger than Lytle, Sill was a West Point graduate. Lytle intended for his attorney brother-in-law Sam Broadwell to share this letter with his legal friends, including his law partner Alexander Todd and Thomas Gallagher and Judge Bellamy Storer.*

H$^d$ Q$^{rs}$ 17th Brigade Huntsville
July 27th 1862

Dr Broadwell. I drafted a reply to the attack on Gen Mitchel by the Journal. This has been signed by the whole of the 17$^{th}$ Brigade with the exception of a few officers in the 15$^{th}$ Ky & some others (including Cols Beatty & Janes) absent at Athens.

I shall forward it to Prentice—care of Judge Pirtle. My impression is it had better not be *published* for fear of injuring the *cause*.

I shall forward you or the Gen a copy by Spencer of the Times, or by my Qr Capt Clarke of Louisville who is about going home on leave. If I send *you* the copy *forward it to Mitchel* of whose whereabouts I am not positive. The question of *publication* I shall leave to Judge Pirtle & Prentice himself. My own case excites much indignation here. The proudest compliment I ever received is a recommendation to the President for promotion signed I believe unanimously (with one exception) by the *whole Brigade.*

I regard my neglect as an *insult a personal affront,* and unless I have different news from home shall resign. The paper to the President has gone to Washington, and I shall wait news from home before I take any decided step.

Believe me that I have no sympathy with officers who resign out of mere pique. I can stand *neglect* but not *insult*— I can interpret the action of the Govt in no other way than as a reflection on my loyalty. To attribute it to anything else when for seven months I have had my present command or a greater one—and always with the approval & commendations of my superior officers is idle.

I have been treated like a dog from the jump. But I repreat to appoint *both* Sill & Turchin, my inferiors in rank, both of whom I have commanded by virtue of seniority to *select them out* and *leave me* in the teeth of Gen Mitchels recommendation—despite the sympathy of every corps I have commanded from Camp Harrison through V$^a$ Ky Tenn—to Huntsville Ala—can only be construed into an *insult.*

Unless this matter is cleared up and amends made I shall *go home*. I am a *stumbling block in the way of officers* who *deserve advancement*. The gallant fellows are willing to sacrifice everything for me, but they shall not wear the crown of martyrdom because a lot of *dogs* at Cin^ati or Columbus or Washington have tracked me like blood hounds.

I believe in private as well as public war and on my return having first settled my private accounts with the cowardly miscreants who have maligned me, I shall then have leisure to look after the country—

I write in great haste. Sincerely y^rs

Lytle

Show this to Todd Gallagher & Storer if you like.
Rosecrans seems a fine fellow *Buell & Staff* have been *marked* in their courtesies.
My Brigade is in tip top condition & after a few drills I have given it manoeuvers splendidly.

### *To Judge Henry Pirtle*

*Lytle believed Maj. Gen. Ormsby Mitchel received unjustified criticism for the lack of discipline in his units. When furor mounted, Lytle rushed to Mitchel's defense, citing the incredible accomplishment of Mitchel and his troops. Presumably he referred to the railroad raid made in northern Alabama by Mitchel's men and civilian James J. Andrews in April 1862.*

Huntsville Ala<br>July 29th 1862

Dr Judge[1]

I take the liberty of forwarding to your care a communication to be handed to M^r Prentice. It is in regard to the article in the Journal[2] concerning Gen Mitchel and is signed as you will see by nearly all the officers of the Brigade. In such cases as these I do not like to see the names of officers figuring in print—as a mere matter of taste—if nothing else. It is unmilitary and the publication of this paper with its array of names *might* injure the *cause might* provoke a newspaper war that would be made use of by the enemy.

I incline to the opinion that it had best be regarded as a private and friendly letter addressed to the Editors of the Journal. The question of its *publication however I am content to leave to you & to Mr Prentice himself.*

I think great injustice was done Mitchel in the article. He has his faults like other men and I can see them, for altho' his friend, I am not blindly his partisan. That the outrages & excesses perpetrated at Athens & elsewhere by a portion of his command grieved him to the *very heart I know.*

That certain officers were not immediately arrested & brought to trial before a military Court arose probably from the almost overwhelming difficulties that encompassed him.

With a mere corporals guard comparatively he did here the work of a whole 'corps d' armíe'—more than men, inferiors in activity energy & *dash* could accomplish with ten times the force.

But he could not spare an *officer* nor a *man* nor in the midst of all absorbing & engrossing labors pause to investigate thoroughly complaints & charges, when struggling for the very *existence* of his little army.

That he had corrupt complicity in cotton or other speculations I cannot believe—and I saw him daily *often,* and have known him from my boyhood.

With my kindest regards to Mrs Pirtle believe me my dear Sir with the highest regard,

Yr Obt Serv

*Wm H Lytle*

Hon Henry Pirtle

Louisville K<sup>y</sup>

1. In writing to Henry Pirtle, the father of his aide Alfred Pirtle, Lytle wrote to a fellow law student of his father's when they studied under Judge John Rowan. The Lytle and Pirtle families remained close, with Lily Broadwell and Ella Pirtle terming themselves "cousins." Henry Pirtle also maintained a close relationship with John Rowan, including service as executor of Rowan's will.

2. Lytle refers to the *Louisville Journal.*

### To Josephine Lytle Foster

*The letters Lytle mentions receiving probably included those from Lily Broadwell writ-ten July 14 and July 26—the only two family letters from July 1862 in the Lytle Collection.[1] Broadwell noted that everyone was relieved to hear her brother's good opin-ion of General Mitchel because they could not believe the slander against him. Broadwell also said Lytle's cheerful tone had relieved the family because they had feared he would resign on impulse. She counseled, "Oh! pray do not Brother for it will do no good & will only engender a feeling of pity for you—among your friends—instead of the respect for the course you are pursuing & indignation at the disregard of your claims by Gov' which they feel now. Besides we are all doing what we can for you & hear that Lincoln says 'he has his eye on you & fully intends promoting you'!" Broadwell also commented that one of Lytle's friends, Colonel Duffield, had been treated badly. And, though Lytle admired John Morgan, Broadwell called him a "perfect fiend" who had burned Lebanon & Danville and was now marching on Lexington with threats to Louisville, Covington, and Cincinnati. With her letter of July 26, Lily Broadwell sent Lytle a box of cigars. Meanwhile, Lytle's unit continued to provide surveillance support.*

H<sup>d</sup> Q<sup>rs</sup> 17 Brigade
August 4th 1862

My dear Josie. Well I have certainly been in luck within a day or two, having rec'd quite a number of letters from home both by private conveyance and mail. Dear Bessie's letter with Johnnie's photograph I have not received. You speak of it in your last letter, written the day before D<sup>r</sup> Muscroft left. Day before yesterday I was presented with two new pair of gauntlets one from Col Burke & another from Lt Wolfe a bottle of delicious [*Arsmankauser*] from D<sup>r</sup> Fries of Cin<sup>ati</sup>—a beautiful flag for my H<sup>d</sup> Q<sup>rs</sup> from Burke, your's & Bessie's cigars (which are *splendid* & most acceptable) and last not least dear Aunties *package*. The last I really needed. My stock of handkerchiefs being almost in tatters. The shirts fit me *exactly*, especially round the throat where I am rarely suited, most ready made shirts being too small for me. The socks too are *just right*. Altogether J. my wardrobe is in a very respectable condition. I had the luck to pick up here a very neat summer blouse and pair of pantaloons—for which I paid only $18— They would have cost more at home so that altogether I am quite *set up*. I return you & Bessie & Aunt a thousand thanks for your thoughtfulness. I believe I wrote you of the great compliment my Brigade officers paid me in recommending me to the Prest. It was very gratifying and under all the *circumstances I want it known at home*. My Brigade well deserves the compliment paid it by [B.]S. in the Gazette. I have not seen so fine a body of men nor one so well equipped & drilled in Buells Army.

Gen Rousseau[2] insists upon another review this week as there a great many ladies here who wish to be present—among the rest Mrs Col [Mundray] a very pretty & lady like woman, D<sup>r</sup> Shumard's wife—Mrs Capt Crittenden Mrs Col Burke & several others. Little Mrs B—— arrived safely a day or two since. I called on her the next day but she was out. Last evening she & Mrs Clemens accompanied by Gen Clemens & Gen Rousseau visited me. She is staying at the Clemens, and I went down there after supper and had a very pleasant time. We are all invited there this evening. D<sup>r</sup> Malone has paid another visit to Huntsville & we had a good long talk over Cin<sup>ati</sup>. He desired to be specially remembered to you all. I enclose you a note addressed him by Mrs Goodman to whom I wished to be introduced to thank her for her politeness during my illness. Is it not beautifully written?

Poor woman! In addition to her mothers death, she has lost an only brother before Richmond. Wilson arrived & seems charmed with Huntsville. He has had a great time in the Regt. The boys volunteering to show him the curiosities of the town. When I telegraphed for him I intended going home if possible, but concluded afterwards to hold on & wait the progress of events at home. I intended to countermand my despatch but in the hurry of business forgot it. I do not need him *here*. If I had gone home I should have needed him as Guthrie is an enlisted man & cannot leave. I will try & get Wilson a place with some of the staff. In fact Capt Fanning wants him—or possibly we may all club & employ him as steward or caterer for the *Mess,* for which he is admirably adapted. Did Sam get my letter enclosing one to Gen Mitchel? I hope so. We commenced fortifying here today. Nearly the whole of Gen Buells army has gone forward to Battle Creek, Nashville, Winchester & other points east. Buell is still here. Rousseau & I get along very well thus far. He is a thorough Kentuckian. Alfred Pirtle is acting as my AAA Gen.

Turchin's case has not yet been decided— At least the finding of the Court has not been announced. The enemy is getting very saucy & prowling all round us. Capt Fanning ventured out two or three miles beyond our pickets the other day & came very near being captured. He had to ride for his life (say nothing of this outside the family—as it bores Fanning to death). I sent this to Sams care fearing you have left town. We hear nothing of Mitchel. I write Todd by todays mail. A great many officers are getting terribly home sick. If it were possible I should like a short leave myself, but do not see how I can leave my command. I hope Uncle Smith is nearly well & shall write him soon. Tell Lily I will send her the money she advanced Wilson by the first safe opportunity.

With kind regard to Foster & Master John & a kiss for Aunt & Nannie I remain

Most Affly<br>Will

1. Elizabeth Lytle Broadwell to William H. Lytle, July 14, 1862, LP, box 31, no. 82 and July 26, 1862, LP, box 31, no. 97.

2. Gen. Lovell Harrison Rousseau (1818-69) commanded the Third Division, Army of the Ohio from July 11-September 29, 1862 and Third Division, First Corps, Army of the

Ohio from September 29-November 5, 1862. He was promoted to major general October 22, 1862, with rank to October 8, 1862.

## To Samuel J. Broadwell

*The Mrs. Lee to whom Lytle refers was a boarder at the Lytle mansion. She occupied Lytle's old room.*

Huntsville 1862
Aug 18th

Dr Sam

Please hand this letter to Mrs *Lee* at the old Mansion.

We expect hot work here before long.

I have not heard from the girls for a long while. Their last letters spoke of having seen Spencers account of the flag presentation. I write in great haste. *Hunter Brooke* is staying with me. Love to all.

WH Lytle

## To Josephine Lytle Foster and Elizabeth Lytle Broadwell

*Though Lily Broadwell's letter of August 10 had not been received by Lytle when he wrote on August 18, it seems probable that he received it and other family letters prior to writing on September 12. On August 10, Lily wrote that Gen. Robert McCook's body lay in state at the Cincinnati courthouse. She also reported reading the full account of General Turchin's trial as published in the Gazette and noted that despite her prejudice against him, it seemed clear that cruelty to his men exceeded what they did to the Confederates. In one letter Broadwell enclosed a copy of a letter to her husband, Samuel Broadwell, from a highly placed friend who had made inquiries in Washington about Lytle's promotion. The letter states that Colonel Sill received his promotion through efforts of a cousin who was a member of Congress and Turchin received his due to his wife's energies. The writer, whose name Broadwell had removed for security purposes, cautioned patience, saying, "Lytle has fine elements as a soldier & there is before him a broad future."[1]*

*Lytle's aunt Joanna Reilly wrote in August,[2] giving local society news. She recalled the prayers for him by Lytle's grandmother and cautioned her nephew to take good care of his watch and money. Reilly also described the once beautiful Cincinnati as having "a Pall thrown over it." No one talked about anything but the awful war, and everything seemed dreary and desolate. Reilly worried about Lytle's health, saying, "do endeavor to protect yourself from taking cold—if possible do not sleep in the wet ground—recollect you have been very differently raised from the Men—what would not hurt them would be your death."*

*Lytle received orders August 29 and 30 to withdraw his force from Huntsville. His*

*instructions called for breaking the railroad and destroying any engines now in shop.[3]
Beginning August 31, Lytle marched the Tenth Ohio from Huntsville to Kentucky
during September as part of the movement of Union forces following Gen. Braxton
Bragg.[4] At Murfreesboro on September 3 Lytle reported that his command was in fine
spirits and condition following the march from Huntsville, driving four hundred heads
of horses and cattle.[5]*

*While Lytle marched across Tennessee, the daring John Morgan and his raiders threat-
ened Ohio. The Lytle Papers contain Lily Broadwell's nearly daily correspondence with
her sister Josephine Foster detailing her view of the "siege of Cincinnati" starting September 2. Broadwell had remained in Cincinnati while Foster, her husband, and their
two small children had gone to Niagara Falls, New York, to escape the heat and find
some relaxation. On September 10 Broadwell wrote to her sister that she feared for
their brother, whom they knew was at Bowling Green, Kentucky. The newspapers had
just reported that Buell's army had instructions to cut off Bragg to prevent him from
reinforcing Kirby Smith. A battle seemed imminent.[6]*

Headquarters 17th Brigade, 10th O.V.I.U.S.A.

Adjutant's Department, Sep 12th 1862

Camp at Bowling Green

My Beloved Sisters

 I reached my present camp yesterday. At Nashville Grover came up
with your letters. You *cannot imagine* what a treat they were, as I had not
heard from you for *six weeks*. I feel profoundly anxious about you all, &
*about Cincinnati* & am in strong hopes that we may be ordered that way.
How long we will be here I do not know—probably not long. I was left in
command at Huntsville & evacuated that place on the morning of the 31st.
Since then we have had twelve days continuous and uninterrupted marching
via Fayetteville Shelbyville Murfreesboro & Nashville. My evacuation of
Huntsville & march I am told elicited high compliments from the H[d] Q[rs] of
the Army. I made the march to Murfreesboro in 4 days, though Buell gave
me six. The heat & dust were almost intolerable—water *very scarce. One* day
we had to march twenty six miles without any for our men or teams. We
had no coffee or sugar or bacon and *lived* on *hard crackers.*

 You can form an idea of the immense contract I had when I tell you
that my command consisted at first of the 15th Ky 10th Ohio Loomis
Battery Kennett's Cavalry, 2 comp[s] Alabama loyal troops, one comp[y] Mich
Eng & mechanics with an enormous train—scores of refugees & suttlers
with their wagons & goods & in addition I had to *drive* between five & six
hundred head of cattle & horses. At Murfreesboro another Battery, the
other two regiments of the 17th Brigade which had marched round, via
Dechard, and an immense supply train of over a hundred wagons were

added to my command. My train was between four & five miles long—but the march was made without the *loss of a wagon* or an animal.

The movement from Huntsville was kept a profound secret not only from the citizens, but from my own officers. And we were out of town & marching before any one knew what was going on. All this cost me however an immense deal of labor & anxiety. Until last night I have hardly slept for more than two weeks. But I feel quite refreshed this morning & am in fine health though *thin & worn*.

*We get the Cin papers here & have all the most* intense anxiety to be ordered home to aid in defending Cin^ati—though my own judgment is a movement in another direction might do more real service— I write in great haste— Love to all.

Most affly
*Will*

1. See Elizabeth Lytle Broadwell to William H. Lytle, August 10, 1862, LP, box 31, no. 98, and name removed to Samuel Broadwell, August [?] 1862, LP, box 31, no. 83 (copy made by Elizabeth Lytle Broadwell).

2. Joanna Reilly to William H. Lytle, August [?], 1862, LP, box 34, no. 669, and September [?], 1862, box 34, no. 668.

3. *O.R.,* ser. 1, vol. 16, pt. 2, 443, 450. Telegraph in Lytle Papers, CHS, CMC, dated August 29, 1862, from J.B. Fry, Chief of Staff to General Buell.

4. See Appendix A, Lytle's testimony at the Buell court of inquiry in which he gives a day-by-day account of his march during September 1862.

5. *O.R.,* ser. 1, vol. 16, pt. 2, 477.

6. Elizabeth Lytle Broadwell to Josephine Lytle Foster, September 10, 1862, LP, box 31, no. 50.

## To Elizabeth Lytle Broadwell

*The same day he wrote this letter, Lytle telgraphed home saying he had arrived in Louisville after a march of twenty-seven days.*[1]

Louisville Hotel, Louisville Kentucky
Friday
Sep 26th 1862

My dear Lily— I arrived here this morning with my Brigade after a most fatiguing march of 27 days from Huntsville. I have run down this morning from camp on business connected with my command & have visited the hotel in hopes of seeing the Steeles but find them gone. I feel *very* weary & am most anxious for rest. We have no tents and as I share with my officers & men the hardships of the bivouac, I do *hope* for a few days here to recuperate— It seems *very hard* to be so near you & not see you.

I trust my telegrams have reached home & that you & Uncle or Sam may be able to see me before I am ordered away— Dear Josie is I suppose absent.

I am expecting every moment an officer on business & must close—

Good by dear dear Sister. With love to dear Aunt & Uncle Sam & everybody.

In great haste

Most affly
Will

We have been marching *27* days *constantly*— Imagine how *tired* & exausted we must be!

Uncle Edward. Where is he? How delighted I should be to see him— If he is in Cin, can he not come down?

1. Telegram, William H. Lytle to Samuel J. Broadwell, September 26, 1862, LP, box 38, no. 39a (one of eight telegrams so numbered).

### To Elizabeth Lytle Broadwell

*Lily Broadwell's letter of September 14, to which Lytle refers, provided a lengthy account of events in Cincinnati on September 10 and 11 when the Provost Guard went to the door of every house telling all able-bodied men to get out and defend their homes. If nothing else the siege of Cincinnati brought its citizens, young and old, rich and poor, together. Requested to hand out flags to welcome the defenders back, Broadwell said, "such a looking set of rowdies you never saw & yet they were all the gentlemen in town as well as all the rowdies. . . . Such a motley crew you never beheld in the ranks—& the beauty of it was they all looked exactly alike!" She continued, saying that all the men, whether young or old, black or white, turned out to dig or drill while the women and servants cooked constantly. Despite her excitement and activity, Lily Broadwell found herself always thinking of her brother, knowing he was on the march.*

H^d Q^rs 17^th Brigade
Camp near Louisville
Saturday Sep 27th 1862

My beloved Sister— I am just in receipt of a letter from *you* & one from dear Josie— Yours dated Sep 14^th & hers, "Niagara Sep 9^th." How *bitterly* I shall be disappointed if we have to march again without my seeing any of you. To meet you here—*some* of the family at least—was the one thing that consoled me on many a mile of the *weary weary* march. I telegraphed the first thing yesterday both to Sam & Uncle but fear that the telegraph office is so crowded with business, that my messages may not get over the lines. I have just been shown (privately) orders from Gen Buell that lead to believe we will march again in pursuit of Bragg today or tomorrow. O Sis! how I shall grieve to leave here without seeing any of you. I cannot even see my friends here as my entire command has to be refitted & I must devote all my time to my duties. Dear Josie's letter gave an account of [ . . . ] interview with Stanton. Gen Mitchel certainly *did* recommend me for he handed me the communication *myself* to take to the Telegraph Operator. I did not read it but know its contents. Afterward, he *withdrew* his recommendation of Turchin.

Gen Rousseau told Shumard (the medical Doctor) that *he* also intended to recommend me, but whether he has or not, I do not know. It is *hard* & bitter dear Sister to be thus maltreated and I *wonder* that my numerous & influential friends can not do me *justice* & *demand* that just shall be done. It is not for *myself* that I am anxious for I have the nerve to make any sacrifice for my unhappy country in this dark hour of her exceeding sorrow, but for the interests of the service itself— I mean that my command can not understand why my promotion is delayed. I fear it may be attributed to wrong reasons & that thus my influence & control over my officers & men may be weakened. Besides I feel *most painfully* that I am a stumbling block in the way of subordinate officers of the 10th Regt. It is a *shame* to see such men as Burke, Ward & Hudson held *down* & held *back* when men far inferior in every way are commanding even Regiments & Brigades. The gallant fellows however back me gallantly & make no complaint.

I have this instant seen the article in the Com¹ mentioning my name in connection with the Congressional nomination in the 1st District. I should certainly feel gratified to be assured that the *people* remember me even though the "rulers" give me the cold shoulder—

I am *told* that Buell spoke of my evacuation of Huntsville as a "masterly movement" and on pretty good authority. Rest assured my dear Sister that I strive late & early to discharge my entire duty to my men & to the Govt and that I shall not shrink or falter, if God spares my health—*anywhere*. By the way did you see the very handsome notice of me in a Sandusky paper? It was from the pen of Dr M'Means Surgeon of the 3d Ohio.

Our march has been a most trying one. Many of the men are bare footed— One soldier of the 10th marched barefoot all the way from Huntsville here! I loaned Hunter Brooke $50 when in Huntsville, which he promised to repay immediately on his arrival home. If he is in Cinati please *ask Sam to collect* it and retain it paying himself the money he advanced Wilson. My health continues good despite the hot mid day suns & the cold night dews & fogs. My staff had to leave our cooks & cooking utensils behind so that on the march we often had nothing to eat. We were really worse off than the men for they had haversacks.

Your letter & Josies were most interesting. I read your account of the alarm at Cinati to a number of officers. It was most graphic and was highly complimented. Your account of "O Higgins charge" on the enemy was received with peals of almost inextinguishable laughter.[1] Remember me most affly to dear Aunt Ann. Do not tell her about the pistols. I *recovered one!* most fortunately—they were stolen no doubt from my holsters on the march by some fellow. He stole them in the dark without knowing whose they were at our first halt, this side of Nashville. When he saw my name on them, he no doubt became alarmed and stuck them in a stone wall. Some troops that followed saw the ivory handle of one protruding from the stone fence. By good fortune it was an Ohio regiment & their Col (my friend Fred Jones) immediately took care of it for me— Jones came up with us at Bowling Green. I pity the thief if the men ever catch him. My love also to Aunt Sallie & Aunt Martha to Sam & Mrs Broadwell. I have many *many* a long story to tell you but must bring my letter to a close. Still hoping almost against hope that you or some of the family may come down before we get marching orders. I remain most affly & devotedly

*Will*

1. Elizabeth Lytle Broadwell to William H. Lytle, September 14, 1862, LP, box 31, no. 83a. Lily wrote, "They have had a good joke on Father O'Higgins—the other day he thought he would ride out & see for himself how near the rebels were— But the first thing he knew he was in the midst of their pickets & fired at from all directions, but he soon made it fire in the *rear*—& made *pretty good time* until he found himself once more within our lines. But that did not help him much for *our* pickets did not know him & fired. In vain were his protestations, they unhorsed him, & dragged him into camp crying 'they'd caught *a long haired rebel spy.'!*"

## To Ezekial S. Haines

*When Lytle wrote this letter, the convergence of troops in Kentucky by the Confederates under Braxton Bragg and Union forces commanded by Don Carlos Buell was leading toward a battle.*

Hᵈ Qʳˢ 17ᵗʰ Brigade
Camp near Louisville
Sep 28ᵗʰ 1862

My dear Uncle— I arrived here with my command (having the advance of "Rousseau's corps d'armie") on Friday morning last. I left Huntsville on the 31st Aug— So that for nearly a month we were constantly on the march. I left Huntsville with the 10th Ohio & 15th Ky, 2 companies Alabama loyal troops, one compʸ with Engineers & mechanics, Loomis' & A[rmis'] Balances & Kennetts Cavalry— At Murfreesboro' I met the 3ᵈ Ohio & 42 Inᵃ of my Brigade which were there added to my command as was also Stone's Battery and a supply train of over a hundred wagons. The evacuation of Huntsville was executed in perfect secrecy. The intended movement was not communicated even to my own officers. To this I attribute the fact that I was not harassed by guerrillas on the march. I moved with great rapidity. I was ordered by Gen Buell to make Shelbyville "inside of four days." We made it in three.

I have the satisfaction of knowing that the march was conducted in a manner entirely satisfactory to the Hᵈ Qʳˢ. I was burdened also by a large number of refugees & drove between 5 & 600 head of horses & cattle. Although the dust & heat were intolerable other water very scarce I lost neither an animal nor a wagon.

The last day my command marched *32* miles! Well, here we are!— Expecting marching orders every moment.

I rec'd your telegram last evening, also letters from Lily, two from Josie and several from Sam. I am profoundly grieved that I can neither visit Cinᵃᵗⁱ nor meet any of the family here— It is very hard to be so near home and see none of the family.

I see by the Comˡ of the 20th that my name is mentioned in connection with Congress. I have just received a letter from Sam which informs me that the suggestion *takes* well & that a large number of prominent Union men have declared in my favor.

I shall accept the nomination if it is offered me. I have made no effort for the nomination, but if the people choose to elect me—it is all right. I am rejoiced to learn that your health is improving & trust that in a few weeks you may be entirely restored. My horse is a good deal used up by hard & incessant work but I shall try & get along without going to the expense of buying another. The *poney* I find useful & shall retain him for the present.

I have a vast deal to say to you, but am very busy to day equipping my men— I hear that *Rousseau* either has recommended or intends recommending me for promotion—We will see.

My best love to Aunt Charlotte.

In great haste
Most affly1
Will H. Lytle

### To Elizabeth Lytle Broadwell

*The sequence of this letter is not clear. It may predate Lytle's letters of September 28. In any event it was written under pressure to begin marching, and contact with the enemy loomed close.*

Thursday 17 miles from Louisville
8 o'clock AM.

We arrived here last night my beloved & darling sister just before dark. Our march was a most fatiguing one. the men suffered *terribly.* I never saw so much straggling.

We have this instant recd marching orders—the enemy is said to be near us.

May the Almighty shield us all Once more Good bye Love to Sam Good bye & send love to all.

your own
Will

The staff send compls.

### To Elizabeth Lytle Broadwell

Taylorsville Oct 3ᵈ 1862

My dear Sister—We lay out here last night under a pouring rain— 30 miles from Louisville. I never was so annoyed on any march in my life—so wearied & disgusted.

The straggling exceeded anything I ever saw—though less from my

command than others—There is *no end* to our labors, cares & anxieties on
these forced marches moving as we do without trains, tents baggage or any
of the few comforts a soldier has—The *battle* is nothing comparatively.
The chances seem we shall soon be engaged. Rest assured that my main
reliance is on the sustaining arm of the Almighty, that he will give me
wisdom & strength to discharge my duties to my men & the country.

If dear Joe has returned give her my warmest love, not forgetting
the children & the Doctor. My best love also to dear Aunt Ann & the
balance of the family. I send this by Mr Ward.

Write me when you can & keep me posted as to events at home.

Most Affly<br>Will

### To Joanna Reilly

Hᵈ Qʳˢ 17ᵗʰ Brigade<br>Sunday morning Oct 5ᵗʰ<br>Camp near Bloomfield

My dear Aunt. We are here 10 miles from Bardstown where the enemy is
reported to be in force. We expect a battle every hour and have been
skirmishing for two days.[1] I sieze the opportunity to send you a line by
my Q Sergt of Brigade whom I send back to Louisville for supplies. My
love to the dear girls and Uncle Smith. I trust we may prove victorious &
thrash Bragg soundly. Do not feel uneasy about me—it will do no good.

A man might almost as well be dead as endure the hardships we
have to undergo constantly, but I hope for brighter days and trust the
people will do justice to those of us who suffer and fall for Liberty & the
Govt of our fathers—

Rest assured dear Aunt that I can never forget the kindness and
devotion you have constantly manifested towards me & believe me ever

Most Affly<br>Will

1. During the battle of Perryville on October 8, 1862, the Third Division, First Corps,
Army of the Ohio was commanded by Brig. Gen. Lovell H. Rousseau. A Kentucky native
who practiced law in Louisville between the Mexican and Civil Wars, Rousseau was acquainted with Lytle socially and through their military service. Along with the Seventeenth
Brigade, the Third Division consisted of the Ninth Brigade, commanded by Col. Leonard

Harris, and the Twenty-eighth Brigade, commanded by Col. John Starkweather. After Lytle's injury at Perryville, Col. Curran Pope, Fifteenth Kentucky, commanded the Seventeenth Brigade for the battle's duration. In his report on Perryville, Rousseau indicated that Lytle fell severely wounded while gallantly maintaining his position on the right. Although Rousseau did not observe Lytle's actions personally, he stated that the country was indebted to Lytle and the brave men of the Seventeenth Brigade. See *O.R.,* ser. 1, vol. 16, pt. 1, 1048.

# 1863

*Lytle's long awaited return to active duty came after his exchange on February 4, 1863.*

Exbland Hotel Nashville
Sunday Feb 15th 1863

My dear Sister,

I arrived here last night without any incident on the road save being *left behind* by the trains at Bowling Green. I stayed there all night (Reardon & I) and came up with my baggage & party last evening— Everything all right— I leave for Murfreesboro tomorrow morning at 6 a m.— am invited to dine to day with Gen Mitchell[1] commanding here. We are old friends, having been captains in the same regiment in Mexico.

To our great disappointment *Carter* our old & excellent cook has left Louisville. Capt Clark moreover, my old Quartermaster of Brigade who has resigned & is here on his way home—informs me that our staff mess chest is lost. It was brand new—very complete and contained all the Hd Qrs cooking utensils, plates &c &c. How I shall *live* the Lord knows.

My horses are all right. This Nashville is I think detestable mud knee deep— What must it be in *the front* at Murfreesboro!

I have met, a great many old friends here—Gen Steedman, Lieut Brooke Capt Yates, Col Davis & a large number of others—[2]

If you hear of my *confirmation* telegraph at once—

In fact I will thank the Doctor or Sam to telegraph me as soon as you know anything definite about my promotion *one way or the other.*

Did you find out who sent *the bouquet*—?

With sincerest love to all believe me dear Sis

Yr affec brother
Will

I will write as soon as I get a little settled at Murfreesboro!

I forgot to say that I spent a day in Louisville. Called on the Pirtles, Miss Rousseau & Judge Lane's family—they all gave me a most cordial reception

If you ever see the *Lanes* be kind to them. I feel heartily sorry for the old people.

The old Judge paid me the money I advanced him like a gentleman—as he is.

[Last] do you & Lil write *often*— It will be my only comfort in this arduous life I am again about to encounter—

God bless you all— & to the Doctor especially give my best regards

I fear you are glad to be well rid of your visitor—as he must have given you so much trouble—

Kiss dear Nan & Sir John for me, not forgetting Auntie & Lil.[3]

Sunday afternoon

P.S. Since writing the above I have had a most interesting visit to Mrs. Polk. It being Sunday her servants were all out & as I approached the door she met me herself. I asked if it was Mrs Polk & introduced myself.

She received me with great grace & cordiality. Said that after receiving Uncle's letter of introduction a year ago she sent her servant down to look for me [in the] Hotel.

She asked all about the family & especially after Aunt & Uncle[4]— She is still *very* handsome & elegantly mannered— I am very glad I called—& hope to meet her in Murfreesboro! where it seems her mother is still living.

Good bye.

1. Gen. Robert Byington Mitchell (1823-1882), an Ohio native, served as a first lieutenant in the Second Ohio in the Mexican War before he settled in Kansas. During February 1863 he was between assignments. From November 5, 1862, until January 9, 1863, he commanded the Fourth Division, Center, Fourteenth Corps, Army of the Cumberland. From March through September of 1863, Mitchell commanded the First Division, Cavalry Corps, Army of the Cumberland.

2. Gen. James Blair Steedman, a Pennyslvania native who had served in the Ohio legislature, commanded the Third Division, Fourteenth Corps, Army of the Cumberland, during the period of January 9 through April 17, 1863. As a brigadier general he commanded a brigade at Perryville, Murfreesboro, and in the Tullahoma campaign. His success leading his troops at Chickamauga through heavy fire to join Gen. George H. Thomas led to him receive a second star.

3. Lytle refers to his niece and nephew Anna Haines Foster and John Moorhead Foster, his aunt Joanna Haines Reilly, and his sister Elizabeth Lytle Broadwell.

4. Mrs. Polk presumably inquired after Charlotte and Ezekial Smith Haines, although she might also have known Lytle's paternal uncle, Edward H. Lytle. However, the Polks would have been well aware of Ezekial Haines in his capacity as surveyor general of the United States from 1838 to 1841. Haines received appointment as surveyor general following the resignation of his brother-in-law Robert Todd Lytle from the position in June 1838 after the disclosure of some financial irregularities.

### *To Elizabeth Lytle Broadwell*

Sunday
Murfreesboro Feb 22$^{d}$ 63

Dear Lily

Josy's letter of last Sunday & your own, have reached me. I arrived here safely last Monday morning, and immediately reported to Gen Rosecrans. The General received me *very cordially*. I am not yet assigned however to any command. I understand that the Gen does not wish to assign me until I am confirmed. As *Col* it is probable I would not have rank enough.

I have as yet recd no notice of my confirmation, though I see by the papers Burke & the other field officers of the 10th have been promoted. I should suppose Tod would not promote Burke unless he had been officially notified of my confirmation.[1]

I do not at all regret Gen Rosecrans delay in assigning me, as the weather has been detestable and the mud is knee deep. Having no tents I addressed a note to M$^{r}$ Lytle on the night of my arrival asking if he could accommodate me with quarters. I am now at his house having come here the night of my arrival. I have a splendid room and the whole family are kind & affectionate as possible.[2]

The old gentleman himself is very ill but I trust is improving. Between the two armies in timber, fencing—stores destroyed and stock stolen he has lost a quarter of *a million* of dollars. He talks of going—if his health will permit to the vicinity of Cin to live—in peace. His wife tell Aunt is a niece of Romania Dashiell. The old gentleman is himself a staunch union man though he has a son & son in law—Dr Patterson—and any number of relatives in the rebel army.

He has two sons at home Robert & W$^{m.}$ The latter D$^{r}$ W$^{m}$ H Lytle is staying here with his wife & family—his property having been burned & his house occupied by the Army.

His wife was also a Miss Dashiell a sister of his step mother— He was regularly educated for his profession at L——e & Phil^a—and is a very clever fellow.[3] His wife is brilliantly educated—a fine latin & greek scholar & a very charming lady—tho in poor health. If you can find the little [*mem*] containing the pedigree of the family please forward it for the amusement of the old gentleman. It may be in my secratary at sisters—in the pigeon hole marked—"family records or papers."

Alf Pirtle & Grover send their best regards. D^r Muscroft is eight miles in the country but has called. I visited my old Brigade yesterday and had a very cordial reception.[4]

The 10th recd me last Monday drawn up in line with three times three & a tiger. I have no doubt these people are *Kin*—the Lytle sticks out all over. One of the little children *Sophy* is as much like one of Uncle Neds children as a photograph[5]— I am glad Hoag was successful—send me a *sample*. My staff of course is not yet organized— Grover & Pirtle will be with me. Gen Granger—commanding 3^d Div in Rousseaus absence[6]—makes his H^d q^rs at my *cousin* D^r Pattersons— the family are exiles.

Is it not *hard*? The house was an elegant one.

I assure you I appreciate my comfortable quarters hugely & look on my coming plunge into the mud with anything but pleasurable anticipation.

The army is *digging, foraging* & doing guard duty— By no means pleasant avocations.

Frank James has been to see me. He has been promoted to a captaincy in his regt— I should like very much to have him on my staff, but fear it is impracticable.

Tell Miss Mary Ann that I have as yet been unable to find the 6th Ohio, but have sent to H^d Q^rs today to find out its camp—& will see [Hosent] as soon as possible.[7] My other commissions have all been executed.

Give my love to Alice T[weed] Jenny Springer & Alice Woodroe & Lizzy Kilgour.[8]

Hoping Sam is better & with affectionate regards to the whole family I remain D^r Bessie

Yr affec Brother
Will

I wish you would write Uncle Ned & tell him to write me all he knows about the branch of the family here— I have promised the old gentleman he would do so.

You do not say how Uncle Smith is— My love to him & Aunt— I will write him as soon as I am assigned— By the way I thought it quite likely I should have to go back to Cin the other day. An order came here for my *recall* before the Buell Court martial, but as I rec'd no official notice of it, I suppose Rosecrans wouldn't let me go. What they could want of me again the Lord only knows.[9]

Pardon my [c . . . y] reply—my pen is too hard. A thousand thanks to dear little Nannie for her valentine. It excited the unbounded admiration of the juveniles here of whom—white & black—there are just a *thousand & ten* & the way they all from seven year old up can play "[ . . . & seven up" is a caution].

Tell Auntie my sabre has been admired by scores of officers— my horses are perfectly well & I lost nothing on the way. I have recd a beautiful letter from Eliza Williams—Clark Williams daughter—in regard to her brother who died in Carolina—thanking me for my enquiries after him &c. It is really splendidly written. I wish you knew her—poor girl her heart seems broken.

1. Ohio Governor David Tod promoted Joseph W. Burke to colonel, Tenth O.V.I., effective January 20, 1863. Twenty-six years old when he entered the service in June 1861, Burke was mustered out with his regiment on June 17, 1864.

2. Lytle made use of the friendship he had formed with David Lytle and his family when stationed near Murfreesboro in 1862.

3. Lytle's abbreviations refer to Louisville and Philadelphia.

4. Though a Kentucky resident, Alfred Pirtle joined the Tenth Ohio on January 28, 1862, to serve with his family friend William Haines Lytle. Pirtle was promoted to first lieutenant on August 12, 1862, and transferred to Company F. The Lytle Papers include a letter from Pirtle written in 1923 in which he reminisces about Lytle's mood just before Chickamauga. In that letter Pirtle confirms Lytle's love for Sed Doremus. James A. Grover was with the Tenth Ohio from its formation. He was promoted to first lieutenant and adjutant on January 28, 1862, and assigned to Company E on January 1, 1863. Charles S. Muscroft was the surgeon of the Tenth Ohio from its inception until his resignation June 9, 1863.

5. Lytle and his sisters often called their father's brother Edward H. Lytle "Uncle Ned." Edward Lytle and his wife, Elizabeth Shoenberger Lytle, lived near Martinsburg, Pennsylvania, and frequently spent winters in Philadelphia. They had six daughters and one son, Edward H. Lytle Jr. (b. 1859). The latter never married, ending the name Lytle as carried by descendants of William Lytle (1770-1831).

6. From July 17 until March 29, 1863, Ohio-born Robert Seaman Granger was brigadier general commanding the First Division, Fourteenth Corps, Army of the Cumberland.

Lovell Harrison Rousseau, a Kentucky native, commanded the First Division, Fourteenth Corps, January 9-17, March 29-July 26, and September 21-November 17, 1863.

7. Mary Ann probably refers to Mary Ann Reilly, the stepdaughter of Joanna Haines Reilly by her marriage to Thomas Reilly. The Sixth Ohio was first mustered into service for three months on April 27, 1861, at Camp Harrison, Ohio, except Companies H and K, which were mustered in on May 10 and 12, respectively. The Sixth Ohio was primarily recruited from an independent Cincinnati military organization known as the Guthrie Gray Battalion.

8. Lytle mentions society friends in Cincinnati.

9. Lytle made a brief return to Cincinnati in March 1863. It was his last time home.

### To Josephine Lytle Foster and Elizabeth Lytle Broadwell

*Lytle returned home briefly in March 1863, possibly expecting to testify a second time in the court martial trial of Don Carlos Buell. He was at Louisville on his way back to Murfreesboro when he received the news that his beloved aunt Joanna Reilly had died. In a letter to their uncle Ezekial Smith Haines dated October 5, 1863, Lily Broadwell recalled that on Sunday, March 22, 1863, the day before Lytle left home for the last time, he said he "had never felt so solemnly on leaving home before, he could not get over it—he felt it so strangely & so deeply."[1]*

Louisville Hotel
March 24th— Tuesday
12 M

My beloved Sisters

Sam's dispatch has just arrived. *Dear, dear Aunty— Why did I not know her end was so near.* That I might have been with her in her last hour. I *cannot* write. I have telegraphed Rosecrans & leave the letter open for his reply—

6 a-m Wednesday morning—

I have received no answer from the Gen.

My orders are imperative—

Good bye my dear Sisters.
Will

1. Elizabeth Lytle Broadwell to Ezekial S. Haines, October 5, 1863, LP, box 31, no. 60.

### To Josephine Lytle Foster and Elizabeth Lytle Broadwell

Murfreesboro April 2[d]

My beloved Sisters

Immediately on the receipt of Sam's dispatch I telegraphed Gen Rosecrans for leave to return home. I did not feel warranted under the stern rules of military discipline to go back without it especially as I had been so long absent, as my orders were imperative and as the delay of a few days might (with the information I then had) have cut me off from the Army for a long time. To this dispatch I rec'd no reply, as I wrote you from Louisville on the the eve of starting. I found on my arrival here that the Gen had *given* me *leave,* but unfortunately his telegram never reached me.

Poor dear Aunt Ann![1] It seems hard that I could not have been with her in her last moments, and been present when her dear form was committed to the dust. Sams letter was rec'd yesterday but I hope soon to receive letters from you giving particulars of the "closing scene." I do not doubt it was calm & peaceful, as her life was holy & crowded with good deeds. How bitter a loss this is to *us* dear Sisters I fully appreciate. I hope if God should ever permit me to return to you, that my coming days may prove that dear Aunts devotion & love for me have not been thrown away.

I *do* hope with Sam that this loss may draw us closer together—we who are left—and that our lives may be such as to render it certain that our little circle will be restored in a brighter world.

I have been staying since my arrival at Mrs Lytle's[2] who kindly invited me here.

Fortunately I have not yet been assigned—*fortunately* because I am much depressed in spirits & have not been at all well. Gen. R—— told me he could assign none of the new Brigadiers until he recd from Washington *official* notice of their appointments & the *dates* of their commissions. I heard this morning at Gen hd qts a *rumor* of my probable position but as it is *merely* a rumor, I do not care to mention it. I found my *glass* (field glass) all safe. It was not in my valise. When will Mrs Lytles mourning be here? the poor woman can get nothing here & is anxiously expecting it.

Mrs Gen Mc'Cook, Mrs Burke Capt Bond Pirtle[3] & a great many other have enquired after you. Give kindest regards to Sam & the Doctor Uncle Smith Aunt Charlotte & all.

Poor Aunt! I had promised that my *first* letter should be to her!

Your devoted Bro
Will

1. Lytle refers to his aunt Joanna Haines Reilly, the sister of his mother who lived with Lytle and his sisters most of their lives. Joanna Reilly, herself a widow with two grown stepdaughters, along with her mother Margaret Haines Lytle, helped fill the maternal void

for her nephew and nieces. Joanna Reilly died March 24, 1863, just one day after Lytle left home for the last time.

2. Mrs. Lytle was part of a Lytle family in Tennessee with whom Lytle had become acquainted in 1862. He considered them to be kin. Quite captivated with Mrs. Lytle, the Union officer asked his sisters to send her clothing and other items unavailable in war-torn Tennessee. She was in mourning for her husband at the time Lytle returned to Murfreesboro in March 1863. It seems possible that the relationship extended beyond friendship to romance, although no firm evidence remains.

3. Wives accompanied a number of officers in the Twentieth Army Corps during the summer of 1863, including those of Maj. Gen. Alexander McCook and Col. Joseph Burke.

### To Josephine Lytle Foster and Elizabeth Lytle Broadwell

*A letter from Josephine Foster dated March 29 and one from Lily Broadwell had reached Lytle by the time he wrote from Murfreesboro on April 4. Both sisters described their aunt's last hours in great detail. The sensitive Lytle must have been deeply moved on learning that his aunt's last words were of him. On her last morning, Reilly asked if Lytle had been there. Thinking she meant his visit of the day before, Foster said, "Yes, Aunty." "But," said Reilly, "I thought he went to Louisville." Foster affirmed that he had gone. "Well, what did he come back for then—for he was here just now." When told she had been dreaming, the dying woman replied, "No—no Josie— . . . it was no dream— I saw him right before me—& he shook hands with me—I saw him plainly. I was not asleep—it was no dream."[1]*

Murfreesboro
April 4th 63

I thank you my beloved sisters from the bottom of my heart for your sweet letters, so sad and yet so full of comfort. I shall carry them along with me and read them often to keep vividly before me, dear Aunts memory, her admonitions her love her calm & peaceful and triumphant death. I remember that when first our father and then our mother died I felt as if I had lost *all* stimulus to exertion. The world seemed a wide dreary waste with no green spot on it—for *you* were then very young, and though I loved you with a boys love I could not appreciate you as I do now. I cannot say that I am affected by the death of dear Aunt Ann as I was by fathers or mothers. An older man I reflect she is now wearing the crown of righteousness, and her troubles all over is mingling with the happy throng forever blessed by the smiles of Heaven. I am sure though that I love her very dearly, that I cannot look upon her as *gone* & *will not* but will always strive to feel that when we are happy she is with us, in our midst, and when we are sad that *then* she is with us still, loving and affectionate & sympathising as of old. It would have been a great comfort to me to have looked once again on her pale brow before I turned my face finally towards the battle field, but I have ever striven to do my duty in the service and felt that I could not turn back without leave. What seems harder still though is that I could not be with her in her last moments—while *she lived*—and that my departure was not delayed for a *few* hours longer.

Dear Auntie!—the dreams or vision of which you speak touched me most deeply.

My beloved sisters I pray God—with you—that she may not have died & lived in vain.

The first news from home was indeed *sad* news.

I am not yet assigned. *Pirtle* was relived from duty on Rosecrans staff & appointed on mine today.

Farewell—write often—for my heart is heavy enough.

Yr devoted Brother<br>*Will*

1. Josephine Lytle Foster to William H. Lytle, March 29, [1863], LP, box 32, no. 259, and Elizabeth Lytle Broadwell to William H. Lytle, [March 28, 1863], LP, box 31, no. 104.

### To Elizabeth Lytle Broadwell

*Lytle probably refers here to Lily Broadwell's letter of April 8, 1863. Broadwell wrote about the void their aunt's death had caused in the sisters' lives. Before her death Joanna Reilly had added a codicil to her will requesting that two hundred dollars be given to the Widows Home. Broadwell stated that she and Foster wanted this to be the first disbursement from Reilly's estate and inquired if their brother agreed. Broadwell also passed along the news that she had been to see the milliners and dressmakers about getting items made for the Tennessee Mrs. Lytle and would do her best to hurry them along. Lily Broadwell further reported that their sister suffered from depression and was not eating.[1]*

*After his long wait, Lytle had received assignment as commander of the First Brigade, Third Division, Twentieth Army Corps in the Army of the Cumberland, where he replaced Brig. Gen. Joshua W. Sill, who had been killed at Murfreesboro on December 31, 1862.[2]*

Murfreesboro<br>Sunday 19th April<br>1863

My dear little Bessie

I delayed answering your last until I could tell you where I was going. The probabilities are that I will not take Matthews Brigade but one in *Sheridans* Div McCooks Army corps[3] & that I will go into camp *tomorrow.* It is like taking a leap in the dark, as I do not know of what troops the command is composed nor am I acquainted personally with a single officer in it—that I am aware of. Rosecrans suggested a command under Sheridan several days since. I am inclined to believe (entre nous) that the Gen wishes to place me where I will be second in command—& thus *in time*—stand a chance for a Division. I look for my orders every moment, as Grover reports they were issued this morning—but the Orderly has not yet arrived. Your last letter disturbed me not a little. I earnestly pray that our beloved Josie is better & also dear Uncle.

You do not know dear Bessie how constantly my sisters are in my thoughts & your names—when I *can* speak of you to a mutual friend—on my lips. It is a great comfort to have Pirtle with me as we can compare notes about *home.*[4]

How feelingly can I apply to each of you *Byrons* lines to *his* sisters
Though human thou didst not deceive me
Though woman thou didst not forsake
Though loved, thou forbarest to grieve me
Though slandered thou never couldnt shake
Though trusted thou didst not disclaim me
Though parted it was not to fly
Though watchful t'was not to defame me
For mute, that the world might belie
*All* the stanzas are I think very touching—*read them*—they were written at just my age—they commence "though the day of my destiny's over."

I am of course still at Mrs Lytle's who has been very kind & polite. If you see Col Kennett tell him I have complied with his request & given her all the advice & assistance in my power. Of course dear Sister in regards to our dear Aunts bequest to the Widows Home, I desire to see her last wishes strictly complied with and trust that her Will will be carried into effect in this particular as soon as practicable.

I need badly Sis a pair of slippers—common ones will do—and a couple of *wash* towels like my old ones. Several were lost in my valise. I have written by the way in regard to *it*—to the R. R. Supt at Louisville—estimating my loss at $130.x but as yet have rec'd no answer. There is some difficulty I fear in sending goods through now—but perhaps you can find some officer to bring me the little articles named as they will not be bulky.

We have heard nothing yet of Mrs Lytle's goods. I trust they will come through in safety & not be delayed by the recent orders of the Treasury Dept. I wrote to Judge Swayne immediately on the receipt of your letter—also a long letter to Uncle.

It will probably be several days before I write again, if I assume command tomorrow.

Tell dear Josie my next shall be to her. I called on Mrs. Burke this morning. She is very pleasantly located at [Mr Kearnys] close by the Camp of the 10th. Mr K——— married a sister of Mr Lytle.

Remember me kindly to Sam, Foster, dear Sis & the little ones—not forgetting the old ladies[5] & believe me

Devotedly Yr Bro<br>Will

Did you see this in the Times?

1. Elizabeth Lytle Broadwell to William H. Lytle, April 8, 1863, LP, box 31, no. 90.

2. Joshua W. Sill, an Ohio-born West Point graduate, was a professor of engineering and mathematics in Brooklyn prior to the war. William H. Venable in his *Poems of William Haines Lytle* quotes a sergeant major in the brigade on the replacement of Sill by Lytle. "'It speedily became apparent that the same lofty courtesies and qualities of mind and heart which had so endeared to us the one, shone out with an equal luster in the character of the other. The same calm breadth of justice, the same high scorn of meanness and baseness, the same rare culture, the same philosophic quiet and studious earnestness to excel, the same genial warmth of manner, the same affectionate tenderness for the comfort of his subordinates, whether officers or men, the same scrupulous care not to offend, the same magnanimity toward foes, and the same magnificent surrender of self toward friends, distinct in individuals, yet alike in their grand resemblances to the patterns and models of the race—it is enough for me to say that the beautiful tribute which General Lytle, in his late speech at Bridgeport, paid to the virtues and valor and wisdom of Sill, is itself the best and truest eulogy that can be pronounced over Lytle.'"

3. Maj. Gen. Alexander McDowell McCook (1831-1903) commanded the Twentieth Corps, Army of the Cumberland, from January 9 until October 9, 1863. During that period Philip Henry Sheridan (1831-1888) commanded the Third Division, Twentieth Corps, Army of the Cumberland.

4. The Pirtle and Lytle families had been close friends since Robert Todd Lytle and Henry Pirtle studied law together with John Rowan between 1822 and 1824.

5. Lytle asked to be remembered to his great aunts Sally Bullock and Martha Brown, along with his brothers-in-law, sister Josephine Foster, and his niece and nephew.

*To Josephine Lytle Foster*

H$^d$Qr$^s$ 1$^{st}$ Brigade 3$^d$ Div
20$^{th}$ Army Corps April 23d
1863

My beloved Sister. Well dear Joe—here I am fairly in camp again, surrounded by all the paraphernalia of busy war. I assumed command yesterday morning. It seemed as if I were entirely cut off from all old associations, as I did not know a single officer in my command—or *man*.

My command is composed entirely of north western troops. My regiments are the 24th Wisconsin Col Larrabee, 21$^{st}$ Mich Col M'Greary, 36$^{th}$ Ill & 88$^{th}$ Ill Col Sherman & Sutermeisters In$^a$ Battery. Maj Gen Sheridan (an Ohio man & graduate of the Academy) commands the Division—M'Cook the Corps. Tomorrow I have my first review. I like the looks of the Brigade very much thus far.

They are all western men & are said to be full of fight. It is poor Sills Brigade. I had a visit today from Col & Mrs Burke, Lt Col Ward, Maj Hudson, Surgeon Shaw & Capt Lacey of the 10th & Capt Shelly & Lt Thomas of the Scotch Fusilers (B. Army)—the two latter gentlemen knew Mr Power intimately.

I expect a number of officers & ladies tomorrow to witness the review. Mrs Burke tells me that Mrs D$^r$ M$^c$Dermott & Mrs Col Goddard (wife of Rosecrans A A Gen) stopped for her the other day to *call on my wife with them*. Mrs B—— had some difficulty in convincing them that I was *not* a married man, and that the Mrs Lytle at whose house I was staying was only a friend or very remote connexion.

The *trunk* by the way arrived safely. I have not seen Mrs L. since but trust she is pleased. When I see her (she will probably be out tomorrow) I will make arrangements for remitting the amount of the bills by express either to the Doctor or Sam

The officers of the 24$^{th}$ Wis waited on me to day in full dress—A remarkably fine looking and gentlemanly set of fellows.

Rosecrans has put me where I am *second* in *command*. I am confident I shall like my regiments & trust *they* will *me*. I *shall do my duty & leave results to themselves.* Sheridan I like very much. *All* have rec'd me cordially. You would like to know my staff. I have retained all the old staff except those crowded out by Grover & Pirtle[1]—this I deemed best (as a temporary arrangement) coming here a stranger. In fact it could not be avoided. I am much pleased with the appearances of the gentlemen. They seem active & efficient.

I have distributed them as follows—

| | |
|---|---|
| J. A Grover<sup>A</sup> | A Gen |
| Lt Trumbull | Brigade Inspector |
| Lt Jackson | Brigade Prov Marshal |
| Lt Boal | Topographical Eng of Brigade |
| Capt Bouton | Brigade Com$^r$ & Q$^r$ |
| Lt Pirtle ⎱ Lt Eaton ⎰ | Aides de Camp |
| Surg Hassé | Brig Surgeon |

I rec'd *your* letter *yesterday* & dear Lily's with the trunk. I am greatly relieved to find you are better & that the children are well.

I think of poor Auntie constantly & can only hope that we will all meet again in the other world. Kiss dear Nannie & Johnnie for me over & over again & tell them not to forget me. It is uncertain when we may get into action.

The very hour I assumed command I found orders to hold my men in readiness to march at a moments notice with 3 days rations. Reconnaissances are made daily with more or less fighting.

There is very little danger however. We may not look for anything of a fight for a long time.

My belt & sash arrived safely—though M'Grews charges are *enormous*. Belt—$40—Sash $30.

I must close my dear Josie, as I much hurried but I knew you would be glad to receive a line even though hurriedly written. With very best regards to the Doctor—whose kindness & attention to me I will never forget & love to the whole family believe me my beloved Sister

Yr devoted—Will

Tell my dear old Aunts that *Mrs Lytle* is *Union* all over.

Kiss them for me. I hear *my Band* playing for parade— It is a splendid one— You know how I love music—

Good bye dear Sister.

---

1. James Grover, an original member of the Tenth Ohio, received promotion to first lieutenant and adjutant on January 28, 1862, and assignment to Company E on January 1, 1863.

*To Elizabeth Lytle Broadwell*

1st Brigade 3d Div 20th Army Corps
Sunday April 26th 1863

Today to my great delight my dearest Bessie I recd today two letters from you, two from Uncle & one from Judge Swayne. I have been anxiously expecting letters for the last three days & was very glad to get them. Poor Mrs Kilgour![1] I was very much shocked to see her death announced in the Com[l] several days ago—of course before your letters arrived, our *paper* mail being very regular.

I do not often read the obituary notices but in these times we lose so many acquaintainces that unconsciously my eyes wandered to them. I deeply sympathize with her afflicted family especially Aunt Charlotte & Miss Lizzie[2] & feel myself as if I had lost one of my best & kindest friends. Be careful by the way dear Lily in writing me to give Brigade—Div & A. Corps (as in the heading of this)—otherwise my mails travel all around the Camp. My review did not come off when I expected. The very night I wrote dear little Sis I rec'd orders at midnight to march the next morning at 5½ to relieve Col Laiboldt's Brigade on a road leading to Shelbyville. I was up nearly all night making arrangements & started promptly to the minute—with 4 pieces of artillery. I took up a strong position and held it for two days when I was recalled. I saw nothing of the rebels, but Gen[l] Sheridan told me this morning that *40* of them made a dash on the very point I occupied just afterwards & drove in our mounted pickets. My expedition was I suppose in conjunction with the move against M'Minnville under Reynolds.[3] I was recalled day before yesterday & yesterday reviewed my command. Everything went off finely. The ceremony was in front of Gen Sheridans H[d] Q[rs]—on the very ground on which I reviewed my old Brigade a year ago. After the review I invited the visitors to my quarters. Among my guests were Gen Sheridan, Col Ducat Ins. Gen on Rosecrans staff[a] Col & Mrs Moore (Miss Van Tramp) Dr & Mrs Patterson—Mrs Lytle in her new carriage & clothes—Col Burke Lt Col Ward Hunter Brooke, Birkham, [Fusé (T.S)] & Curry—a son of Olivar Curry (reporters) all the field officers of the Brigade—a wagon load of officers of the 10th & many others—so you see I had quite a party! Well dear Lil—I have bad news to tell you. *I must lose Joe Guthrie & Reardon!* There is an order it seems forbidding men to be detailed from their regiments into other corps or divisions as orderlies. I made application for them which was refused by the Adjt

Gen & today I saddled my horse & rode in & saw Rosecrans personally. *It was no use.* The Gen was like flint—said he had refused a similar application from Lew Wallace[5] "& wouldnt do it for his own brother." I fear that after I left him I swore a little though it is Sunday. *I really dont know how I shall get along. It is as heavy a blow as I could get—so far* as my personal comfort is concerned. The two men are *invaluable* to me. I fear *indispensable* to my comfort—so far as a man *can be comfortable* in campaign. Please send for old Wilson & see if he will come as my *groom & body servant* & on *what terms* & write me as to whether you think he had best come. Please act speedily.

Poor Joe! He will be heart broken. I have not yet told him. He was more delighted when my commission arrived than I was myself & was as *proud* a man yesterday at the handsome manner in which things went off, as you ever saw. Reardon too is a most sterling fellow. They are both so neat & tidy & so soldierlike that it was a real pleasure to have them about.

My poor horses too—their splendid grooming is I fear a thing that will excite no more the admiration of the Army. In a months time I expect to have no horse to ride on & no shirt to my back—for a great army is full of pilferers & Joe watches everything like a hawk—However a soldier must not complain & I hope for the best.

I will send Mc'Grew his money when I *get ready.* His charges were outrageous. He sent me a pair of shoulder straps which I didn't order & will return.

Mrs L——'s wardrobe pleased her very much— I called there today & she handed me the amount of the bills $146.25/00 which I have directed my Quartermaster to invest in a Govt draft or certificate payable to my order. I will forward it as soon as possible to you care of M^r B—— You said the bills would amount to more, but were I suppose mistaken. I added them up myself & am sure this is correct. Mrs L—— expresses herself as under great obligations to you & so am I dear Sister. I am afraid you & dear Josie have had a great deal of trouble. The dresses are I think elegant & the young widow looked yesterday quite attractive & "a la mode." There would be no end Bessie of all the amusing things I could tell you—if I could only *talk* to you—but to write long letters consumes too much of my time just *now* at *the start,* when every moment is precious. I am entirely willing to leave the matter of the monument or vault entirely to your taste & that of the family & I am disposed to think I should agree with you in preferring the monument.

With best love to dearest Joe the little pets, Jack & Nan & kind regards to Sam the Doctor Mrs Broadwell & the old ladies.

Ever your devoted<br>
Will

*Miss* Rousseau is here[6]— Pirtle visited her this morning—

Col Ward tells me the officers of the 10th are getting me up a testimonial.

Poor Guthrie & Reardon I must now *break the ice* to them

Write me about Wilson immediately. I will pay him $20 or even $25 if his *health is good*[7]— I will write Uncle this week.

Uncle's letter mentions dear Aunt Ann very feelingly— You know his peculiarities & should pass them over.

Camp in the field<br>
April 28th—

Just in from Picket dearest Lil. I enclose Mrs L's note— I have not yet been able to buy a draft but expect to have one tomorrow—

All well<br>
Love to all<br>
In great haste<br>
Most Affly Will

1. Lytle refers to Elizabeth Coles Higbee Kilgour, a New Jersey native and sister of Charlotte Higbee, the wife of his uncle Ezekial Smith Haines. The Kilgour, Lytle, and Haines families were among Cincinnati's elite, and they lived in the Queen City's most prestigious neighborhood close to the central business district and Ohio River. (See Doris Dawn Dwyer, "A Century of City-Building: Three Generations of the Kilgour Family in Cincinnati, 1798-1914" [Ph.D. diss., Miami Univ., 1979].) The Haines family was originally from New Jersey. Daniel Haines, governor of New Jersey from 1847 unitl 1850, was the first cousin of Lytle's mother, Elizabeth Smith Haines Lytle. Sarah Doremus, the sister of Daniel Haines, was the mother of Sed Doremus, for whom General Lytle held great affection.

2. Lizzie refers to Elizabeth Kilgour, the niece of Charlotte and Ezekial Haines, born in 1843.

3. Joseph Jones Reynolds (1822-1899) was with the Fourteenth Corps, Army of the Cumberland, during 1863. He was a Kentucky native, West Point graduate, and former professor of engineering at Washington University in St. Louis. McMinnville is forty miles east-southeast of Murfreesboro; Shelbyville lies twenty-five miles south of Murfreesboro.

4. Arthur C. Ducat was lieutenant colonel and inspector general.

5. Lewis Wallace (1827-1905), an Indiana native, served in the Mexican War as a second lieutenant, and like Lytle later became a lawyer and served in the state legislature. *Who Was Who in the Union* by Stewart Sifakia (New York: Facts on File, 1988) does not give any command for Wallace during 1863. However, from the Lytles's viewpoint, he is best known as being responsible for the defense of Cincinnati in 1862. After the war he became famous as the author of *Ben Hur*.

6. Lytle presumably refers to a daughter of then Maj. Gen. Lovell Harrison Rousseau, a native of Kentucky whom both Lytle and Pirtle would have known prior to the Civil War.

7. Lytle inquired about the health of his elderly personal servant John Wilson, then in Cincinnati. Lytle was considering paying Wilson to return to the front.

## To Lewis J. Cist

H<sup>d</sup> Q<sup>rs</sup> 1<sup>st</sup> Brigade 3<sup>d</sup> Div
20<sup>th</sup> Army Corps
Murfreesboro 29<sup>th</sup> April

Lewis J. Cist Esq.
St. Louis

My dear Sir.[1] I rec'd a letter from you before leaving for the front propounding certain questions which at that time I was unable to answer—not having rec'd my commission until after my arrival here.

My commission is dated March 17<sup>th</sup> 1863—with rank from Nov 29<sup>th</sup> 1862.

Trusting that at some future days our old acquaintance may be renewed I remain Sir Yrs very truly

W<sup>m</sup> H Lytle (Brig Gen Vols)

1. Lewis J. Cist was a member of a prominent Cincinnati family. This letter is in the Gratz Manuscript Collection, Historical Society of Pennsylvania.

## To Samuel J. Broadwell

*Lytle normally wrote to his brother-in-law Sam Broadwell, an attorney, when he had financial or legal affairs to conduct. In this instance he thought Broadwell had gone to Sandusky, Ohio, on business and therefore addressed the letter to the care of his physician brother-in-law, Nathaniel Foster.*

Hd Qrs 1<sup>st</sup> Brigade 3<sup>d</sup> Div 20<sup>th</sup> A. C.
May 3<sup>d</sup> 63

Dr Sam. Yours of April 29th is rec'd. Make the best arrangement with M<sup>r</sup> Haines you can & buy the property you speak of if you think proper. I enclose you draft for $146.25, with Mrs Lytles *bills*. Lily or Joe can pay them.

All well
In great haste
Truly yrs
WH Lytle

D[r] Doctor— Sam being probably at Sandusky I will address this to you. In writing me my friends must be careful to give my *Brigade—Div* & Army Corps as above.

Let Joe keep the receipts as I have receipted to Mrs L——

### To Josephine Lytle Foster

*As the Army of the Tennessee and the Army of the Cumberland enjoyed a lull from battle, Rosecrans rotated brigades on outpost duty.*

[Undated but probably May 5, 1863]
1st Brigade

My dear little Joe— I can only dash you off a line— my Brigade has just rec'd orders to go on outpost duty & I expect to be absent four or five days. If during that time I can communicate with you by mail, I will do so. Tell the Doctor I shall not need Wilson at present.

Lily & Sam are I suppose at Sandusky. *Do* write often—it is the only luxury I have. Good bye my dear Sister.

Kiss the children for me & give kind regards to Nat— I send slip from Chicago Tribune— In great haste.

Yr devoted brother—Will

### To Josephine Lytle Foster

*At the time Lytle wrote this letter, Rosecrans held the Army of the Cumberland near Murfreesboro as he tried to garner needed supplies for his army. In the East Hooker had just led Union forces in their defeat at the battle of Chancellorsville, although word of the loss had not reached Lytle and his forces at the time this letter was written.*

H[d] Qrs 1st Brig 3 Div 20th A.C.
On Outpost—May 8th 1863

My dearest Joe. We have been here two days on this duty. I have my brigade here and two pieces of artillery. We are near *Salem*—a point southwest of Murfreesboro! I expect to be relieved tomorrow. Everything quiet, thus far—though the enemy has a cavalry brigade only 9 miles off, and his videttes & mine are in sight. Guthrie & Reardon are still with me— It is quite possible I may get into a row about them, but I shall hold on to Guthrie at least—as long as possible. Your last letter (speaking of Wilson) arrived day before yesterday. It was a great treat—here in the woods. We are looking in anxious suspense for the news from Hooker. Another reverse in the East would be a calamity indeed.[1] I have no news to tell you as I have not had any time of late—being constantly occupied.

Miss Rousseau is in Murfreesboro, but I have not been able to see her— How are the children? I would give a $50 bill to take a ride with Miss Nannie & Capt Jack this morning.

I hope dear Bessie is enjoying herself & that her trip will benefit the poor child.

Tell Uncle I received his letter & will write him on my return to camp. My black horse is improving. The weather out here has been *awful.* Rain—all the time & the nights *cold.* I put on a woolen shirt to day—instead of my white one. My men have the little shelter tent (tent d'abri) which they carry in their knapsacks—two men to a tent.

Give my best love to Uncle & Aunt & the old ladies not forgetting Nat.

Farewell dear Joe. I must make up my daily report which I have to send in by courier to H$^d$ Qrs of the Army. Three deserters & three contraband came in yesterday from the enemys lines—but brought no intelligence of interest. Good bye. We expect stirring times soon but there is no telling. Our hope is that they will attack.

I knew that you would be glad to get even a few lines—so steal a moment from Uncle Sam to dash off this.

Most Affly<br>Will

1. Gen. Joseph Hooker commanded the Army of the Potomac during the Union loss at Chancellorsville, May 2-4, 1863. Though the South gained a victory, it proved costly in Confederate casualties, including the death of Gen. Stonewall Jackson.

### To Josephine Lytle Foster

H$^d$ Qrs 1st B——— 3Div 20 A C<br>Monday May 11th 63

My beloved Sister

I recd your letter yesterday while on Outpost duty announcing the death of poor Aunt Sallie. My dear Josie am I never to hear ought but bad news from home! Grief after grief & sorrow after sorrow! Poor old lady! I had fondly hoped that her life might yet be spared for many years and that I might greet her on my return home. I was very much attached to her. She was certainly a most remarkable woman, but I doubt not, her suffering all over, has made a happy exchange for this life of trouble & sorrow.

I sympathize with dear Aunt Martha[1] deeply. I doubt not the family by redoubling their attentions to her will endeavour to lighten her load as much as possible. Please give her my warmest best love & say I will have many a long story to tell her of my campaigns when I get back.

Poor dear Bessie I am afraid the sad news will mar all the pleasure of her little trip— My heart bleeds for you my sisters. Aunt Ann, Aunt Sallie, Mrs. Kilgour, Mrs Davis & Mrs Thompson all gone! What a wide chasm it makes in our pleasant circle.

Yet dear Sister we shall be the easier weaned from *this* life when our closing scene shall come, and will gladly look "across the river" to the loved hands that beckon us on. I do beg that you & Lily for my sake as well as that of others so near & dear to you will bear up bravely under these successive shocks.

Should either of *you* be ill I must be by your side & *nothing* can keep me away—if I have to throw up my commission, for the world without my sisters would be to me a desert. I write in great haste dear Joe as my duties are incessant & laborious. My health is good as usual thank God.

Guthrie is still with me. My love to the dear little ones the Doctor & *all*. I will soon write again.

Yr devoted brother<br>
*Will*

1. Martha Brown was the last surviving sister of Lytle's grandmother Margaret Smith Haines Lytle.

## To Samuel J. Broadwell

*While the Union forces in the West continued the Vicksburg campaign, the Army of the Cumberland prepared to pursue the Army of Tennessee deeper into Tennessee.*

H^d Qrs 1^st Brig 3 Div 20th AC<br>
Sunday May 17th 1863

Dear Sam,

Make such an arrangement with Pool as you deem best. I leave the whole matter to M^r Haines the Doctor & yourself. Whatever course you pursue will meet with my entire approval.

I write in great haste, as my military duties are entirely absorbing. The army is being rapidly mobilized and we *may* be on the eve of *events*.

I cut down my baggage & sent my sick to the rear this morning.

Love to all<br>
[signature cut off]

## To Elizabeth Lytle Broadwell

H^d Qrs 1^st Brig 3 Div 20th A C
Thursday—May 20th 1863

My dear Sister Lily. I have recd your letter written since returning from Sandusky, but was much disappointed in not hearing from any of the family either yesterday or the day before. I look for the arrival & distribution of the mail every day with the utmost anxiety & always feel sadly disappointed unless I receive a letter from *somebody*—if even a [*dash*], so that it comes from *home*. I have had *hard* work dear Lil since I assumed command.

I not only came among strangers & had to overcome if possible the very natural dissatisfaction among the friends of an old & meritorious "Col Com^g"[1] at his being *superseded* but I found also a *drill of the Brigade* which was entirely new to me—the drill of *Casey*[2] instead of that of Scott & Hardee[3] to which I had been accustomed—a drill in *two* lines, instead of *one* & a drill *combining* movements of artillery infantry of the line & skirmishes. I have finally mastered it but it required *intense* application for a commanding officer must not only know the *tactics* but know them *better* than any one else. My officers are most of them *remarkably* intelligent men & my brigade the best drilled brigade I *ever saw*—that is so far as its Brigade drill is concerned. There are four ladies in the 88^th Ill—Mrs Col Sherman, Mrs Quartermaster Cushing, Mrs Surgeon Pearce & Mrs— somebody else (I forget her name)[4]

My staff & I invited them over last night to my H^d Qrs to meet Col & Mrs Burke. We had a tea fight & a good time generally, with music by the band & singing by Burke & Alf Pirtle. To my amusement *Joe* Guthrie & Capt Bouton (Brig Q^r) being at a loss for a table cloth had borrowed the *sheets* of the Gen Cous^l & the first thing I knew had them spread on the table. I peremptorily ordered their removal, much to the disgust of both Bouton & Joe who were viewing their fine effect with great satisfaction. After a pleasant evening however came hard work—for before daylight this morning (being field Officer of the Day for the Corps) I had to visit the picket lines—a hard ride of twelve miles. My escort & I returned to breakfast at 7 this morning.

At 11 with my Staff & Col Larrabee Com^g 24^th Wis, I rode through Murfreesboro to Gen Negleys[5] H^d Qrs in front of which the old 10^th was reviewed by Gen Rosecrans. The old regiment looked & marched splendidly, but is a little behind in drill having had no drill in battalion

movements for a long time. After the review Gen Negley invited Rosecrans
& staff & myself & staff to the handsome house he occupies—where
*Mrs* Negley made her appearance & we were invited to partake of an
elegant collation with wines &c.

Old *Rosey* was very cordial in his greeting & devoted most of his
conversation to your humble servant. He has promised to ride out & see
my next drill & witness some new evolution of my own. Good bye dear
Bessie. I have no time for more— I could fill a score of sheets— Do *all*
of you write often.

We may have stirring times *now* at any moment. Love to dear Sister
Uncle & Aunt C Sam Doctor Mrs B & all[6]— Most devotedly

—Brother Will

1. Lytle refers to Brig. Gen. Joshua W. Sill, killed at Murfreesboro on December 31,
1862.

2. Silas Casey was a Union general and author of *System of Infantry Tactics* (1861). The
United States Army adopted Casey's system in 1862.

3. William Joseph Hardee, C.S.A. general, had taught infantry, artillery, and cavalry
tactics at West Point. The Confederates made some use of Casey's system but generally
favored Hardee's.

4. As is apparent throughout Lytle's letters of 1863, some women accompanied their
officer husbands in the Army of the Cumberland.

5. James Scott Negley, a Pennsylvania native, was like Lytle a volunteer officer. He
survived the battle of Chickamauga but was relieved of his duties. Although a court of
inquiry cleared him of charges of cowardice and deserting his men, he never held command
again.

6. Along with his usual references to Charlotte and Ezekial Haines and his brothers-in-
law, Lytle mentions his great aunt Martha Brown.

### To Ezekial S. Haines

*Ezekial Haines had been in a generally weakened condition since mid-1862. Though
few of Haines's Civil War letters remain, Lytle considered his uncle a good core-
spondent.*

H[d] Qrs 1st Brig 3 Div 20th A C.

May 21st 1863

My dear Uncle. I do not think you are as good a correspondent as you
were formerly. My own letters have to be written at rare intervals, my
time being entirely occupied by military duties. I have had many
difficulties to encounter since I assumed command here. Amongst other
matters I had to master a *new drill*—entirely different from that to which

I had been accustomed. There is a great deal of intelligence among my officers. You have probably heard of Col Larrabee com^g 24^th Wisconsin.[1] He was formerly a member of Congress from that state & had a wide spread reputation as *Judge* Larrabee, the leader of the Douglas party in Wisconsin. He is an accomplished lawyer and a man of great ability.

Col Sherman of the 88^th Ill is a son of the present Mayor of Chicago.[2] His regiment is one of the "Board of Trade" regiments & his officers represent the élite of the young men of Chicago, the other two regiments are ably officered, the 36^th Ill—being one of the famous "Pea Ridge" regiments.[3]

We are under orders today to be ready to move "at a moments notice" (this confidential). —An advance at any hour would not surprise me & we cannot go *far* without a desperate fight. I trust your health is improving & that Aunt is well. I have been wanting to write her but really I have not had the time.

Almost every letter from home has brought me sad tidings. I earnestly trust that those remaining may be spared from further affliction.

Guthrie is still with me—the black horse is so terribly hard mouthed that I find him of little use. Neither Guthrie nor myself can ride him a few miles without being utterly used up. In action I could not get along with him at all. I will try & trade him off. I have a tip top staff— excellent men—active brave & laborious. My Brigade Com^r & Qu^r is a large [grain] merchant of Chicago—a thorough going business man & first rate manager. He has had a very happy influence on my *purse,* as my *mess* bills are not one half what they were at Hunstville & I believe better. I was amused yesterday at *Bouton.* He asked me if I liked *eggs.* I said "yes"—So he bought a *barrel* at 25 cents per doz of a Sutler in town—sold *half* at 45 cents per doz and informed us last night that he had realized *the purchase money*—had 35 *doz of eggs left* & could declare a *div—— of 15 cents!*— Please tell Lil & Joe this. Bouton is from N. Hampshire!

Please give my love to Aunt Charlotte & remember me most kindly to Judge Swayne & Miss Lillie—and to all my friends who remember me.

Good night my dear General. How delighted I should be to meet you all this summer. Hoping soon to hear from you. Believe me most affly

Will

1. Charles Hathaway Larrabee (1820-1883) served in the Union army from April 17, 1861, until his resignation in September 1863. *Bigraphical Directory of the United States Congress* (Washington, D.C.: GPO, 1989), 1345.

2. Francis T. Sherman, colonel of the Twenty-eighth Illinois, was the son of Francis

Cornwall Sherman, who served as mayor of Chicago from 1841 throuh 1842 and from 1862 until 1865. *Biographical Dictionary of American Mayors, 1820-1980* (Westport, Conn: Greenwood Press, 1981), 330.

3. Union forces under the command of Samuel R. Curtis won the battle of Pea Ridge near the Arkansas-Missouri border on March 7-8, 1862.

## To Samuel J. Broadwell

*As of this writing Lytle had heard good news from the Vicksburg campaign, where Ulysses S. Grant was leading the ultimately successful siege against the Confederates.*

Nashville May 26th, 1863

D[r] Sam

I enclose deeds & Power of Attorney to Todd—

[To Com[r] for Ohio, here]

I trust the authentication will be satisfactory.

I had to come here on purpose & the trip & acknowledgements will cost me about 25.[x]—about my interest I suppose in the *purchase money*!

*Pirtle* is with me. He came up last evening & leaves for Camp tomorrow morning. We are all jubilant over the news from Vicksburgh.[1] Pirtle & I propose calling on Mrs. Polk this morning. I am in fine health. Everything going well here. Hope to find letters from the family at Murfreesboro— Love to all.

Sincerely yrs

W[m] *H Lytle*

This letter is in the Gratz Manuscript Collections, Historical Society of Pennsylvania.

1. Lytle had probably heard that Grant had Vicksburg under siege. On May 24, 1863, Grant had informed General Halleck that the fall of Vicksburg was only a matter of time. McPherson, *Battle Cry of Freedom*, 633.

## To Elizabeth Lytle Broadwell

*In an undated letter, probably written May 18 or May 25, 1863, Josephine Lytle Foster wrote to her brother about their sister Lily Broadwell's severe "bilious attack." Almost apologetically, Foster told Lytle she felt it essential for Broadwell and her husband to spend most of the summer in the mountains or at the seashore because they had been home all of the past several summers. She added that her family would probably join the Broadwells at some point, despite their unease at the increased distance it would take them from him, mail, and the activities of the Army of the Cumberland.[1]*

Hd Qrs 1ˢᵗ Brig 3ᵈ Div 20ᵗʰ A C.
June 1ˢᵗ 63

I seize my dearest Bessie the first moment of leisure since my return from Nashville to express my heartfelt delight to hear that you are better. I fear you have been far more ill than I supposed at first. Do not conceal anything from me if unhappily you should ever be sick again. If I thought you or dear Sister were ever in *any* danger no earthly power could keep me from your side.

I am *very* weary to night. It is 11 o'c— Tomorrow at day break my brigade starts again on Outpost duty—where we were before—or near there.

Sam's few lines acknowledging the receipt of my letter from N——e arrived today. Also one from Uncle to whom I will write soon. Everything has gone well thus far & pleasantly. We are anxiously awaiting the news from Grant.

I feel that if Providence should spare me to be with you all at home once more I should be very happy. Do not show *all* of my letters to any one but Josie.

I have very much to say to you my beloved Sister but am too weary & must have rest after I attend to some matters tonight yet indisposed of. May God grant that you may have better health hence forward.

*Do* make arrangements—both you & Sister—to visit the sea shore or some pleasant watering place. You both need such a trip after your sad spring. God bless you.

I send you a good night Kiss.

Yr own Will

Tell Josie that her letters arrived safely & to kiss Nannie & Johnnie for Uncle.

1. Josephine Lytle Foster to William H. Lytle [May ?, 1863], LP, box 32, no. 266.

### To Ezekial S. Haines

Hᵈ Qrs 1ˢᵗ Brig 3ᵈ Div 20 A. C.
On Outpost June 3ᵈ 1863

My dear Gen. We have been here now for two days, about 4 miles from town. Expect to return to camp day after tomorrow. I acknowledge the receipt of your letters & seize the earliest moment I have had to reply to them. There is nothing new here to tell you. We have been looking for marching orders daily for some time, and may move at any moment. I have gotten along very well & pleasantly thus far with my Brigade.

The weather is quite cool. I sleep under blankets & oftentimes a buffalo robe. The nights are much pleasanter than with us.

Tell Aunt C—— that the forest in which we are camped is filled with mocking birds. One splendid fellow kept me awake last night until midnight.

I see Nat M<sup>c</sup>Lean has been appointed Prov M. Gen[1]— I would not have the place on any consideration. It will suit him, however, exactly.

We receive our mails regularly from Cin<sup>ati</sup>. Newspapers of Monday we get on Wednesday—though we never see anything but the *Com'*— now & *then* a *Times*. In fact there is no other Cin<sup>ati</sup> papers we care much for—the *Enquirer* I believe is prohibited. Our old friend Tom Lewis paid me a visit a few days since—looking cheerful as ever. He always enquires after you very particularly. My horses are well. The sorrel is greatly admired everywhere. He is certainly a game little animal, entirely too pretty a horse to have in this service—though I *hope* to bring him home. I ran up to Nash last week to acknowledge some deeds. It is now a stupid place.

Pirtle & I called on Mrs Polk but she happened to be in Murfreesboro! I notice that her mother has died within a few days.

You must pardon this very dull letter but there is nothing in our routines of daily duty (laborious as it is to me) to interest outsiders & it is very near my hour for visiting the picket lines. Good bye General.

My affectionate regards to Aunt. Sincerely & Affly

*Will H. Lytle*

1. Nathaniel Collins McLean, Ohio native and Union general, held the position of provost marshal general, Department of the Ohio (May 1863-ca. May 1864).

### To Samuel J. Broadwell

Outpost near Salem
H<sup>d</sup> Qrs 1<sup>st</sup> Brig 3 Div 20 A.C.
June 4th 63

Dear Sam

I have no objection to selling the Warren & Union County tract if you all deem it advisable.

I trust my power to Todd may answer as it is quite likely we may soon move forward & I shall have no opportunity to attend to business. In great haste & trusting dear Lily is entirely recovered.

truly yrs<br>WH Lytle

## To Elizabeth Lytle Broadwell

*Although no letters written by Lily Broadwell or Josephine Foster from late May through the end of July survive, General Lytle indicated he received mail occasionally during that period. Meanwhile, as summer's heat set in, the Army of the Cumberland was either on the move or anxiously observing the Confederates' movements.*

H<sup>d</sup> Qrs 1<sup>st</sup> Brig 3 Div 20th A.C.<br>June 5<sup>th</sup> 63—Outpost near Salem

My dearest Bessie. Your cheering letter was rec'd two days ago, but until today I have not had time to carefully read it. I am *very thankful* that you are convalescing and trust sincerely that you will rapidly improve in strength.

By all means I think you & Jodie should avoid the hot months in the city and start as early as practicable for the seashore or some pleasant watering place or summer resort where you can have plenty of fresh air and change of scene & society. Do not fear for me I beg of you as I shall feel far happier if I know you are pleasantly located for the summer.

Well dear Lil, we have had stirring times within the last two days. In truth for *four* days I have scarcely slept. On Wednesday I rec'd orders that indicated a forward movement next day. I was riding my picket lines about half past 5 P.M. when I got the orders—to have camping inspection throughout my whole command—at 6 P.M—men to have 40 rounds in boxes, three days rations in haversacks and four in knapsacks—five days in wagons & five days forage. Being out in the woods on Outpost I had to send in to camp for my teams to come out with supplies and then distribute them to the command. This kept me up nearly all night but at daylight we were ready. The best laid plans however "aft gang astray" We *did not* march yesterday. My cavalry pickets were attacked early yesterday morning near Salem—or rather the cavalry pickets, in front of my infantry line. *My* boys they did not venture to assail— About 10 A.M the rebs came up on the Shelbyville Pike a few miles from Murfreesboro on my left and attacked Carlin's Brigade and about three we heard furious cannonading in the direction of Franklin. So that all day yesterday on

this advanced post we had cannon in front "cannon to the right &
cannon to left of us." I had ordered my Brigade yesterday to shift slightly
its position & stand to arms this morning at day break. Before light an
officer came in (in a hurry) from my picket line reporting a regiment of
rebel cavalry & *ten thousand* infantry advancing against my brigade. I
immediately formed line of battle on the ground I had selected last night
and with a few of my staff rode out to the exterior picket lines to
reconnoiter for myself. It turned out to be a mistake at least so far as the
inf$^y$ was concerned. The cavalry made no attack this morning &
everything today has been quiet. We *have not marched* however, and I
think the general rebel advance against us yesterday on so many roads
rather astonished folks in Murfreesboro. (All I say about military matters
is confidential in the family.) The whole thing on their part was probably
a reconnaissance in force to see what we were about.

So you see dear Bessie we have lively times. Yesterday was quite
exciting. I have a fine battery & had they come in this morning would
have given them a warm reception. Tell Jodie *the box* has not yet arrived.
I look for it daily.

The 10$^{th}$ I hear is going to make me a handsome present. I wish it
would come before we move that I might send it home.[1] Please tell Sam
that I have written Ripley in case the R.R. should pay me anything for
my luggage to mail it to *him*. I want Sam to deposit it to my credit in
one of our banks.

Well dear Bessie it is nearly dark & they are waiting supper for me.
Kiss dearest Joe & the children. Write me often when you get stronger
but do not fatigue yourself now. Tell me all about *the people*. Is Charlie
Pendleton going to marry *Flitz*? or *Splitz*?[2] I hear so. God bless you dear
Sister. I trust that Providence has many happy days in store for us all in
the future.

Good bye. Yr own

Will

Saturday morning.[3] Here we are still. It seems we were really
threatened by a considerable force on Thursday. Scouts assured me last
night that two brigades of infantry & a regiment of cavalry came up to
within six miles of my pickets. This morning [two] deserters came in and
corroborated the story.[4] The dash on the cavalry pickets was made by
300 rebels with two pieces of artillery. The *rebs* were every where
repulsed. Alf Pirtle sends his regards.

1. Lytle refers to the jewel-encrusted Maltese cross presented to him by the officers of the Tenth Ohio on August 9, 1863, near Bridgeport, Alabama. His speech on receiving the cross is included in Appendix B.

2. Lytle refers to his friend and correspondent Charlotte Pendleton. The question marks regarding the names of her potential husband are Lytle's. Though the Lytle Papers collection includes none of Pendleton's letters to William Haines Lytle, there are some by Pendleton written to Lily Broadwell after his death.

3. Lytle remained on outpost Saturday, June 6, 1863.

4. Lytle means deserters from the Confederate Army.

### To Josephine Lytle Foster and Elizabeth Lytle Broadwell

*On June 24 Rosecrans ordered the Army of the Cumberland to resume its advance to the south. He had supplied his army well with animals and wagons so they could move off the main roads to gain surprise in the rugged terrain, with its natural passes and fortifications. Known as the Tullahoma campaign, the maneuvers of June 23 through July 4 ended with the Confederates retreating from Tullahoma and Federal forces in control of the approaches to Chattanooga.[1]*

(Private)
Murfreesboro June 23<sup>d</sup> 1863
Tuesday 3 P.M

My beloved sisters

I have been on Court Marshal duty for several days. My brigade is out on Outpost on Salem Road. I have not yet rec'd marching orders but am *told* unofficially that *our division moves in the morning*. My *cross* arrived yesterday and we were to have had a grand time, a great many officers invited &c &c—but this is all knocked on the head of course for the present. It was my intention to have sent it immediately home for you to keep it for me. The *box* arrived safely and Mrs Lytle *paid* me the am't of her bills. It was my purpose to have sent her money home, along with my own bills for towels &c but I was waiting for the paymaster. *That* individual I have not seen for some time, and being *flat broke* I shall use Mrs L's money (about 30$) until I get paid off. I wrote Charley Ripley that when the L.&N R. R paid for my luggage he should remit the money to Mr Broadwell.[2] Out of this you can pay Mrs L's bills & my own

The Govt will owe me at the end of this month, two months pay—about $600+. I will write you my dear sisters every chance I get but you must not feel uneasy about me if you do not hear regularly—as our mails will necessarily be *irregular.*

Give my love to Uncle S & Aunt Charlotte, to Sam & the Doctor.

Everything today is stir & bustle. It looks like a general movement.

I trust the Lord God of battles will be upon our side. My position *here* today is a bad one for a start as I cannot be present to oversee matters, my command being away out in the woods & under the command of a junior Col. I expect to be at work all night. Give my love to dear little Nannie & Johnnie. Also my sincerest regard to my very dear friend [Frances] Burchett if she is still with you. When you write *Sed* say to her that I will never forget her, and if I survive the wars hope to meet her again. I trust God will vouchsafe to her a happy & peaceful life.[3]

My best love to Aunt Martha. Write me dear girls whenever you can. Your letters I hope may reach me. Rest assured that I shall rely on our *father* to give me strength & wisdom to guide my command on the march or in battle to the best advancement of our great Cause.

Hoping that my dear Sisters will remember me in their hearts & prayers I remain

Yr devoted brother
Will

1. Patrick Abbazia, *The Chickamauga Campaign: December 1862-November 1863* (New York, Gallery Books, 1988), 29-34.

2. Lytle indicates that the Louisville & Nashville Railroad lost his luggage and he expected to be reimbursed.

3. Sed Doremus and William Haines Lytle had a long history. Although she said no to his marriage proposal, probably in 1855, by the time of his death they had reaffirmed their devotion to each other. Doremus kept an all-night vigil by his coffin prior to his October 22 funeral in Cincinnati and mourned Lytle for the rest of her life, never marrying. Her father, Thomas C. Doremus, was the brother of Professor R. Ogden Doremus. Her mother, Sarah Platt Doremus, was the sister of Daniel Haines, a governor of New Jersey. Sarah Doremus founded the Woman's Union Missionary Society and served as the manager and director of more benevolent and religious institutions than any other woman in New York City. She died January 29, 1877, at age seventy-four. (Taken from an undated newspaper clipping in a scrapbook in the Lytle Papers.)

### To Samuel J. Broadwell

June 24th 1863

D<sup>r</sup> Broadwell

I write in great haste. Please say to *Joe* that I rec'd the box of goods & will send the money to pay bills in a few days.

I write you to know what chance I have of securing a command in the 30,000 new Ohio troops recently called out by the Governor. My command here is a fine one but I would of course swap it for the command of 30,000 men or even a *Division*. If you deem it *advisable* please have Tod[1] written to by some friends. Of *course* I *prefer* to command (other things being equal) troops from my own State. The command of a *Division* would probably soon increase my *rank* and candidly I believe myself to be as well qualified as *any other man* to assist in the organization, drill & disciplining of new troops.

The Gove *must*, if he raises this new levy, call experienced officers from the army to drill & prepare them for service. If the Governor *should ask the President to have me sent to Ohio for this purpose I have no doubt the request would be granted.*

Please see a few of your leading Union men & agitate the question. We must act promptly.

Write me as soon as you can.

I am now on Court Martial duty. I *hear* "the Cross" has arrived safely.

There are rumors again of a *move—somewhere.*

Love to All
[bottom of letter cut off]

1. Lytle refers to Ohio governor David Tod.

### To Elizabeth Lytle Broadwell

*At the time Lytle wrote this letter, Union troops in Pennsylvania had turned back the Confederates at Gettysburg after fighting July 1-3. Though the Army of the Cumberland was engaged in the battleless Tullahoma campaign in the mountains in south central Tennessee, Lee's defeat at Gettysburg made for optimism in the North.*

H<sup>d</sup> Qrs 1<sup>st</sup> Brig 3 Div 20th A C
*Cowan* Tenn July 4th 1863

My beloved Lily. I wrote Josie a long letter from our camp beyond Tullahoma. We reached this point yesterday about 4 o'c P.M. via Tullahoma and Winchester crossing the Elk river about five miles from Winchester. We have been close up on the enemy's rear guard all the while, of course with more or less fighting. Polks corps[1] passed through here a few hours before we got in—they left at 11 a m. Our march has been a severe one, drenched with incessant rains obliged to ford swollen streams, on half rations and with all or nearly all our tents & camp comforts left behind. Yesterday I had the advance infantry column. As we approached we saw from a height plainly visible to the naked eye, the enemy's line of mounted skirmishers. Our cavalry (new troops) hesitated a little about going in and Sheridan ordered me to throw forward my skirmishers & drive the enemy out. The cavalry finally was brought to the scratch & charged driving the rebels through town. We had hardly got in & been bivouacked for a few minutes when a considerable force of the enemy was reported at a creek on the Cowan road about a mile & a half from town. Sheridan immediately ordered me forward with instructions to drive him across the creek. I marched down—in a pitiless rain—& threw two of my regiments covered by a skirmish line on the west of a hill commanding the creek.

—The principal part of their force fell back on a few shots being fired.

To my great regret during the skirmish a poor little boy was accidentally shot dead by one of our sharpshooters. He ran out from a cabin (as we discovered afterwards) to put up some rails in a fence. Some rebel soldiers were near him, and being dressed in gray he was mistaken for a soldier. He was at an enormous distance from us—in fact I was looking at the group myself with a glass when our skirmish line opened fire and thought it entirely out of range. Our men are armed—at least the two companies then on the front with colts repeating rifle and the poor little fellow was killed instantly. I saw a man run out of the cabin to drag him in. Through my glass I discovered him to be in citizens' dress & made the men cease firing—*fortunately* for it was his father. What made it more painful was, that his father has always been a union man. As our column marched by a sister cried out from the window—the tears streaming down her cheek *"Hurrah for the Union,* but oh you have killed our dear little Freddy." The father did not censure our men at all, but swore vengeance on the rebels who had thus been the cause of his disaster. Such is war! A heavy cavalry fight is said to be now progressing on the road we take tomorrow. There will probably be a stand made by the enemy at Bridgeport which is naturally a very strong position though they may not halt until they arrive at Chattanooga.[2] *Winchester* you will remember is the town where I had a bitter fight last spring. Our march has been a severe one but our men have stood in nobly. The tremendous storms have retarded our progress and made our marches very difficult— all the water courses being much swollen. The last two fords we crossed were nearly breast high—& the current very rapid. The men crossed however splendidly—cheering—and holding their cartridge boxes above

their heads to keep the powder dry. *Cowan* is at the foot of the mountains—
a spur of the Cumberland range.

Tomorrow we will probably commence our mountain march but
by what route I do not yet know. We have picked up a good many
prisoners—as a matter of course—stragglers & shirks, but I am inclined
to believe that the rebel army of Bragg was never in better condition as to
discipline, spirit and equipment, than it is now. They were out flanked
& have fallen back to their strongholds, but will give us ultimately sharp
& hot work. Our own army however is in fine condition & the men full
of enthusiasm.

Would to God dear Sister this unhappy war were honorably
terminated—as it can only be by the restoration of the supremacy of our
Govt and that I were with you all again in our happy home. I long for
peace & quiet after all my weary marches & hardship—for *rest.* And yet I
feel it my duty as long as I *can* to share with my generation its heavy
burden and to stand along side of my brave comrades in arms to the last
gasp. I write in great haste but know you will be glad to receive even a
hurried scrawl. I do not know either when I may have a chance to write
again, so you must not be uneasy if you do not hear from me for sometime.
I expect a mail tonight and *hope* most earnestly it may bring a letter from
you or dear Sister.

The band this instant before my tent strikes up "Hail Columbia"
and the thunder of a national salute from my battery, mingled with the
grand reverberations of the artillery of heaven has just died away among
the mountains, but alas how the day awakens memories of the past when
our dear country stood forth united before the nations and was the
admiration of the world. God help the old flag! In no nobler or holier
cause can a man's life be offered up.

Farewell dear Bessie until my next. Remember me to Sam & Mrs
B——³ most kindly & to the whole family.

> In great haste
> Yr brother
> *Will*

1. Lieut. Gen. Leonidas Polk commanded the corps, Army of Tennessee, from November 20, 1862, until October 23, 1863. The Confederates were retreating from Murfreesboro.

2. General Rosecrans had established his base at Stevenson near Bridgeport, Alabama. Stevenson was a juncture point for the Nashville & Chattanooga and the Memphis & Charleston Railroads; Bridgeport lay on the Tennessee River. Chattanooga, a transporta-

tion hub and supply center, had Lookout Mountain on its outskirts. The surrounding countryside is rugged with many ridges and mountains.

3. Mrs. B refers to the mother of Samuel J. Broadwell, who resided with her son and daughter-in-law.

*Lytle filed a report covering his march from Murfreesboro to Cowan, Tennessee, with Capt. George Lee, the Third Division's assistant adjutant general.[1]*

HDQRS. FIRST BRIG., THIRD DIV.,
TWENTIETH ARMY CORPS,
*Camp at Cowan, July 6, 1863.*

CAPTAIN: In compliance with orders from division headquarters, I have the honor to report that my brigade, with Sutermeister's battery (Eleventh Indiana) attached, marched from Murfreesborough on Shelbyville pike June 24, 1863, at 7 a. m., Bradley's and Laiboldt's brigades, of this division, being in advance. About 11 a. m. the column was halted at Walnut Grove Church, A point 9 miles from Murfreesborough, and two of my regiments were thrown forward to support the enemy, on the arrival of Brigadier-General Brannan's column, our division resumed its march at 3 p.m., and went into camp at 6 p. m. at the junction of the Fosterville and Old Millersburg roads. Distance marched June 24, 13 miles.

June 25, still in bivouac. Cannonading in direction of Liberty Gap.

June 26, marched at 6:30 a. m. Infantry column in rear of general train. The route being rendered almost impracticable for teams on account of heavy rains, I found it impossible to-day to make more than 3½ or 4 miles. Bivouacked in timber, about 3 miles from Manchester pike.

June 27, moved about daylight; struck Manchester pike and marched to Beech Grove; marched thence to Fairfield, where there was skirmishing between our advance and the enemy. After a short halt, during which the enemy was driven back, the column resumed its march toward Manchester pike. Bivouacked on the roadside at Walker's house. Distance marched June 27, 18 miles.

June 28, my command (to-day in rear of column) moved at 7 a. m.; reached Manchester at 10:30 a.m. Distance marched, 6 miles.

June 29, moved at 11 a. m.; camped on right of road in timber at 5:30 p. m., having previously been in line of battle on same ground, immediately on our arrival. More or less skirmishing toward our front. Distance marched, 7 miles.

June 30, in same camp.

July 1, moved at 1 p. m.; reached Tullahoma at 4:30 p. m., and camped.

July 2, my brigade moved at 4 a. m.; at 10 a. m. halted at Winchester Springs. The bridge over Elk River having been burned, were compelled to take an upper ford. Move again at 2 p.m., and forded Elk River. Bivouacked on left bank. Marched to-day 13 miles.

July 3, moved at 4 a. m., my brigade in advance. Reached Winchester at 7 a. m., our cavalry advance driving on detachment of rebel cavalry. The enemy having been reputed in some force at ford of Boiling Fork, was sent forward with my brigade by Major-General Sheridan with orders to drive him across the river. Found on arrival that the enemy had fallen back. Crossed Boiling Fork of Elk River about noon, and arrived at Cowan at 4 p. m. Distance marched, 12 miles.

I have no casualties to report. It need hardly be stated that nearly the entire march from Murfreesborough was conducted in the midst of a storm, probably without precedent in these latitudes, and that the roads in consequence were rendered in many instances almost impassable. It affords me great pleasure to be able to report that the officers and men of my command endured their extraordinary exposure and fatigue with the utmost cheerfulness; that there was little or no straggling on the march, and our one matter of regret—that the enemy was not met in force.

I am, captain, most respectfully, your obedient servant,

W.H. LYTLE
*Brigadier-General, Commanding*

1. *O.R.,* ser. 1., vol. 23, pt. 1, 517-18.

## To Joseph W. Burke

[July 10, 1863]
Hd Qrs. 1st Brig 3 Div 20th A.C.
Camp at Cowan Sunday Night 10th July

My dear Col.

I was very happy to receive your note last night. The news is indeed most glorious so far thus far. It seems to me that the Confeds are "gone up," so at least the *dawn begins* to *break.*

After these brilliant successes I think that without any impropriety, and in consonance with the practice of our Gov. in other wars, Mr.

Lincoln might proclaim an amnesty to all rebels who would lay down their arms and return to their allegiance, and all states or parts of states that would proceed at once to elect members of Congress—reserving perhaps from the scope of the proclamation the archleaders of the rebellion—though even as to such men as Jeff Davis, Slidell, Mason and others, on the principle that "it is well to have a giant's strength but not to use it *like* a giant" a magnanimous policy might be the one most befitting a mighty nation which has crushed out the most formidable rebellion in history.

By the end of the war, the South will have been punished seriously enough God knows. Her fields desolated, her people impoverished, her pride humbled, her currency worthless rags, and the blood of her best and bravest shed in vain. A magnanimous and human policy towards the rebels after this overwhelming display of the power of the Federal Gov't, would in my judgment, be more dignified, would exalt us in the eyes of all foreign states, and would render easier the task of restoration of good feeling between the sections when the war is over.

Meanwhile however the work so well begun is to be vigorously pushed, without giving the enemy time to "get his wind" or rally, until his great armies are completely routed, scattered and dispersed.

We came in here only two hours after the enemy's rearguard left. He was drawn up in line of battle, and had we not been delayed in fording Elk we should have measured swords with him.

I had the advance of the Div—— My men marched splendidly— In fine spirits, with little or no straggling. We had more or less skirmishing at several points.

Tomorrow or the day after it is rumored we will probably move to "University"[1] I hope to see you ere long. The letter you were so kind as to forward informed me that Mrs. Foster had been dangerously ill but was much better.

With best regards to Ward, Hudson, Father O'Higgins[2] and the rest

believe me, my dear Col.

Most sincerely yours
Wm. H. Lytle

My kindest regards to Gen Rosecrans.
Col Harrison is with me at present acting as Vol. Aid.

The letter in the Lytle Papers from Lytle to Col. Joseph W. Burke, Tenth Ohio, dated

July 10, 1863, is a typescript, not the original. In July 1863 the Tenth Ohio, under Burke's command, was assigned to the general headquarters, Department of the Cumberland, commanded by General Rosecrans.

1. Lytle refers to the location of the University of the South at Sewanee, Tennessee.

2. Lytle asked to be remembered to officers of the Tenth Ohio, including Lieut. Col. William M. Ward, Maj. John E. Hudson, and Chaplain William T. O'Higgins.

*To Josephine Lytle Foster*

Cowan
July 10th [1863]

My dear Sister Josie

Lily's letter of the 25th June by Sister Anthony was forwarded to me from Gen Rosecrans Hd Qrs last night by courier from Tullahoma

I am terribly distressed about your illness & most earnestly pray you are now better— I wrote you a long letter on the march which I hope you have rec'd.

Do write immediately & let me know how you are—

Your own *Will*

*To Josephine Lytle Foster*

Hd Qrs 1ˢᵗ Brig 3ᵈ Div 20 A.C.
Camp at Cowan Tenn
Thursday July 16th 1863

To my great relief my dearest Josie I rec'd yesterday your letter of the 9th written in pencil from your sick bed.

I had been terribly anxious about you as a letter from Lily had informed me of your relapse after coming down stairs. Most earnestly do I hope my beloved Joe that by this time you are *very* much better and able to take the jaunt you so much need after the trying ordeal you have passed through this spring. My letters have no doubt been delayed by Morgan's raid, as I have written *three long* letters since we marched, one to you from camp near Tullahoma, one to Lily & one to Uncle. Perhaps by this time you may have rec'd them.

We are still here, as you see and what is to be the programme for this army during the summer is yet in darkness. It will probably be some time before we can move but *whither* I know not.

The news of Jno Morgans raid in Ohio reached us yesterday. What would I not have given to have been at home! The excitement among the Ohio troops is intense. We are all profoundly anxious to hear whether he has succeeded in getting out of the State. It will be an indelible stigma on Ohio if he is not cut to pieces. If there are not men enough in Ohio to do it I shall feel ashamed of my State and hope Morgan will take her with him into the confederacy.

Rousseau's Division came up yesterday.[1] I rode over with my Staff & called on the General. We had a very warm welcome from the officers of my old Division. It seemed quite like getting home again.

Findlay Harrison is now with me. He walked into my quarters the other day somewhat to my surprise. He conducts himself with much propriety.

Having no commission he is at present serving as Vol. A.D.C. I have written to Gov Johnston to try and secure for him a commission as Col in the Tenn line. I am very much annoyed that dear Lily should have had to pay Mrs Lytles bills. Mrs L—— paid me the money promptly but as we have not seen the paymaster since last April I was *broke,* and preferred using the $30 to borrowing. It is an outrage & very contemptible that the R. R. Coʸ has not paid me for my luggage. If I ever live to get home I will sue them, but have to wait as Guthrie is my only witness as to the contents.

Write Bessie that as soon as we are paid off I will remit the amount. I am greatly indebted to you for the slippers—they are a very great comfort.

I am sorry Lily & Sam can not take you with them as I fear you will be lonely in their absence but trust you will not long be separated.

There is nothing new here to write of. We had more or less skirmishing all the way down but I lost no men either killed or wounded. My Division had the advance & was highly complimented for the celerity of its movement.

No wonder—I observed yesterday when I visited Rousseau that Cols Comᵍ Brigades in that Div travel with *seven* head Qʳ tents. I & my whole Staff have but *one*—small wall tent. Of course we move *light* & with rapidity.

Now my dear Sis you must cheer up and get *well* & come back *hearty* in the fall. If our armies continue victorious I shall begin to hope that we are approaching the happy end of all our trials & labors & hardships.

Kiss the dear children for me and remember me most kindly to

Nat. Please tell him if he ever meets Muscroft[2] to give that old & sincere friend of mine my best regards.

And now good bye dearest Joe. You cannot tell how *anxiously* & *impatiently* I await every mail to hear from you & Lily. Write whenever you *can* without fatiguing yourself.

With love to all
I remain yr affec bro
*Will Lytle*

1. Lovell Harrison Rousseau commanded the First Division, Fourteenth Army Corps, Army of the Cumberland, at various times during 1863, including the period from March 29 through July 26.

2. Dr. Charles S. Muscroft was the surgeon of the Tenth Ohio until his resignation, June 9, 1863.

*To Josephine Lytle Foster*

H[d] Qrs 1st Brig 3[d] Div 20th A. C.
Wednesday July 22[d] 1863
Camp at Cowan

I was so fortunate dear Sister as to receive two letters yesterday, one from you & one from Bessie. I am truly happy to hear that you are getting better, as I have been feeling most uneasy about you. The letters were those written on the eve of Lily's departure. I am sorry my Tullahoma letter miscarried as it was a very long one & gave a history of the march to that point. It is no easy task to find time to write when on the march and *very* provoking to have ones letters lost after all. Should you leave the city, do not forget to write me often & keep me informed of your whereabouts. I was amused to hear that Jno Morgan had cut off your *line* of *communication* with the *babies,* but am very glad the little ones have come home in such fine condition. My compliments to Master John & Miss Nannie. Tell Johnnie I consider it very lucky for Morgan that Dixie[1] did not get after him.

Well here we are the whole army at a halt. What the next move will be I cannot tell. The road is now open to Stevenson, perhaps to Bridgeport. My brigade is the only one of our Division here. The *second* being at *Stevenson* and the *third* at University. The latter point is on the mountains. It is the site selected by Bishop Polk for the great southern university, which was to have in it each southern state represented by a college. The cornerstone was laid in 1860 with great ceremony. The design was to educate the southern youth *in the South* instead of sending them North to be contaminated with social & political heresies.

Cowan you know is just at the base of the mountains, and from the Hd Qrs I can see this morning our signal station at University—seven miles distant. The Signal station communicates away back to Winchester & Tullahoma, with the H$^d$ Qrs of the Army. Two of my staff rode out to the mountain top a few days ago & report the view as magnificent. The climate here is very fine. Much like that of Huntsville. We have pure mountain air & delicious spring water as clear as crystal & cold enough to make us forget the luxury of ice. The old 10$^{th}$ marched into Winchester yesterday from Tullahoma—following the H$^d$ Qrs of Gen R——. *Burke* sent word yesterday that he would dine with me today. Winchester is seven miles from here. The *cross was* to have been presented at Manchester, but on the day *set* we all got marching orders. If we remain here any time it will probably be presented here and when I get it I will send it home by the first safe opportunity. By the way the Paymaster has just made his welcome appearance & commences paying off my regiments today.

In the course of a few days I will send home a draft for my surplus funds to Foster—there will be several hundred dollars which Nat will please deposit to my credit in the Lafayette Bank—remitting Bessie the am't of Mrs Lytle's bills ($28 or 30) if I remember correctly). There will also be a draft of Joe Guthries for about $200 which I want put to *his* credit.

Please send me dear Joe in your next letter, a plain black silk necktie or two, *narrow* & modern style. You had better get them at McKee & Roths.

I should not be surprised if our Div moved in a few days to Stevenson. I have been fighting hard to get back to Huntsville & Gen Sheridan is quite in the notion of going there if he can get leave. (*Strictly between ourselves Harrison* has behaved very badly since he has been here & I fear he is utterly lost and shall get rid of him as soon as possible— but *say* nothing to any *one* unless it be the Doctor. I felt great sympathy for the poor fellow & was anxious (as I explained to Gen Sheridan) to give him a foothold in the army & another chance—but my kind intentions are all, I fear thrown away. Be careful I repeat to *say* nothing of this. While there is life there is hope for all.)

I wrote you the other day that Rousseau's Div was here. Rousseau & Gen King$^2$ called on me last week as did also many of their officers. The letter in the Com$^l$ *was* Pirtles'. He writes a very good common sense letter.

I enclose you a note *recd only a few days since* from Mrs *Mary Farrell Moore*.[3] It is very flattering is it not and gracefully written too. *Grover*[4] says his parents know her & that he has heard them speak of her in the highest terms. I wrote her a reply which I wish you might see. How would it do for you to call on her. I am told she is somewhat advanced in years & in reduced circumstances. Perhaps you might help her. It is all very good in the poor woman I am sure. Our band master has arranged the music for the band & it is very much admired.

Why does not Uncle write? I have not heard from him for a long while & he was formerly a capital correspondent.[5]

How delighted I should be to be able to join you in a visit to the sea shore this summer. We are all looking anxiously for the termination of our troubles, though our noble Army of the Cumberland is full of high & stern resolve never to sheath the sword until the rebellion is trodden down. Rumors have been quite of prevalent of late that *our* Corps was to be sent to the Potomac. I trust *not*. It is *said* Mc'Cook is quite anxious to get there. I am rejoiced to hear that Morgan has been so roughly handled in Ohio. The loss of *Basil Duke*[6] will be a terrible loss to Morgan, even if the *Gen* should escape. Morgan can do nothing with out him & is said to be indebted to him for much of his reputation. A sad accident happened yesterday in one of my regiments. A sharpshooter was cleaning his revolving rifle. He had taken it to pieces & while handling the *chamber* in some unaccountable manner one of the barrels exploded. The ball passed through a tent killing almost instantly one of the men. The poor fellow was asleep at the time. He was one of the bravest & best soldiers in the regiment.

*Grover* has just entered my tent saying that in the absence of Gen Mc'Cook, *Sheridan* will assume command of the Corps & I of the Division.

Gen Sheridan has just left camp on an engine for Stevenson with a guard of 30 sharp shooters. Alf Pirtle accompanied him. So that I shall have my hands full probably in his absence— *There* I have written you a *long* letter, if not an interesting one. If opportunity offers try & send me a good french novel. Ask Aunt C—— to select one or two for me with a small french pocket dictionary[7]— Perhaps you may have a chance by some officer. I would not object either to a pocket edition of *Horaces* Satires—in the original—with a small latin dictionary. Send the french anyhow by the first chance, perhaps you can *express* them through to Winchester care Col Burke.

The Doctor can find out how far the Express lines extend without difficulty. I have *nothing* to read but a few military books—pretty well exhausted & thumbed by this time.[8]

I feel quite as well as usual. I keep regular hours—always busy am careful as to diet & drink little but cold water.

Remember me most affly to Nat, Uncle S & Aunt C—— & Aunt Martha—also to Cousin Carrie Alston. Dont forget if you see any of them to give my best regards to the Taylors—Cousin Sallie & all.

Hoping dear Jodie that you may be entirely restored & quite *blooming* in the fall.

> Believe me
> Yr Affec brother
> *Will*

P.S. Uncle's letter with.

P.S. from Aunt C—— arrived last evening.

I will reply soon.

Grover & Pirtle send Com[ls].

I trust the news of Maj Mc'Cooks death may be a mistake[9]— Burke rode over to see me yesterday. He expects soon to go home on leave.

---

1. Lytle refers to his horse Dixie, which he had left in Cincinnati.

2. Brig. Gen. John Haskell King (1820-1888) commanded the Third Brigade, First Division, Fourteenth Corps, Army of the Cumberland, from May 6 until July 26 and from August 24 until October 10, 1863. Between July 26 and August 23, 1863, he commanded the division.

3. There are two letters from Mary Farrell Moore to William H. Lytle in the Lytle Papers.

4. James A. Grover was the adjutant in the Tenth Ohio.

5. Ezekial Smith Haines and his wife, Charlotte, passed the summer and fall of 1863 in the East, where he sought medical treatment. Haines was in New York City when Lytle was killed and his health did not permit his attendance at Lytle's funeral.

6. Basil Wilson Duke was the brother-in-law of John H. Morgan. A Kentucky native, Duke took part in Morgan's raid north of the Ohio River in the summer of 1863. He was captured at Buffington Island, Ohio, but not exchanged until August 3, 1864, just before Morgan was killed. Duke took over Morgan's brigade for the remainder of the war and gained promotion to brigadier general.

7. Charlotte Haines spoke and read fluent French. William Haines Lytle studied French from an early age. His mother, Elizabeth, wrote Robert Todd Lytle on July 26 [1834] that Lytle's English studies had advanced so well that she expected him to begin French that winter when he would have been just eight years old. See LP, box 25A, no. 197.

8. At the time of his death, Lytle had with him *Infantry Tactics or Rules for the Exercise*

*and Manouevers of the United States Infantry,* new edition, by Major General Scott, United States Army (New York: Harper & Brothers, 1861), and *The Field Manual of Evolutions of the Line* by Capt. Henry Copeé (Philadelphia: J.B. Lippincott, 1862). The latter was a gift of Lytle's uncle Edward H. Lytle. These books are included with the Lytle Papers at the Cincinnati Historical Society Library.

9. Lytle probably refers to Daniel McCook, who was killed July 19, 1863, attempting to capture John Hunt Morgan.

## To Josephine Lytle Foster

H$^d$ Qrs 3$^d$ Div 20th A. Corps
Wednesday July 29th 1863
Camp at Cowan

I write you my beloved sister from Gen Sheridans H$^d$ Qrs. I have been commanding Division for about ten days, Gen S—— being in command of the Corps during Gen McCooks absence. The duties are delicate & responsible as the command is scattered and I have to keep a great many *strings,* well in hand. The 2$^d$ Brigade is at Stevenson. The 3$^d$ Brigade is 10 miles off on the mountains and I am at this very moment signaling it to march immediately to Bridgeport.

This latter move & various other rumors indicate another grand forward movement of the whole army. The enemy is fortifying at Chattanooga and his cavalry pickets are distributed all along the southern shore of the Tenn$^{ee}$.

Two of my own regiments with a section of artillery are at Anderson & Tautalari guarding the R. R, and doing outpost duty. I sent day before yesterday a letter to the Doctor enclosing two drafts one for $500 & one for $190—$10 in money & a due bill for $150. I hope they arrived safely. If desirable you can pay Bessie Mrs Lytle's bills out of the money. When you have read my letters please forward them to Bessie as I do not know her address.

I hope most earnestly dear Joe that you are better and able to be about. When you leave home be careful to send your address to me.

I had occasion to write Gov Dennison a few days since and rec'd from him a *very* kind & cordial letter in reply. Nothwithstanding the Camp Harrison affair I am disposed to believe the Gov is a warm friend.

I have heard this moment that in all probability the whole Div will move to Stevenson & Bridgeport in a day or two. This is as I expected this morning—we having the advance. I have given Harrison one more chance. He has pledged me his honor to drink *no* more while with me and as I know if he leaves me he will go straight to ruin, I will give him another trial. He *could* be most valuable both to me & the service.

The war is by no means over. God knows when the end will be. I am most anxious once more to be with you all & would desire no thing more after all my hardships & exposure & wounds than to lead a calm & peaceful life in the midst of my friends & family. How long however before the condition of my unhappy country will allow this we cannot tell.

I shall be most anxious to hear of the condition of your health & that of the children *frequently* and hope that when you get away you will take special pains to have a real *good time.*

You must not worry about me at all as it can do no good and I shall be far happier to feel that you are out of that hot, noisy town.

I cannot thank you too much for the slippers and towels. They are indispensable to my health & comfort.

I am glad Jno Morgan tripped up in Ohio. I had bet $20 to $1— that he would never get out.

Kiss the little ones for me. Remember me to old Arthur & *Wilson* if you ever see him. Please ask the Doctor whether he & Sam made the sales we spoke of in Marion & Union— Also what has been done in the matter of the *Will* of Uncle Elias. Sam has neglected to write me. Farewell Dear Joe. Remember me most kindly to Foster & Uncle & Aunt C.[1]

Most affly
Will

11 o'c P.M. Good bye again dearest Sis—another move!—I leave in the morning at daylight with the balance of the Div for Stevenson.

1. Arthur and Wilson were former Lytle family servants. The property Foster and Broadwell were trying to sell in northern Ohio was inherited by Lytle and his sisters from their uncle Elias Haines and aunt Joanna Reilly.

*To Josephine Lytle Foster*

H^d Qrs 3^d Div 20th Army Corps
Stevenson Ala Tuesday
Aug 4th 1863

Your letter my dear Joe enclosing Lily's from Niagara reached me last night. I wrote you I think on the even^g of leaving Cowan. I am still commanding the Division and have had a very stirring time I assure you. Two of the regiments of my command proper are still at Anderson.

Laiboldts Brigade Rasweks & Sutermeister's batteries[1] are here & two companies of cavalry.

Bradleys' Brigade[2] & two of my regiments are at Bridgeport. I had a heavy load of responsibility on my shoulders. It was a very difficult matter to keep the several commands supplied with rations, forage &c &c. Everything however has worked smoothly thus far and as I have repaired the rail road I have now cars running from Cowan to Bridgeport. This valley of the Tenn is by no means as pleasant as our post in the mountains. The nights are cool to be sure, but the heavy fogs & mists from the river render them unhealthy. My clothes in my tent this morning were saturated with dampness. The days are *very hot*. Our Division is in advance. So you see I have had the honor of commanding the advance of the Army. Day before yesterday Gens Thomas & Sheridan rode down to Bridgeport on the first train that went through. I accompanied them. The rebels are distinctly visible on the opposite side. They are said to have a brigade there watching us.

Yesterday I rode down to the Tenn River to Capertan's Ferry 3 miles south of this with a cavalry escort. Leaving my escort hidden in the timber I advanced with Col Laiboldt & two of my staff on foot to the high bluff commanding the river & the opposite bank. We no sooner came in view than a rebel picket sprang to their feet immediately opposite us. Lt Dunning of Gen Sheridans Staff (who is with me) called out that we would not fire, and we had quite a conversation across the river.

It was quite a pretty picture, our little group of officers on the high bluff, the rebels in their grey uniforms on the south bank of the Tenn[ee] and between us the romantic river peacefully flowing through forests & mountains. The river at the ferry is about 400 yds wide so that we were within range of each other with our long range arms.

The rebs however made no hostile demonstrations, and we made a very cool & leisurely examination of them through our glasses. Gen Sheridan ordered me to establish an outpost there, & I went down to put it in position myself. My tent today is *hot as an oven*. I hope you rec'd my *drafts*—or rather I hope the D[r] did— Perhaps I may hear from you again tonight. Please let Uncle see these if in town. I would write him today but feared he had left the city. I enclose you another note from Mrs Moore in reply to mine. The publication of my letter is somewhat of a *bore,* but I suppose I can stand it.

I shall probably send home today by the Brigade baker (who is going to Cin[ati]) for a new *hat*. My old one is the most delapidated looking institution you ever saw—so intolerably shabby that my staff protest I must lay it aside

It seems to me that the whole *Lytle* family must be in the army—on one side or the other. I never heard of so many before. There is a D$^r$ Lytle a Surgeon in my Brigade, a Lt Lytle in the 3$^d$ Brigade a Lt Lytle in the 2$^d$ Tenn Cavalry (Union) besides any quantity in the rebel service. Where is Uncle Edward? I wrote him from Cowan but have rec'd no answer.

This whole country around us swarms with *bushwhackers. Gurley* who killed M'Cook has an organized gang between here & Bellefonte.[3] They are perpetuating the most horrible barbarities on the loyal people shooting & hunting them down like wild beasts. The terrified women & children are flocking in to us from all quarters. How little do our people at home know of *war* & its attendant horrors. A young man came into our lines at Anderson who had been a Union refugee for nine months. During all that time he had been living in caves in the mountains. The rebels had hung his father & killed his brother because they were loyal men. He himself with two or three companions had fled to the mountains for refuge. They made many attempts to capture him & his comrades— even trailing them with dogs. His comrades in one of their many fights with their pursuers were killed or captured, but he, though badly wounded, managed to escape. Sometimes he managed to steal down to his cabin & visit his wife. When it was not safe for him to do so she would *lay a rail* across the path. The lynx eyed rebels discovered the *sign* & he narrowly escaped capture. Then she struck on another plan when all was right at home she stuck a half dollar in a crevice in a tree—when it was *not* there he was to be on his guard. The bloody villains found this out also! His story is as interesting as a romance. At last one fine morning he heard somehow or other of our advance. Weary & faint & suffering terribly from his wounds he managed to crawl rather than walk to the neighborhood of the camp at Anderson. He heard away off in the mountains our drums at reveille *"And oh!* said he, his features *glowing* with happiness." *When I heard the drums I knew it was you uns!* He is a very bright intelligent young fellow & swears bitter vengeance against secession—

In fact all these East Tennesseans are bitter as gall & fierce as wild cats—no wonder—they have been hunted out like wild beasts & their crops & homes & household goods all given to the torch—

farewell

Most affly

Will

Love to Capt John & Nannie & kind regards to Foster & Uncle & Aunt

Harrison is behaving splendidly— I made him take the pledge— I hope soon to hear from Bess—Dear child! I hope she is enjoying herself. Tell her to write long *gossipy* letters— Alf Pirtle & I favor each other with extracts now & then from our mutual correspondence.

When Gen Sheridan is relieved he tells me he will make his H$^{dqrs}$ here & send me to Bridgeport— My letters are *confidential in the family.*

1. Bernard Laiboldt, a Missourian, commanded the Second Brigade, Third Division, Twentieth Army Corps, from March 3 until October 9, 1863.

2. Luther Prentice Bradley, who lived to be eighty-eight years old, commanded the Third Brigade, Third Division, Twentieth Army Corps, between January 9 and September 28, 1863. He was wounded at the battle of Chickamauga.

3. Frank B. Gurley, a member of Brig. Gen. Nathan Bedford Forrest's cavalry, killed Union general Robert I. McCook on August 5, 1862. This brought him much trouble over the years and he twice narrowly escaped being hanged. On November 23, 1862, he was mustered in as captain, Company C, Fourth (Col. Alfred A. Russell's) Alabama Cavalry, at which time he rejoined Forrest.

*Between his letters of August 4 and August 16, Lytle submitted several reports to General Sheridan. From Bridgeport on August 12, he provided information supplied by two deserters from the Forty-fourth Mississippi reporting five rebel regiments and one battalion of sharpshooters and battery. Lytle estimated the Confederate force at two thousand and noted that the bridge had been prepared to burn. After some firing on Island Ford the previous evening, all was quiet that day.[1] Three days later Lytle reported rebel activities. "Just before dark we discovered what may be working parties, with three wagons, on edge of timber" slightly less than one and one-half miles from Federal batteries. "Dispatch from old Kelley, brought by negroes, reports rebel cavalry to-day 4 or 5 miles east of Jasper. Kelley says 200 or 300. Information so indefinite I hesitate to send out, say without orders from yourself. Rebels may be too strong for Second Tennessee. Large bivouacs this evening at locality of supposed working party." After receiving Lytle's information from Sheridan, Rosecrans issued orders for Lytle to watch the rebels' motions carefully. "Movement will begin tomorrow by all corps. Tell General Lytle to have the fires counted and watched to see if they are not a humbug."[2]*

1. *O.R.,* ser. 1, vol. 52, 14.
2. *O.R.,* ser. 1, vol. 52, 39.

### To Elizabeth Lytle Broadwell

*While General Lytle remained engaged in military matters, his sisters vacationed in New Hampshire. The Lytle Papers include Broadwell's letter of August 7, 1863, in which she noted that Smith and Charlotte Haines had rented out their Cincinnati home until December. On their return from Rye Beach, New Hampshire, the Broadwells planned to visit relatives in New York and Philadelphia, including the Doremus and Macalester families. The Lytles' cousin Lily Macalester, whom Will had wanted to marry in the early 1850s, had married a Belgian diplomat, and Lily Broadwell wanted to meet him.[1]*

*Shortly before writing to his sister Lily on August 16, Lytle received a letter from Richard Realf, a sergeant major in the Eighty-eighth Illinois Volunteer Infrantry, one of the regiments in Lytle's brigade. Realf thanked Lytle for the gift of two books—Miles Standish and Tannhaüser.[2] Always a lover of literature and poetry, Lytle delighted in someone who shared those interests.*

> Hd Qrs U.S. forces Bridgeport Ala
> "Camp Roberts" Sunday
> Aug 16th 1863

I seize a moments leisure my beloved Bessie to acknowledge the receipt of yours of the 7th from Rye Beach. It is the first I have had from you for a *long* time and was joyfully welcomed. I hope that the sea bathing and the fresh sea breeze will speedily restore you and dear Joe also, who by this time has probably joined you. Ah! how I envy you sweltering as we are here in our shifting tents. Rather, how I wish I could be *with* you for I am rejoiced that you have escaped from the hot town & so many depressing influences. Truly dear Bess I *have* had my hands full ever since we moved from Murfreesboro on the 24th of June. I commanded the Division until McCook returned making my Hd Qrs at Stevenson. When Gen Sheridan was relieved of the command of the Corps I was sent up here where (Since the 5th of August) I have had command of the *advance* of the Grand Army.

5. P.M.— I was interrupted this morning dear Lil at 11 o.c. and have been busy ever since conducting negotiations under a flag of truce from Gen Patton Anderson[3] of Florida the rebel commander opposite. We are in full view of the enemy or at least of his Pickets on the opposite side of the river. The Tennessee runs through a valley here bounded on every hand by mountains. Across the river lies a rebel Brigade composed of five Miss. regiments, a battalion of sharp shooters and a regiment of cavalry with a battery of napoleons. In the middle of the river is an island some seven miles long. A splendid railroad bridge spanned the Tennessee

at this point. It is over a mile from bank to bank but the island is only about five hundred yards from us. This island was held by the rebels until night before last and was crowded with their men. My own H^d Qrs are within easy range of their sharp shooters to say nothing of their cannon. You would not suppose it very agreeable to lie down at night with the comfortable assurance that any "gray back" has it in his power to put a rifle ball through your tent or cot when one is asleep yet after awhile a fellow becomes accustomed to it. Bragg on his retreat burned the bridge on *this* side the Island but the bridge from the Island to the eastern side was standing until night before last. On Friday night the rebels got scared at something and concluded to burn it— It had been carefully prepared for burning—filled with combustible matter so that a single match on a few moments would set it all ablaze. I had slept badly that night and after awakening several times had just fallen into a light sleep again when I heard the startling announcement (7 P.M— "Well here goes for another start for I am *determined* to finish my letter) *"tell the General the bridge is on fire."*

I sprang out of body cot, got into my clothes as well as I could in the dark and rushed out to find the bridge just bursting into a blaze, calling my staff together I ascended the high hill in the side of which I live and mounted the parapet of the redoubt. From there the scene was grand beyond description. The immense bridge rammed full of dry resinous wood and saturated with turpentine was soon enveloped in flame. The river could be seen for miles lighted up like molten lava, whilst in the background the tall mountains looked down on the scene like black and stern old giants. Soon to all this was added the roar of artillery. My orders were to open fire as soon as they attempted to burn the bridge. At the signal, my two batteries gave tongue and woke up with their thundering music the midnight echoes of the Tennessee hills. The whole scene was one of the grandest I ever beheld. I do not think that even by the glorious sea you can behold anything so awe inspiring as this picture torn from the stern history of the war. It may interest you to know that my command here consists of the 1^st + 3^d Brigades of my Division, two Batteries of artillery & a regiment of cavalry. Oh Yes, the cigars by Sister Anthony arrived safely—for which a thousand thanks— also dear Josies french books which are another great treat. I almost forgot to say that my *cross* was presented in due form a few days since by the officers of the 10th a delegation of whom came away down here for the purpose. My old friend Major [Heilpin] 15^th Ky intended to write an account of the affair & publish it in the Commercial. I trust you may see it and may like the style of what I had to say. All present *seemed* to enjoy themselves hugely. A movement is again near at hand. I can only hope my dear Bessie that Providence will take care of me in the future as heretofore and that I may again meet after "this cruel war is over" my beloved little sisters whom I love so much.

You must get a map and try and follow my movements. Do not be alarmed or uneasy my dear Sister but do your utmost to strengthen & benefit your constitution during your summer trip and always look on the sunny side of all things. You speak of Mrs. Neff in your letter. Please enquire if Miss Williams ever rec'd mine from Murfreesboro. Findlay Harrison has not touched a drop since he left Cowan and is making hosts of friends. He is a splendid officer and if I succeed in making a man of him I feel that I shall have done a good work. You say the Macalesters and Doremus' are at Long Branch—*who* of the latter is there?

I might write pages more but have already encroached I fear on time that should be otherwise appropriated tonight. Remember me affy to dear Uncle—*Do* for I know not where I can write him. I want to send home my present from the 10th, but I dont know *by* whom or *to* whom in Cin[ati] to forward it. Tell me who to send it to, to keep for me. This valley must be very sickly, the days are intensely hot & with night comes a dense, permeating fog, that saturates everything with dampness. I keep well enough however and have not been really *ill* this summer despite all our exposure.[4] Ah how *little* do the gay throngs in the 'salons' at home know of what we daily endure. The *battle* is nothing. It is the march, the sickly camp, and worst of all, with an officer of rank, the wearing sense of responsibility. Where is Charley Pendleton? Tell me all about Seddie Doremus and Lily Macalester when you see them. I cant help away down in these Alabama hills feeling a slight choking sensation about the throat when I look back on happy hours *long gone*—*Yet* I am strong in heart thank God, and bow humbly to His will & hope I may do my work.[5] Good night. Love to all. Tattoo just sounds from camp to camp.

Your devoted<br>Will

1. Elizabeth Lytle Broadwell to William H. Lytle, August 7, 1863, LP, box 31, no. 87. Lily Macalester Berghmans had one daughter, Camille Leontine Judith Macalester Berghmans, who married a Spanish marquis. After Berghmans's death, Lily Macalester married a Mr. Laughton, who died about one year later in Algiers, where they had gone for

his health. (Information provided by Marie Page Edgerton from information that had been copied from notes in the possession of Josephine R. Foster.)

2. Richard Realf to William H. Lytle, August 10, 1863, LP, box 34, no. 661.

3. Tennessee native James Patton Anderson (1822-1872), then a Florida resident, commanded the brigade, Withers's-Hindman's Division, Polk's Corps, Army of Tennessee (December 1862-September 20, 1863).

4. Lytle suffered from a severe cold during the battle of Chickamauga.

5. Lytle was particularly concerned about Sed Doremus. His continuing affection for Doremus, however, did not prevent him having a "love affair" in Murfreesboro, Tennessee. Although the lady is never named, a letter written by Emily Perkins on November 13, 1864 (LP, box 34, no. 626), requests that Lytle's sisters return any love letters written to Lytle by her Tennessee friend. Though Perkins indicates that the lady in question married someone else ten months after Lytle's death, she also records Lytle's last words to the woman: "And you will *never never* forget me!" And her response—"Never, Never!" Given that Lytle was a romantic and that he enjoyed relationships with women, it is understandable that he had at least a serious flirtation if not more during his two tours of duty near Murfreesboro. Although it is conjecture, the lady in question was likely Mrs. David Lytle, who was widowed by the time Lytle returned to Murfreesboro in March 1863.

In an undated note to one of his sisters—most probably from 1862 when Lytle was stationed in Kentucky (LP, box 33, no. 507), Lytle talks about a flirtation that was taken more seriously than he had intended:

(Private) This evening [Maynard] & I called on Jennie Springer [a member of one of Cincinnati's elite families]. she gave me her photograph & asked me for a military button which I sent her next morning. In my note I ask her if she didn't want an 'army correspondent.' I was sorry afterwards I had done so but it was too late. It was merely a piece of *badinage* in *my style* that no other young lady would have thought a *very* serious matter. What I heard *here* a month after from *friends* of mine led me to believe that Mrs *[Jones]* considered it a *formal proposition to commence a* courtship—of which God knows I had no idea. So I felt bored & wrote *another* letter to Miss Jennie (care Mrs Foster)— very polite & courteous assuring her that I had only *hoped* now & then to receive a line from her in a friendly way—as I had several lady correspondents at the north &c &c.

I am *told* that Mrs *Jones conducts Miss Jennies correspondence & neither document has rec'd the slightest notice—which I consider ill bred. At* least I think my character & position should have ensured a respectful declination. You may laugh if you choose but I confess I am somewhat *bored*. If you have a chance when you see Jennie try & find out for me how the case *stands*—Will (Burke & Alf Pirtle are much amused at the whole performance).

## To Josephine Lytle Foster

*Between August 16 and August 31, when he wrote his last letter, Lytle was constantly involved in surveillance, dealing with deserters, and bridge building. When Lytle wrote home for the last time, or at least the last letter that survived, he had just received a letter from Lily Broadwell dated August 21, 1863. She wrote that the mail had arrived in Rye Beach with the August 18 Cincinnati Commercial, which contained a transcription of Lytle's speech on accepting the cross. The Broadwells planned to leave New Hampshire about September 7 to stop in New York to see Sed Doremus on their way home. Josephine Foster and her family expected to remain at Rye Beach until early October. Broadwell, who had wanted to congratulate her brother on his speech, promised she would write a longer letter soon. Her next letter, dated September 2, 1863, and describing vacation activities and travel plans, was found in Lytle's pocket after he was killed at Chickamauga.[1]*

H<sup>d</sup> Qrs U S forces  
Bridgeport Ala Aug 31<sup>st</sup> 63

A year ago today, my dear Sister since we evacuated Huntsville! How rapidly time has passed! Dear Bessie's letter advising me of your arrival at Rye Beach reached me yesterday. I am *very* glad you got there safely & hope that ere this you are much benefitted by the sea bathing of fresh air. Probably ere this reaches you we shall all be over the river, en route for Chattanooga or Atlanta.

We are all hard at work here night and day—cutting roads to the fords, bridge building, boat building and devising all possible contrivances for putting the army on the other side. The trestle bridge from the western shore to the Island will be completed I think day after tomorrow.

I built a foot way across the [*Wither*] Channel yesterday out of the 'debris' of the old railroad bridge and tomorrow I think we will commence laying the pontoons. From my tent on the hill the camp presents a busy appearance. Railroad trains rolling in & out, locomotives whistling, long wagon trains loaded with timbers for the bridges, "engineers and mechanics" busy as bees, regiments of infantry & cavalry passing and repassing— fatigue parties in every direction in short, all the stir and bustle and note of preparation indicative of another grand advance of the Army of the Cumberland.

I send you two or three slips from newspapers which perhaps you have not seen.

The *reconnaissance* alluded to was conducted under my orders & it was my battery that did the shelling. I was also with the party when the rebels opened on us from their picket station & came so near hitting the Generals little boy. The Gen came up that day & insisted on visiting a ferry on foot at Island Creek about five miles from here. Our party consisted of the Gen [Com<sup>g</sup>] Maj Gen McCook Maj Gen Stanley, Chief of Cav——[2] Your humble servant a dozen or so of Staff officers & five or six mounted orderlies. After a gallop through a wild & deserted country we were approaching the ferry, when off on our left toward the river we heard a shot— Then after riding a little further came another & another and the *party halted*. I never felt half as nervous in a battle as I did that day. As commandant of the post I felt myself responsible for the safety of the party. It occurred to me that the enemy *might* have thrown across the river a small cavalry force and the thought flashed across me that if old Rosey & M<sup>c</sup>Cook & Stanley should be *bagged* that I would be censured for not bringing along a stronger escort and catch the d——l generally!

M<sup>c</sup>Cook asked me if I had any force at the ferry— I told him no! The fact was all my disposable cavalry was watching another ford higher up the river. I began to feel tolerably *bilious*. If I had been alone it would have made no difference. However after listening a minute we plunged boldly forward old Rosey & all, and to my great delight after riding a few rods I saw the videttes of a federal car regiment their carbines poised on their saddles and beyond them near the river quite a strong detachment of the 1<sup>st</sup> Tenn Union Cavalry. I was very much relieved I assure you. We found that the rebel pickets had that day commenced firing, and it was during our reconnaissance that day of the ferry that one of their balls came so near hitting the Generals little boy. I am glad you liked my speech. I see that it is having quite a *run* at home. What do you think old Rosey asked me the other morning?— why *bluntly* in the presence of a number of officers says he "Lytle was your father a better orator than you"? I felt like a fool, as you may imagine.

The *cross* I sent this morning by Col Larrabee (who has resigned) to Louisville to Mrs *Pirtle* to keep for me until you or Bessie returned. I did not know what else to do. If you or Lil want it you can have it expressed through to you.

How do you like my *cartes*? They were taken in my *camp* & we all *here* consider them admirable likenesses.

In truth as works of art I have never seen better at home. One of them is taken sitting in a chair. Some how the picture looks as if I were *tilting* forward. This spoils it—but otherwise it is a very fine specimen of photography. Notice especially how capitally the hand & sword hilt are given. I do not like the expression though as much as that of the other two. I merely call your attention to the *work* which for a camp artist I think is most creditable. The fellow would not take any pay either! However he can afford it as I am told he has already orders for *800* copies. I *do* hope you will like them.

The H<sup>d</sup> Qrs of the Army are at Stevenson. The Telegraph operation advises me that the Generals special train will be here in a few moments so that I must abruptly close.

Where my next letter will be from I can hardly tell. I will *try* &
drop you or dear Lillie a line before we march. *Do* write *when* ever you
can. My old friend Mrs Milton (S. Adams) has written me two beautiful
letters lately.[3]

Kiss Bessie & the little pets & kind regards to all

God bless you

*Will*

I wrote recently to Uncle—care Mrs Doremus.

1. Elizabeth Lytle Broadwell to William H. Lytle, August 21, 1863, LP, box 31, no. 88,
and Elizabeth Lytle Broadwell to William H. Lytle, September 2, 1863, LP, Lytle Scrapbook.

2. Lytle accompanied Gen. William S. Rosecrans; Maj. Gen. Alexander McDowell
McCook, then commanding the Twentieth Corps, Army of the Cumberland; and Maj.
Gen. David Sloane Stanley, who commanded the Cavalry Division, Army of the Cumberland,
from March through September 9, 1863, and again November 9-20, 1863.

3. Lytle refers to a Louisville friend, Sallie Adams Milton. Her two letters mentioned no
longer exist. However, the Lytle Papers contain two of her letters written after Lytle's death
to Elizabeth Lytle Broadwell. Milton and Lytle shared an interest in poetry and literature.
Although married, she mourned Lytle deeply, indicating that her husband had promised to
take her to Chickamauga if Lytle survived his wounds. In December 18, 1863, Milton
wrote that if she could manage it with her two babies she would come to Cincinnati to visit
the cemetery to "see how he sleeps." Milton described Lytle as having a *"beautiful* face,
animated & lovely as a woman's" along with "a delicious *gushing* voice" (see LP, box 34, nos.
594 and 595).

*Lytle lived twenty days after writing his last family letter on August 31,
1863. During those three weeks, the Army of the Cumberland moved toward
Chattanooga. Both the Army of Tennessee and the Army of the Cumberland
maneuvered large numbers of troops close to Chattanooga, which controlled
access to the lower South along with the railroad and the river. After days of
uncertainty, fighting began on September 19 near Chickamauga Creek, the
"river of death," in the northwest corner of Georgia, short miles from Chattanooga and Lookout Mountain. Lytle's actions during the battle are detailed by
several authors, including Cozzens and Morris. In* This Terrible Sound: The
Battle of Chickamauga, *Cozzens eloquently captures Lytle's moves and moods
during his last days, while putting them in the context of the battle.*

*During the second day of fighting, sleepless and suffering from a cold,
Lytle was ordered to bring his brigade to a point on the line of battle where the
Union had given way. With Confederates converging from three sides, he ral-
lied his brigade to go forward. He and his staff rode right behind the center of*

the *Twenty-fourth Wisconsin as they advanced under heavy fire.*[1] *Lytle, on horseback, was an obvious target for the Confederate soldiers and was shot several times in the exchange of bullets. Although his counterattack did little to gain time for the rest of the division, Lytle had done his duty to his country. He had stayed true to himself and his sense of honor through his last bold, brave act. When the fighting ended, Lytle lay dead.*

*Though immediately mourned by his men, they continued to perform their duty. Following Lytle's death, Findlay Harrison, volunteer aide to the fallen general, and Alfred Pirtle, Lytle's aide de camp, reported for duty to General Sheridan. Seldom given to praise, Sheridan later said both Harrison and Pirtle "subsequently behaved very handsomely."*[2] *Though Lytle reportedly encouraged his men with the words, "If we beat them today boys, we will be home for Christmas,"*[3] *even those who survived the battle did not see home that year. Rather, the South's success in holding at Chickamauga rallied its spirit, possibly prolonging the war. After Chickamauga, Lytle's beloved Tenth Ohio saw further action at Missionary Ridge in November 1863 and several Georgia battles, including Resaca in May 1864. Surviving members of the Tenth Ohio were mustered out in late June 1864. The First Brigade was reconstituted under the command of Col. Francis T. Sherman, Thirty-sixth Illinois, as part of the Second Division, Fourth Army Corps, under Sheridan at the division and Gordon Granger at the corps. It too participated in the Chattanooga campaign, including the battle of Missionary Ridge.*[4]

1. Edwin B. Parsons to Elizabeth Lytle Broadwell, August 14, 1888, Lytle Papers, box 34, no. 615, CHS, CMC.

2. *O.R.,* ser. 1, vol. 30, 82.

3. Parsons to Broadwell, August 14, 1888.

4. *Battles and Leaders of the Civil War,* vol. 3 (New York: T. Yoseloff, 1956), 727.

# Epilogue

AFTER WILLIAM HAINES LYTLE DIED on September 20, 1863, during the bloody battle of Chickamauga, the Confederates retrieved his body and buried it carefully in a marked grave. When Lieut. Col. William Ward, then commanding the Tenth Ohio, requested that General Rosecrans ask for Lytle's remains from the Confederates, General Bragg rapidly acceded. Under a flag of truce Confederate soldiers transported Lytle's body to Union hands. A guard of honor led by Ward met the fallen hero's remains at the picket line and escorted them to the chapel tent. Maj. John Hudson, Tenth Ohio, arranged for the coffin to be placed on a raised dais and draped with velvet and white linen. The American flag decorated the opened outer coffin; Lytle's sword and scabbard lay over the flag in the form of a cross. Flowers, evergreens, drooping willow, and other greenery surrounded the coffin and filled the hall, while burning incense and candles perfumed it. The Tenth Ohio then held a memorial service in the chapel tent before sending Lytle's body to Cincinnati and its final resting place.

Colonel Ward's moving eulogy brought tears to the eyes of many. Citing the special grief felt by members of the Tenth Ohio, Ward echoed the tribute drafted by members of the Tenth Ohio on September 30, which said, "those who knew him best, loved him most. The blood chills at the thought that, that voice, 'loud as a trumpet with a silver sound,' shall be heard no more for ever, nerving the failing arm, and dressing the shattered ranks; that, that heart in which throbbed in singularly witching harmony, the tenderness of woman, with the daring of the hero, shall never again soothe our griefs or nerve our arms to emulate his valor.— Trunk of the Elephant wert thou Lytle! pliant and gentle to lift a lady's glove, strong and brave to break the gnarled oak, or scatter an armed host!" Ward closed by saying that Lytle, gifted and eloquent in life, was not mute in death. His example of bravery and patriotism would live after him. "He did not die in vain."[1] Had the Seventeenth Brigade, Lytle's former command, not been away on duty, many of its members undoubtedly also would have been present.

Following Colonel Ward's address, a procession formed and the cortege accompanied the coffin to the wharf to begin its long river voyage to Cincinnati. An accompanying guard of honor consisted of Lieutenant Donahue and one man from each company in the Tenth Ohio.[2] Although his sisters had preferred privacy in their sorrow, they agreed to allow the general's body to lie in state in the Cincinnati courthouse for one day. As Josephine Lytle Foster observed, "a few hours there would gratify his many friends and ensure us quiet & privacy, when brought home—so that finally we yielded for the first day."[3] The *Commercial* noted that while the body lay in state in the rotunda at the courthouse, Wilson, Lytle's "aged colored servant . . . the faithful sharer of his campaigns" was observed "weeping at the foot of the coffin . . . refusing to be comforted."[4]

Cincinnati paid its last respect to its native son William Haines Lytle October 22, 1863. Lytle's death was a loss for the whole community, not just his family. He was the heir to the proud legacy of his civic-oriented father and grandfather, their names intertwined with Cincinnati's history. With the death of the last male Lytle, a chapter symbolically closed on the Queen City's collective heritage. More citizens turned out to watch the funeral procession than any in the city's previous history. The military display, too, was the largest ever at any Cincinnati funeral. The funeral procession featured Lytle's orderly Joe Guthrie leading the general's riderless horse with the boots turned backwards. The distinguished pallbearers surrounding the hearse included future United States president Gen. James A. Garfield, Gen. Jacob Cox, and Col. John Kennett. Lytle's staff and relatives rode in carriages.[5]

Lytle's family and friends gathered to help his sisters through their dark hour. Edward Lytle and his wife came from Pennsylvania to be with their nieces. Sed Doremus, the distant cousin on the Haines side who loved and had hoped to marry Lytle, came to share her grief with Josephine Foster and Lily Broadwell. Only Ezekial Smith Haines and his wife, Charlotte, were unavoidably absent because Haines was in New York seeking medical attention for his failing health. Normally undemonstrative, Haines wrote that he read accounts of Lytle's last moments through tears.[6] Like many others, Haines expressed sadness at never hearing Lytle's much-loved voice again. To his nieces, "fellow sufferers in a sad & crushing calamity," he admitted his grief, saying " . . . tho in life I loved our dear one much I hardly knew how much until I have lost him— Dear boy— He was affectionate, brave & gallant— True hearted & generous."[7]

Many tributes had been paid Lytle in life, and more came in death.

D. Thew Wright, a friend of Lytle's from childhood, spoke to the Cincinnati Bar. Wright termed Lytle "a patriot of incorruptible integrity," "a child of light," who "possessed the fire of true genius" and totally lacked fear for his personal safety. Lying wounded after Perryville, Lytle had told Wright "it was a glorious day & I turned to see the last sun go down in this magnificent setting. I felt that I had done my duty & that I could put my armor off, as one lying down to pleasant dreams."[8] His comrades, however, did not share Lytle's tranquil acceptance of his fate. The Tenth Ohio drafted an emotional tribute to their beloved former commander before Lytle's remains left Chattanooga.[9] Lytle's friend Charlotte Pendleton wrote a poem about "Columbia's bravest son," Carnifex Ferry, and Faugh-a-Ballaugh, Lytle's beautiful horse, who became a war casualty in his master's fearless quest for glory:

> Where death and danger lead the van
> There Lytle rides the foremost man. . . .[10]

Letters continued to pour into the Foster and Broadwell homes in late 1863 and early 1864 with unabashed tributes from those who had known and loved Will Lytle. In December 1863, Lily Broadwell sent Lieutenant Colonel Ward a memento of her beloved brother. She noted that the ties between herself, Will, and Josephine had always been exceptionally strong. Becoming orphans at an early age had served to deepen their bonds further. She added that then more than ever, she and Foster would hold his friends and enemies as their own.[11]

The sad times for his sisters did not cease with Lytle's death. The next two years, 1864 and 1865, brought more deaths in the immediate family. Their uncle Edward H. Lytle died in Philadelphia in April 1864. Ezekial Smith Haines died just one year later. No letters survive that record the sisters' emotions on the deaths of Edward Lytle and Smith Haines. Yet, those written at the deaths of Joanna Reilly and their brother Will suggest that Foster's and Broadwell's grief must have caused near paralysis. So many deaths in such a short time would have devastated anyone. Even the end of the war in April 1865 must have been bittersweet as Lytle's sisters mourned their "vacant chair"[12] and dwindling family. On a happier note, Foster gave birth to a son, William Lytle Foster, in 1867, and a daughter, Lily Foster, in 1872. But little John, "Sir John" to his uncle Will, died from heart trouble in 1872. Neither Anna Haines Foster (little Nannie) nor William Lytle Foster ever married. Of his sister's children, only Lily Foster, who never knew her famous uncle, married and raised a family. It is through

Lily Foster, her husband, Charles J. Livingood, and their three children, that the Cincinnati Historical Society received the Lytle Papers.

The many letters and papers include later letters and documentation concerning the final moments of William Haines Lytle and some correspondence concerning the publication of the book of Lytle's poems edited by William H. Venable and his memoir of Lytle. Throughout her life Lily Broadwell remained passionate about her brother's memory, poems, and achievements. After Broadwell died in early 1890 at age fifty-five, Josephine Foster began efforts to publish their brother's poems. Foster dedicated the volume "to the memory of a beloved sister, Mrs. Elizabeth Haines Broadwell, with the hope that in its accomplishment her cherished wish has been fulfilled."[13]

Dr. Nathaniel Foster died in 1881. Sam Broadwell, surviving his wife, remarried briefly to a distant Lytle cousin, Marie Nixon, before succumbing to illness in August 1893. Both Foster, a physician, and Broadwell, an attorney, were highly respected within their professions. Despite the ardent Democratic politics of William Haines Lytle and Ezekial Smith Haines, Foster and Broadwell both held Republican viewpoints.

Josephine Foster and Lily Broadwell, meanwhile, took leadership roles as permitted for women of their time and class. Both were very active in church and missionary endeavors. Broadwell served as president of the Cincinnati Orphan Asylum and supported several missionary societies, including one for Freedmen of the Presbyterian Church. Her husband's will left money to the Woman's Union Missionary Society of America to found a memorial in her honor.[14] Foster gained renown for her charitable and religious interests. She served as president of the Women's Society of Christ Episcopal Church, president of the Helping Hand Society, a lady manager of the Orphan Asylum, president of the Cincinnati Branch of the Woman's Union Missionary Society, and vice president of the New York Society.[15] At her death in 1898, the *Cincinnati Commercial Tribune* credited Josephine Foster with being the center of her church's social life and having "much of the philanthropic work of the city circ[ling] around her."[16] Three children survived Foster's daughter and son-in-law, Lily Foster and Charles Livingood. They and their descendants have continued the public-spirited tradition of their forefathers and have made valued intellectual and historical contributions to Cincinnati and the country at large.

William Haines Lytle was the gifted heir to a proud tradition of leadership. His great grandfather Capt. William Lytle, his grandfather William Lytle, and his father Robert Lytle set outstanding examples of personal bravery, enterprise, and public service to follow. Born into all the advantages of culture and education, the brilliant Lytle internalized his forefathers' values and combined them with his own. These men of the West, antebellum Cincinnati, and Kentucky indelibly influenced their scion. Combining gentility and toughness, compassion and integrity, education and horsemanship, writing poetry with a military spirit, free spending of money with a disinclination to worry about making it, and above all personal courage and integrity, William Haines Lytle epitomized a southern cavalier rather than a Yankee. Cincinnatians, who often had honored him in life, paid unbounded tribute after he fell heroically at Chickamauga. For, as General Lytle had hoped, the people understood that their native son had given his life willingly for a noble cause. He had, as he had admired, "died with [his] harness on, in the great war for Union and Liberty."[17]

Notes

1. Undated newspaper clipping from *Cincinnati Daily Commercial* in October, 1863, giving report dated Chattanooga, October 15, 1863. LP, Lytle Scrapbook. William M. Ward, Tenth Ohio, was promoted to lieutenant colonel from captain, Company I, March 15, 1863. He was mustered out with the regiment on June 17, 1864. John E. Hudson was promoted to major from captain, Company C, on January 20, 1863. He was mustered out with the regiment on June 17, 1864.

2. Lieutenant Donahue may have been Joseph Donahue, initially a corporal in Company D, Tenth Ohio. He is the only Donahue listed for the Tenth Ohio in the *Official Roster of the Soldiers of the State of Ohio.*

3. Josephine Lytle Foster to Ezekial S. Haines, October 31, 1863, LP, box 32, no. 246.

4. *Cincinnati Daily Commercial,* October 23, 1863. The *Commercial* refers to John Wilson who had been with Lytle in several campaigns prior to Chickamauga.

5. Accounts of William Haines Lytle's funeral procession in the *Daily Gazette* and *Daily Commercial,* October 23, 1863. The *Commercial* indicated that Wilson had formerly been the waiting man of Commodore Perry and thus followed "the dead body of his second hero master to the grave."

6. Ezekial S. Haines to Josephine Lytle Foster and Elizabeth Lytle Broadwell, [October ?, 1863], LP, box 32, no. 306.

7. Ezekial S. Haines to Josephine Lytle Foster, October 16, [1863], LP, box 32, no. 304.

8. D. Thew Wright's remarks to the Cincinnati Bar dated October 15, 1863, enclosed in letter D. Thew Wright to Josephine Lytle Foster, November 5, 1894, LP, box 34, no. 731.

9. Handwritten copy of the tribute from the Tenth Ohio. LP, box 34, no. 769.

10. "The Last Ride of the Good Steed Faughaballa," in Charlton [Charlotte Pendleton], *Songs of the Year and Other Poems* (Cincinnati: Robert Clarke & Co., 1875), 44-48.

11. Elizabeth Lytle Broadwell to Lieut. Col. William Ward, December 15, 1863, LP, box 31, no. 63.

12. D. Thew Wright's remarks to the Cincinnati Bar on October 15, 1863, used the

"vacant chair" phrase when he noted, "And in that sad circle of home, where he was the light & the idol, the 'one vacant chair,' stands as a silent monument of eloquent woe."

13. *Poems of William Haines Lytle,* edited, with memoir, by William H. Venable (Cincinnati: Robert Clarke Co., 1894).

14. *Cincinnati Commercial Tribune,* August 1, 1893.

15. *Cincinnati Enquirer,* December 22, 1898.

16. *Commercial Tribune,* December 22, 1898.

17. William Haines Lytle speech, August 9, 1863, at Bridgeport, Alabama. See Appendix B for the complete speech.

# Appendix A

Buell Court of Inquiry
Testimony of Col. W. H. Lytle

Transcript from Phonographic Notes
of the Buell Court of Inquiry

Cincinnati, December 1, 1862.

Col. W. H. LYTLE (a witness for the Government), being duly sworn by the judge-advocate, testified as follows:

By the JUDGE-ADVOCATE:

*Question.* What is your position in the service of the United States, colonel?

I have been in the three-months' service, but was commissioned in the three-years' service on or about June 6, 1861.

*Question.* Will you state to the court what part of that time you were in service under command of Major-General Buell in Tennessee and Kentucky?

I reported for duty in the Department of the Ohio on or about January 2, 1862.

*Question.* You will please state to the court what you know of the operations of General Buell at the time of the invasion of the State of Kentucky by General Bragg.

I can only give the movements of that portion of the army with which I was connected. On the 31st of August, 1862, I was in command at Huntsville, Ala. and under orders from General Buell conducted on that day the evacuation of the town. My orders were to make Shelbyville inside of four days. I made the march inside of two days and a half. I camped 4 miles from Nashville on the evening of September 5, having halted nearly a day at Murfreesborough for orders. From thence we marched to Perryville via Louisville.

*Question.* During that time what division were you attached to?

I commanded the Seventeenth Brigade of General Rosecrans' division.

*Question.* State to the Commission what you know of General Bragg's position during the march of the rebels.

I was not specially informed as to his movements, my attention being directed generally to my own command. I had the general idea that Bragg was marching in a direction parallel, or nearly so, to that of our own army.

*Question.* Could you point out the parallel movement of General Bragg?

I am not able to do so; I had no opportunity at the time to observe.

*Question.* Do you know anything, colonel, about the surrender and failure at Munfordville:

I know nothing of it; I know only of the movements of my own command.

*Question.* You know of the surrender of that place?

Yes, sir.

*Question.* Can you state to the Commission as to the probability of its being relieved?

I do not know; I do not recollect the date of the surrender of Munfordville. My command reached Bowling Green September 11. We halted there several days, and did not arrive at Munfordville until after its surrender.

*Question.* What was the cause of your delay at Bowling Green?

I do not know.

*Question.* Do you recollect how many days you were there?

My impression is we were there three or four days. Of course I have no opportunity now to refer to any official document, but my recollection is that we were there three or four days.

*Question.* I understand you to say that Munfordville was surrendered before you arrived there?

The town, I think, was surrendered either during our halt at Bowling Green or during our march thence to Munfordville. The march from Bowling Green to Munfordville command (including the halt at Horse Well) six or seven days. We were at Horse Well about two days.

*Question.* What was the cause of the slow march you made between Bowling Green and Munfordville?

I do not know.

*Question.* Could you produce any reason for your delay?

At Horse Well we were drawn up in line of battle, fronting toward Munfordville.

*Question.* Had you any evidence of a large force in the neighborhood at the time?

I saw none. There was more or less skirmishing reported during our halt there. As general officer of the day I rode to the extreme outposts; the enemy's pickets could be seen.

*Question.* What position had General McCook's corps in the army?

It had at that time, I think the advance on that road. My impression is that it was the first to arrive in Louisville.

*Question.* You stated that you do not know the reason of the delay at Bowling Green or why the march was so slow from Bowling Green to Munfordville.

I do not know.

*Question.* What was the rate of marching previous to arriving in Bowling Green?

I made rapid marches to Nashville with the command left at Huntsville. The march thence to Bowling Green, as was also the march from Munfordville to Louisville, was a rapid as possible.

*Question.* Were you engaged at the battle of Perryville?

I was.

*Question.* Will you state, as near as you can, the circumstances of the affair?

Cincinnati, December 2, 1862.

Col. W. H. LYTLE's examination continued.

(Map produced by the judge-advocate, that the movements and positions of the Union and rebel armies might be pointed out by the witness.)

The witness then proceeded and said:

Our column (McCook's army corps) moved by the way of Taylorsville, Fairfield, Bloomfield, and Chaplin, encamping the night before the fight at Mackville. There were but two divisions of the army corps at that point—Rousseau's and Jackson's. The Third Division (Sill's) was not with us. My original orders at Mackville were to move at 6 a.m. Before daylight, however, I received orders to move immediately. My own command was in motion in twenty minutes. I had no tents. My brigade had the right of Rousseau's division, which had the advance of the corps.

We arrived on the field of battle about 10:30 a. m., to the best of my recollection. As we reached the ground I saw a column of our troops on the Springfield road, which I ascertained subsequently was a portion of Gilbert's corps. [Witness points out Springfield road on map.]

Having been directed by General Rousseau to place a good skirmishing regiment in advance, the Tenth Ohio occupied that position, and on our arrival on the field was at once deployed as skirmishers.

General Rousseau's original line of battle was considerably in the rear of the line he actually occupied during the fight. Our march had been accelerated when we heard cannonading.

by the JUDGE-ADVOCATE:

*Question.* Where was that cannonading?

I do not know exactly; think it was from a battery on the right of my position during the fight. General Rousseau's original line was nearly at right angles with the road, his right resting near Russell's house.

I will remark here that my recollection of the topography of the field may not be accurate, as I saw it only during the fight and afterwards from an ambulance on my return from the enemy's lines.

On our arrival on the field at 10:30 a. m. a section or more of artillery was thrown forward and opened fire. No response having been elicited, General Rousseau directed me to move with my brigade toward Perryville. At this time the Tenth Ohio Infantry, thrown forward as skirmishers, had not returned, though I had sent a staff officer and several orderlies to recall it. My orders being imperative, however, to march, I sent an order to Lieutenant-Colonel Burke, commanding, to fall in the rear of my brigade, and directed Colonel Beatty, with his regiment (Third Ohio Infantry), to take the advance.

*Question.* How far was your right from the next corps on your right?

I saw no line of battle on my right at all. My own command was composed of the Third and Tenth Ohio Infantry, Fifteenth Kentucky Infantry, Forty-second and Eighty-eight Indiana Infantry, and Loomis battery.

In compliance with orders about 12 o'clock I resumed the march, the Third Ohio having the right. The impression at this time seemed to be that the enemy had retired. My column was in motion, as directed, when my attention was directed to a [scattering tire] on the left of the road. It immediately struck me that it proceeded from the skirmishers of the Tenth Ohio, which, as I have said, had not yet reported. Riding up to the eminence where our artillery had been posted in the morning, commanding a ravine, an officer of my staff approached me and said he discovered the enemy on the opposite side of the ravine. With my glass I saw heavy masses of rebels apparently deploying into line of battle. The morning was bright and clear. General Rousseau directed me to form line of battle immediately. My column, then in motion and descending the hill into the ravine, was marched by the right-about, and the order was complied with. Cannot state the precise distance from the enemy.

My brigade had the right of Rousseau's division in line of battle. Harris' brigade was on my left. Jackson was on the left of Rousseau. We had then an artillery duel, which lasted perhaps two hours.

*Question.* Could you see the enemy's line at the time from that eminence? They were screened by the timber. In the ravine which separated us from the enemy was the rocky bed of a creek. The men had suffered much from thirst. One of my regiments (the Forty-second Indiana) had been ordered to the ravine in the morning by General Rousseau to supply the men with water, but there was little or none there.

After the fire of the artillery had been prolonged some time Captain Loomis reported that his long-range ammunition was nearly expended. I accompanied him and reported to General Rousseau. The general and Loomis rode off together, as I supposed either to have Loomis' ammunition replenished or another battery sent forward to take its place. I returned immediately to the front.

*Question.* During this time did you receive any orders from any other officer? Had General Rousseau received any orders from General McCook from 12 to 2 o'clock?

I received no orders during that time from any other officer. As to whether General Rousseau received any orders from General McCook or not during the time mentioned I cannot state. The position of my regiments was reported to General Rousseau when the fight opened, and my general instructions were to hold my ground there as long as practicable, and in case it became impracticable to hold it to retire in good order. Shortly after my return to the front I saw Loomis' battery being withdrawn, the general desired any change in the position of my line. To this message I got no answer, nor can I say whether or not it ever reached the general. Shortly after 2 o'clock p. m. the fire of the rebel artillery slackened and his infantry advanced. The Third Ohio was immediately ordered from the slight depression of ground that

partially screened it from the artillery fire to the crest of the hill. The
Fifteenth Kentucky was ordered to support it. The Tenth Ohio was
on the left of the Third Ohio, from which I had not felt at liberty to
withdraw it. The Eighty-eighth Indiana was held in reserve.

We held our position for two hours or more after Loomis was
retired, and finally, being without our battery and exposed to a severe
fire of artillery as well as that of an infantry force greatly superior in
number, the brigade fell back in good order and reformed, as I am
informed, in the neighborhood of the original line selected in the
morning near Russell's house.

*Question.* Did it appear from the sound of the cannon that the enemy was
on the left?

The rattle of small-arms was so deafening that it would have been
hard to tell. I could see only two regiments on my left, such was the
conformation of the ground. While the fight was progressing I became satisfied, between 2 and 3 o'clock, that we were outnumbered.

My battery had been withdrawn, and the brigade was exposed not
only to a severe fire from the enemy's infantry posted in the ravine,
but from a heavy fire of his artillery, which swept the crest of the
ridge. I accordingly sent back a staff officer for re-enforcements. He
returned with the message that I should hold the position as long as I
could, and if it became impracticable, should retire; that Jackson was
very hard pressed, and no re-enforcements could be spared. Between
3 and 4 p.m. I renewed my application for re-enforcements, but to
this second application received no response.

Meanwhile my whole line, after a most obstinate and resolute
struggle and severe loss, had been retired, with the exception of one
regiment, the Tenth Ohio.

*Question.* How many rounds of ammunition had you?

Forty rounds. The ammunition train was, I think, in the woods near
the Russell house, though of this I am not certain. Our line was so
suddenly formed that I had no time to ascertain its location. I had
finally sent back for the Eighty-eight Indiana, being determined to
hold our position if possible until re-enforcements came up. I could
not believe but what they would finally arrive from some other corps,
having seen the column on the Springfield road in the morning. Before the Eighty-eight got up, however, the Tenth was nearly enveloped by the enemy and was obliged to fall back. A most destructive
fire was poured on the regiment's front and from the flanks, and

while endeavoring to cover its movement to the rear with skirmishers I was wounded and captured. There are the material points that came under my observation up to the time that I was taken prisoner.

It is my impression that after Harris was obliged to retire for want of ammunition the attack of eight or ten regiments of the enemy was concentrated on my brigade, or rather on the three regiments—the Third Ohio, Fifteenth Kentucky, and Tenth Ohio—which were the last to retire.

*Question.* Did you know the headquarters of General Buell?

I did not. I saw General McCook and General Rousseau. After the battle began General Rousseau's attention, as I gathered from his official report, was mainly directed to the left of the line. My loss was very heavy. The orders to the brigade were executed to the letter as I understood them. I am informed the loss of the brigade was between 700 and 800 killed and wounded. Have not yet seen official report.

*Question.* How far to the right was the army?

General Gilbert's corps, on the Springfield road, could be readily seen with the naked eye. I do not think the Springfield road was more than a mile from my position. There was a battery on my right, on a wooded eminence, probably a quarter of a mile distant, but there was no infantry between my right and the battery.

*Question.* Which way was the wind blowing?

I remember that when a barn near the right of the Third Ohio was fired by the enemy's shells the whole line was almost enveloped in smoke. The wind must have been, I think, a southerly wind; it blew from right to left of my line.

*Question.* Was it known that the enemy was in force at Perryville:

That I do not know. I remember meeting General McCook in the morning, and that the General remarked there would be fun before night or some remark to that effect.

*Question.* With the exception of Gilbert's column were you not aware of the positions of the other corps?

I was not.

*Question.* You had no knowledge of the force of the enemy?

Nothing definite.

*Question.* When you were taken prisoner could you form any estimate of the numbers of the enemy?

I could not.

*Question.* Did you know their line of retreat, what roads they went by, where their force lay, and where they arrived that night?

I have some delicacy in testifying to these points under the terms of my parole. I can state that I was very much surprised that we were not re-enforced that day, and also that no advance was made the next morning.

*Question.* What reason can you give that prevents you answering these questions?

My impression is that there is a provision in the terms of the parole "that I shall not reveal anything that I might have discovered within the line of the enemy." I therefore decline to testify on these points.

*Question.* How many days were you in the hands of the enemy?

The battle was fought on Wednesday, the first week of October. I was paroled the next day, and returned to our lines on Friday night and immediately reported at General Buell's headquarters.

*Question.* Where were General Buell's headquarters?

They were on the Harrodsburg pike, beyond the position we occupied, near the road. When I returned I was in a buggy; I returned by way of Danville.

*Question.* Where were you at the time you received your parole?

I was at Harrodsburg.

*Question.* For how long were the men provided with provisions?

They had provisions for three days.

*Question.* During the battle the men threw away their haversacks, sometimes their knapsacks. Had you noticed anything of the kind in your corps?

I did not observe that they did so; I noticed that they were very cool.

*Question.* When you were at headquarters did you see Gen. Bragg?

I was not at the headquarters of the enemy.

Here the court desired the witness to produce the parole, to which the witness assented.

The day following the colonel produced the parole.

*Copy of the parole.*

Hdqrs. Army of the Miss., *Harrodsburg, Oct. 9, 1862.*
I, Wm. H. Lytle, Army of the United States, having been taken prisoner by the Confederate States Army and this day paroled, whereof this is witness, do swear that I will not bear arms against the Confederate States, nor will I in any way aid or abet its enemies, until I am regularly exchanged, under

the penalty of death; nor will I disclose anything that I have seen or heard in said Confederate States Army to its prejudice.

WM. H. LYTLE
Colonel, Commanding Seventeenth Brigade, Third Division
Sworn to and subscribed before me October 9, 1862

SAM'L K. Hays
Major, C. S. Army

The Commission adjourned to meet December 4, at 10 o'clock a. m.

CINCINNATI, *December 4*, 1862—10 a.m.
Examination of Col. W. H. LYTLE continued.

Cross-examination by General BUELL:

*Question.* On leaving Huntsville did you received orders to proceed directly to Nashville:

I did not. I received orders to proceed to Murfreesborough by way of Fayetteville and Shelbyville, my orders being to reach in four days.

*Question.* When did your division leave Nashville on the march toward Kentucky?

My brigade left its camp near Edgefield and joined the main column. September 7, 1862, halted at Gee's Tavern.

September 8, marched to Tyree Springs.

September 9, marched to Sharp's Branch, near Franklin

September 10, marched to Cave or Sinking Springs, near Bowling Green.

September 11, marched to Bowling Green.

September 16, march late; camp 3 miles from Barren River.

September 17, bivouac near Dripping Springs, 9 miles from Glasgow.

September 18, to Prewitt's Knob.

September 19, to Horse Well.

September 21, to point 3 miles from Munfordville.

September 22, march late; camp at Munfordville.

September 23, to Nolin.

September 24, Burlington (or Bloomington).

September 25, cross Salt River; halt; at 2 march resumed.

September 26, marched to Louisville.

*Question.* Do you know what the orders were under which your division marched?

I do not.

*Question.* Do you know what its immediate destination was?

I do not.

*Question.* Did you know any circumstance which made it necessary for it to reach any particular place at any given time?

I was not personally informed of any.

*Question.* Did any division leave Nashville in advance of it!

I do not recollect.

*Question.* On what road did it march?

We marched on the Bowling Green road by way of Tyree Springs.

*Question.* Was your march continued from the time you left Nashville until you arrived at Bowling Green?

The march was continuous, making only the necessary halts.

*Question.* When did you arrive at Bowling Green?

On the 11th September.

*Question.* Was your division first to arrive at Bowling Green?

My impression is that our division was not the first to arrive. I think there were several before us.

[NOTE BY GENERAL BUELL—"It was the first division that arrived."]

*Question.* When did you march from Bowling Green?

We marched from Bowling Green on the 16th, in the afternoon.

*Question.* How far did you march that afternoon and on what road?

We marched on the Dripping Springs road, and camped 3 miles from the Barren River.

*Question.* What time in the afternoon did you encamp?

I cannot remember.

*Question.* Before or after dark?

I cannot remember.

*Question.* On what road did you march the following day?

We marched to Dripping Springs; that was the termination of the second day's march from Bowling Green.

*Question.* Where did you encamp the second day?

Upon a high hill at Dripping Springs.

*Question.* Where did you encamp the third day?

At Prewitt's Knob.

*Question.* Where did you encamp the fourth day?

At Horse Well.

*Question.* Did you that day make the march you expected to make?

I have no reason to think we did not.

*Question.* Where did you arrive at the end of the fifth day's march?

At Bear Wallow, quite early in the forenoon.

*Question.* When did you leave Bear Wallow?

On the afternoon of the seventh day out from Bowling Green.

[NOTE BY GENERAL BUELL.—Marched from Bowling Green late on the "16th," and arrived at Munfordville on the 21st—five days instead of "seven."]

*Question.* Did you know of the immediate destination of the army when leaving Bowling Green?

I did not.

*Question.* Where did you suppose Bragg's army was?

My impression was that it was moving in a line parallel with ours, but know nothing of his position.

*Question.* Who was in command of your column?

General Rousseau.

*Question.* Of what troops was it composed?

His own old division and General Smith's.

*Question.* Were there any detachments from your column at Bear Wallow?

There was a detachment moved in the direction of Glasgow to cut off a train, as I supposed.

*Question.* Did it return before the column left there?

It did not.

*Question.* For what point did you march?

We marched on the pike, turned to the left, and halted within 3 miles of Munfordville.

*Question.* On what day of the week and month?

I cannot give the day of the week; it was on the 21st of September.

*Question.* When did you reach Louisville?

On the 26th September.

*Question.* What is the distance between Louisville and Munfordville?

Between 70 and 80 miles.

*Question.* How many encampments did you make between Munfordville and Louisville?

I remember but four.

*Question.* Was there any unnecessary loss of time?

The marches were made promptly. We had good marches up to the time of arriving at Bowling Green.

*Question.* Do you know anything of the amount of supplies on hand at the time of leaving Bowling Green?

I do not.

*Question.* At what hour on the morning of the 8th of October did McCook's column leave Mackville?

I moved about 5 o'clock.

*Question.* Was the line of battle formed by McCook's corps a continuous line or did it consist of detached positions taken up at the moment?

I can make no statement except as to that portion attached to my command.

*Question.* Could you judge of the position of the line by the firing?

I could not.

*Question.* Was the engagement throughout the entire line during the principal part of the action?

I inferred it was a general one.

*Question.* Did you know where the headquarters of General McCook were during the engagement?

I did not.

*Question.* Did you know where the headquarters of Rousseau were during the battle?

I had no express information where they were.

*Question.* In your evidence you express surprise at the enemy's not being pursued next day; did that surprise arise from the knowledge you obtained while a captive or from other circumstances?

Among other reasons, I had supposed no other division but ours had been engaged. I was surprised no attack was made the next day because I understood the enemy's attack had been repulsed by our corps.

I decline to state anything I saw within the lines of the enemy.

*Question.* Was that attack made by the whole of the rebel army upon this one corps?"

That I cannot state.

*Question.* Is it true that no other part of the lines was attacked except General McCook's corps?

I believe other portions of the army were engaged before the battle was over.

*Question.* Did you know that any division of the army was in the rear and on the march to join its corps?

I did not: I supposed there was a general concentration of the army at that point.

*Question.* Did you know what the strength of the army at Perryville was on the 8th?

I did not.

*Question.* What did you suppose it to be?

I supposed we had 60,000 or 70,000 men.

*Question.* Did you know what the condition of our army was?

I did not know its condition.

*Question.* Did you know what loss it sustained in the battle of the 8th?

I had no means of ascertaining.

*Question.* Had you formed any estimate of the loss.

No; it would have been impossible.

*Question.* What did you suppose to be the strength of the rebel army, independent of Kirby Smith's force?

I supposed General Bragg had 40,000 or 50,000.

*Question.* Was that the general estimate among persons who had opportunity of knowing?

I cannot say what opinion others had; estimates differ.

*Question.* What did you suppose to be the force under Kirby Smith's command; by that I mean the whole rebel force in Kentucky, not including Bragg's army, and including that of Humphrey Marshall?

I had no knowledge of any other corps except of that portion under command of Kirby Smith. I estimated that at from 15,000 to 20,000.

*Question.* Does that include the force under Humphrey Marshall?

It does not. Any force under him I know nothing of.

Lytle's testimony at the General Don Carlos Buell Court of Inquiry is found in the *O.R.,* ser. 1, vol. 16, pt. 1, 67-75.

# Appendix B

*Last Speech by Brigadier General William Haines Lytle*

On August 9, 1863, in camp at Bridgeport, Alabama, William Haines Lytle received a jeweled Maltese cross from the officers of the Tenth Ohio Regiment. Colonel William M. Ward made the presentation speech. He concluded with these words:

> We, now, your old comrades in arms, witnesses of your conspicuous gallantry in the field; witnesses, also, of your skill in council, and thoroughly conversant with your accurate knowledge of military duty—present to 'our Colonel' the cross I have placed, General, upon your breast, knowing as we all do—and also anxious to tell your dear brothers in arms—gentlemen of whose gallantry I would have been assured, even if you had not told me of it—that our Colonel's cross will be like the white plume of the hero of Ivry—seek it where the fight is thickest.

## General Lytle's Speech

Colonel, and Gentlemen of the Tenth Ohio Infantry—My old Friends and Comrades:—I can not tell you how deeply I am touched by this beautiful testimonial. I am very glad to learn that, although you have not for a long time been under my command, you have not forgotten me: and I feel it also an honor that you have taken the trouble to visit me in our camp in the mountains to make me this present in the midst of a campaign, and I fear, at great personal inconvenience. In all sincerity I can say to you that never did the heart of a soldier of the Old Guard beat higher—no, not even when at the hands of the "Little Corporal" himself he received the Cross of the Legion—than does mine today. Come what may to me tomorrow or in days beyond; come what may, as under the leadership of our gallant chief, the invincible Rosecrans, this Army of the Cumberland follows his happy star through the eventful drama of the war, at least for me this token, from the cherished comrades with whom I entered the service, is secure.

So long as in God's providence, my life is spared, I shall look on it, gentlemen, and be reminded of many a stirring incident, both in your experience and mine. It will recall the pale and troubled faces with which men stood in the black shadows that strove before civil war, and the horror that thrilled our breasts when the rebellion first proclaimed itself by overt acts; the revered and holy flag of the nation was fired on by parricidal hands at Charleston. It will bring back to me the fiery and tumultuous gatherings of armed men that rallied to defend the flag. I will remember, as I gaze on it, a thousand incidents connected with our camps at Harrison and Dennison. It will remind me of the long and weary marches when our solitary column threaded the mountain defiles of West Virginia, of the memorable 8th of October at Carnifex Ferry, when your ranks, plowed by shot and shell, stood fast and firm until the enemy fell back across the Gauley under cover of the night, the movement masked by darkness and the roar of the mountain stream. It will remind me of the brave Milroy; of Fitzgibbon, the color-bearer; of Kavanaugh and Kennedy, of many a hero soldier whose name we will keep green in memory; of that red autumnal day, at Chaplin Hills, when Jackson, Terrill, Jones and Campbell fell, their names crowned with the deathless laurel, when in your own brigade, the chivalry of Ohio and Kentucky, and Indiana and Michigan, added a new and glorious leaf to the somber annals of the Dark and Bloody Ground.

I will be reminded too, as I gaze upon its emerald and its shamrock, the significant emblems with which your taste and the craft of the artisan have enriched it, of that gallant and beautiful island of the sea, the devotion of whose children to my country and their country, has been so gloriously manifested in this hour of her bitterest travail.

String with fresh cords the Irish harp, worn with recounting the triumphs of your race, to breathe in new and yet loftier strains of minstrelsy their deeds in arms and deeds of noble daring during this rebellion. Let the pale cheek of Erin, as she watches across the deep, crimson with exultation at the names of Corcoran and Meagher, and the records of your own gallant regiment, the armed witness before this, your generation, to the undying fame of Richard Montgomery.

I will not deny, gentlemen, that when on reporting to this department, I found you were to be no longer in my command, I felt that sense of loneliness and isolation natural to one whose old army associations were broken up. My present command will pardon me for saying this, I know, for in my judgment, no man who forgets his old friends deserves to make new ones. But long since I have felt perfectly at home, and I can not let this the first occasion that has presented itself pass by without expressing to the officers and men of the First Brigade my heartfelt thanks for the warm and generous welcome they have awarded to a stranger. Gentlemen of the Tenth Ohio, you see around you your brethren in arms, the men of Sheridan's division; men from the Northwest, from the clans of the people, who pitch their tents on the prairies of Illinois and Michigan and Wisconsin, and by the shores of the great lakes,—veterans of Pea Ridge, Perryville, and Stone River. When the next fight comes on, may they and the Old Tenth stand shoulder to shoulder, and see by whom, in glorious emulation, our battle-flags into the ranks of the enemy can be flung the farthest and followed the closest. Nor will it diminish your interest in this brigade to tell you it was once commanded by the pure and heroic Sill—Sill, whom you knew so well last year, during your campaign in Northern Alabama. Than his, the war has developed no nobler spirit. The Military Academy at West Point might point to his name alone, and stand fast in the affections of the people. Ohio in no braver or better blood has sealed her devotion to the Union.

> Him shall no sunshine from the field of azure,
> No drum beat from the wall—
> No morning gun, from the black fort's embrasure,
> Awaken with its call,

But his name will be embalmed in the praise of states, and this, his old brigade, at Chattanooga, or Atlanta, or in Eastern Tennessee, or wherever its proud banners flaunt the sky, will cherish his memory and avenge his fall.

But, gentlemen, I know your time is limited, and that I must not detain you too long. Rest assured that I shall follow the military career of each and all of you with the deepest solicitude. The third year of the war is upon us. How fierce has been the struggle, our vast national debt and shattered ranks bear witness. Whether the end is near or not, I can not tell. The past months will be forever memorable for the splendid triumphs of our arms, and to the eyes of hope the sky is flushed with faint light and the morning seems near at hand. But come victory or come defeat, come tri-

umph or come disaster, this I know, that against rebels in the field or traitors at home, despite the plots of weak-kneed and cowardly politicians of
the North and the machinations of foreign despots and aristocrats, the
scarred and bronzed veterans of the warlike West, the men on whose banners are inscribed Mill Springs and Donelson, Pea Ridge and Vicksburg,
Shiloh, Carnifex and Stone River, will make no terms, accept no truce,
indorse no treaty, until the military power of the rebellion is crushed forever, and the supremacy of the National Government acknowledged from
the Potomac to the Rio Grande.

Am I told that Union restored by force of arms is not worth having?
Am I told that if the states now in revolt are whipped in fair fight—beaten
and humiliated—they will be unworthy and degraded members of the
Union? We must have peace first, says a certain school of politicians, and
then, if we can, we will argue the South into a reconstruction. In other
words, these gentlemen would have the Government and the loyal masses
of the country drain to the dregs the bitter cup which they would dash
from the hands of traitors and rebels. The territory you have occupied is to
be abandoned, the public property, the dockyards, and fortresses you have
recaptured after two years of war, are to be surrendered, the victorious
armies of the Mississippi, the Cumberland, and the Potomac, followed by
the jeers and scoffs of the enemy, are to sneak, with arms reversed and flags
trailed in the dust, across the Northern border; and your Government—
the Government of Washington, and Jefferson, and Jackson—is to cower,
dishonored and disgraced, a byword and hissing among the nations. If the
rebel armies (I will not say the rebel States, for it is not against the States,
nor their constitutional rights, we wage war), if the rebel armies, and the
oligarchs who control them, have their pride broken, and their prestige
humbled, let them blame themselves. They have sown the wind, let them
reap the whirlwind, till the bloody problem is finally worked out; eye to
eye, foot to foot, sword to sword, bayonet to bayonet; if need be, for ten
years longer, with iron hearts, and iron fleets, and iron hail, this generation
of loyal men will, by God's grace, endure its heavy cross, and until the
broad daylight of peace and order and victory shall come, will stand to
arms.

And then for you, soldiers—soldiers, but freemen and armed citizens
of the Republic—it will be for you to remember the Roman saying, *"Vel
pace, vel bello, clarum fieri licet,"* or, as old Milton has paraphrased it "Peace
has her victories, no less renowned than war." It will be for you to look to
it that those arbitrary war measures, justified by the awful presence of a

rebellion, whose like the world never saw before; justified by the maxim that "the safety of the Republic is the supreme law," die, with the necessities which gave them birth. It will be for you to see that the powers of the Government are restricted to their lawful and appropriate channels; that each State has its full and perfect rights under the constitution, awarded to it; and, finally, through the instrumentality of the ballot box, it will be for you to put the seal of eternal political damnation on those subtle and designing demagogues, whose disaffection and disloyalty to the country have already prolonged the war, and today, more than all other agencies, feed the unholy fires of treason, riot and insurrection. Mark the prediction, that when the war is over, it will be to the men of this human army, more than to any others, that the people of the Southern States will look for a wise, generous, patriotic conservatism.

They will trust you because of your unflinching and unwavering loyalty to your great cause; they will respect you as one brave man, even though overcome, respects another with whom he has measured swords. The government of Jefferson Davis may flatter the political apostates of the North for military purposes, but I mistake the character of Southern men, if, while they hug the treason, they do not scorn the traitor.

It will be for you, above all others, when this rebellion has spent its strength, to recall to the minds of the people, the admonition:

"It is well to have a giant's strength,

But, oh, 'tis tyranny to use it like a giant,"

To heal up the sores and scars, and cover up the bloody footprints that war will leave; to bury in oblivion all animosities against your former foe; and chivalrous as you are brave, standing on forever stricken fields, memorable in history, side by side with the Virginian, the Mississippian, or Alabamian, to carve on bronze or marble the glowing epitaph that tells us of Southern as well as Northern valor.

That the day of ultimate triumph for the Union arms, sooner or later, will come, I do not doubt, for I have faith in the courage, the wisdom, and the justice of the people. It may not be for all of us here today to listen to the chants that greet the victor, nor to hear the brazen bells ring out the new nuptials of the States. But those who do survive can tell, at least, to the people, how their old comrades, whether in the skirmish or the charge, before the rifle-pit or the redan, died with their harness on, in the great war for Union and Liberty.

# Appendix C

*Mexican and Civil War Letters Written by William Haines Lytle*
*in the Lytle Papers at the Cincinnati Historical Society*

To aid future researchers and library staff at the Cincinnati Historical Society Library, the following list provides box and letter numbers for the letters from William Haines Lytle in the Lytle Papers that are included in this book. In some cases Lytle wrote more than one letter on the same day.

All of the letters in the index are in the Lytle Family Papers, Mss q L996P, Cincinnati Historical Society, Cincinnati Museum Center.

| Date of Letter | Box No. | Letter No. |
|---|---|---|
| [early October 1847] | 30 | 10 |
| October 30, 1847 | 30 | 5 |
| October 31, 1847 | 30 | 6 |
| November 10, 1847 | 30 | 7 |
| December 8, 1847 | 30 | 8 |
| December 12, 1847 | 34 | 562 |
| January 15, 1847 [i.e., 1848] | 30 | 11 |
| January 26, 1848 | 30 | 12 |
| February 21, 1848 | 30 | 13 |
| February 29, 1848 | 30 | 14 |
| April 7, 1848 | 30 | 15 |
| April 8, 1848 | 33 | 457 |
| May 8, 1848 | 30 | 16 |
| [May ? 1861] | 33 | 476 |
| [May ? 1861] | 33 | 477 |
| [June 1861] | 33 | 504 |

| Date of Letter | Box No. | Letter No. |
|---|---|---|
| June 26, [1861] | 33 | 532 |
| June 26, 1861 | 34 | 569 |
| [late June 1861] | 33 | 529 |
| July 4, 1861 | 33 | 555 |
| July 5, [1861] | 33 | 511 |
| July 8, [1861] | 33 | 533 |
| July 16, 1861 | 33 | 512 |
| August 2, 1861 | 33 | 513 |
| August 2, 1861 | 34 | 570 |
| August 9, 1861 | 33 | 514 |
| August 9, 1861 | 34 | 571 |
| August 20, 1861 | 33 | 515 |
| August 24, 1861 | 33 | 556 |
| September 7, 1861 | 33 | 516 |
| January 1, 1862 | 33 | 546 |
| January 6, 1862 | 33 | 519 |
| January 11, 1862 | 33 | 517 |
| January 14, 1862 | 33 | 518 |
| [January 16, 1862] | 33 | 528 |
| [January 19, 1862] | 33 | 506 |
| January 23, 1862 | 34 | 572 |
| [January 27, 1862] | 33 | 502 |
| February 3, 1862 | 33 | 479 |
| February 7, 1862 | 33 | 520 |
| February 11, 1862 | 33 | 521 |
| February 26, 1862 | 33 | 480 |
| February 28, 1862 | 34 | 574 |
| [March 1, 1862 ?] | 33 | 531 |
| [March 6, 1862 ?] | 33 | 524 |
| [March 11, 1862] | 33 | 503 |
| March 16, 1862 | 33 | 547 |
| March 23, 1862 | 33 | 573 |
| March 29, 1862 | 33 | 523 |
| [March 30, 1862] | 30 | 34a |
| April 2, 1862 | 30 | 31 |
| April 6, 1862 | 30 | 32 |

| Date of Letter | Box No. | Letter No. |
|---|---|---|
| [April 14, 1862][1] | 30 | 37 |
| May 6, 1862 | 33 | 481 |
| May 28, 1862 | 33 | 525 |
| June 1, 1862 | 30 | 33 |
| June 5, 1862 | 30 | 34 |
| June 19, 1862 | 33 | 482 |
| June 30, 1862 | 33 | 526 |
| July 4, 1862 | 30 | 35 |
| July 12, 1862 | 33 | 483 |
| July 27, 1862 | 33 | 534 |
| July 29, 1862 | 34 | 565 |
| August 4, 1862 | 30 | 36 |
| August 18, 1862 | 33 | 555 |
| September 12, 1862 | 33 | 527 |
| September 26, 1862 | 33 | 484 |
| September 27, 1862 | 33 | 485 |
| September 28, 1862 | 33 | 557 |
| October 3, 1862 | 33 | 486 |
| October 5, [1862] | 34 | 575 |
| February 15, 1863 | 30 | 52 |
| February 22, 1863 | 33 | 487 |
| March 24, [1863] | 33 | 522 |
| April 2, [1863] | 33 | 530 |
| April 4, 1863 | 30 | 40 |
| April 19, 1863 | 33 | 489 |
| April 23, 1863 | 30 | 41 |
| April 26, 1863 | 33 | 488 |
| May 3, 1863 | 33 | 536 |
| [May 5, 1863] | 30 | 48 |
| May 8, 1863 | 30 | 42 |
| May 11, 1863 | 30 | 43 |
| May 17, 1863 | 33 | 537 |
| May 20, 1863 | 33 | 490 |
| May 21, 1863 | 30 | 44 |
| June 1, 1863 | 33 | 491 |
| June 3, 1863 | 30 | 45 |

| Date of Letter | Box No. | Letter No. |
|---|---|---|
| June 4, 1863 | 33 | 538 |
| June 5, 1863 | 33 | 492 |
| June 23, 1863 | 30 | 46 |
| June 24, 1863 | 33 | 539 |
| July 4, 1863 | 33 | 493 |
| July 10, 1863 [?] | 34 | 568 |
| July 10, [1863]² | 30 | 48a |
| July 16, 1863 | 30 | 47 |
| July 22, 1863 | 30 | 49 |
| July 29, 1863 | 30 | 50 |
| August 4, 1863 | 33 | 548 |
| August 16, 1863 | 33 | 494 |
| August 31, 1863 | 33 | 549 |

Notes

1. The date of the letter box 30, no. 37, is in dispute. Although it appears to read September on the manuscript, that is not possible in the context of Lytle's movements during 1862. He went to Huntsville, Alabama, in April 1862 and left there at the end of August to march to Kentucky. On September 14, 1862, Lytle was between Bowling Green and Barren River, Kentucky.

2. Lytle wrote Sunday July 10 on this letter and did not include the year. However, July 10 was not a Sunday in 1861, 1862, or 1863. The context of the letter places it in 1863.

# Bibliography

*Selected Sources—Books, Articles, and Dissertations*

This list contains sources, exclusive of manuscripts and newspapers, cited or consulted heavily in the preparation of this book. There are many more sources that pertain to the Civil War and the life and times of William Haines Lytle. Unless otherwise indicated biographical information about the Union and Confederate officers was taken from Stephen Sifakis's two compilations. Information concerning members of Ohio units, unless otherwise specified is taken from the *Official Roster of the Soldiers of the State of Ohio in the War of Rebellion, 1861-1866*.

Aaron, Daniel. *Cincinnati, Queen City of the West, 1819-1838*. Columbus: Ohio State Univ. Press, 1992.

Abbazia, Patrick. *The Chickamauga Campaign: December 1862-November 1863*. New York: Gallery Books, 1988.

Barnett, James. "Forty for the Union: Civil War Generals Buried in Spring Grove Cemetery." *Cincinnati Historical Society Bulletin* 30 (2): 91-121 (Summer 1972).

*Battles and Leaders of the Civil War: Being for the most part contributions by Union and Confederates officers, with new introduction by Roy F. Nichols*. 4 vols. New York: T. Yoseloff, 1956.

Bauer, K. Jack. *The Mexican War, 1846-1848*. New York: Macmillan, 1974.

Bowles, John. *Chickamauga and Chattanooga: The Battles that Doomed the Conferederacy*. New York: Avon Books, 1995.

Brill, Ruth. "Cincinnati's 'Poet-Warrior': William Haines Lytle." *Historical and Philosophical Society of Ohio Bulletin* 21 (3): 188-201 (July 1963).

Capps, Randall. *The Rowan Story: From Federal Hill to My Old Kentucky Home*. Cincinnati: Creative Co., 1976.

Carter, Ruth C. Brill. "The Lytle Family of Antebellum Cincinnati: Everyday Life, Kin, and Values of Elites in the Urban West." Ph.D. diss., Univ. of Pittsburgh, 1993.

Coggeshall, William Turner. *Poets and Poetry of the West: with Biographical and Critical Notices.* New York: Follett, Foster & Co., 1864.

Cohen, Stan. *The Civil War in West Virginia: A Pictorial History*, rev. ed. Charleston, W.Va.: Pictorial Histories Publishing Co., 1976.

Coles, Harry L. "Ohio Forms an Army." *Publications of the Ohio Civil War Centennial Commission* 5: 3-26 (1962).

Connelly, Thomas L. *Civil War Tennessee: Battles and Leaders.* Knoxville: Univ. of Tennessee Press, 1979.

Cozzens, Peter. *This Terrible Sound: The Battle of Chickamauga.* Urbana: Univ. of Illinois Press, 1992.

Dwyer, Doris Dawn. "A Century of City-Building: Three Generations of the Kilgour Family in Cincinnati, 1798-1914." Ph.D. diss., Miami Univ., 1979.

Eisenhower, John S.D. *Agent of Destiny: The Life and Times of General Winfield Scott.* New York: Free Press, 1997.

———. *So Far from God: The U.S. War with Mexico 1846-1848.* New York: Doubleday, 1989.

Fisher, Noel. "Groping toward Victory: Ohio's Administration of the Civil War." *Ohio History* 105: 25-45 (Winter-Spring 1996).

Ford, Thomas J. *With the Rank and File: Incidents and Anecdotes During the War of the Rebellion, as Remembered by One of the Non-Commissioned Officers.* Milwaukee: Press of the Evening Wisconsin Co., 1898.

Hafendorfer, Kenneth A. *Perryville: Battle for Kentucky.* Louisville: K.H. Press, 1991.

Harlow, Alvin F. *The Serene Cincinnatians.* New York: Dutton & Co., 1950.

Harrison, Lowell H. *The Civil War in Kentucky.* Lexington, Ky.: Univ. Press of Kentucky, 1975.

Hessler, Sherry O. "'The Great Disturbing Cause' and the Decline of the Queen City." *Historical and Philosophical Society of Ohio Bulletin* 20 (3): 169-85 (July 1962).

Hodges, Fletcher, Jr. "Stephen Foster—Cincinnatian and American." *Historical and Philosophical Society of Ohio Bulletin* 8 (2): 92-93 (April 1950).

Horn, Stanley F., *The Army of Tennessee.* 1952. Reprint, Norman, OK: Univ. of Oklahoma Press, 1993.

Kemper, Dr. Andrew C. *A Paper Read before the Loyal Legion, on William Haines Lytle . . . Burnet House, June 6, 1883.* Cincinnati: Peter G. Thomson [1883].

Kerr, Charles, ed. *History of Kentucky*, vol. 2. Chicago: American Historical Society, 1922.

Klement, Frank L. "Sound and Fury: Civil War Dissent in the Cincinnati Area." *The Cincinnati Historical Society Bulletin* 35 (2): 99-114 (Summer 1977).

Long, E.B., with Barbara Long. *The Civil War Day by Day: An Almanac, 1861-1865.* Garden City, N.Y.: Doubleday, 1971.

Lowry, Terry. *September Blood: The Battle of Carnifex Ferry.* Charleston, W.Va.: Pictorial Histories Publishing Co., 1985.

Mansfield, E.D. *Personal Memories: Social, Political, and Literary with Sketches of Many Noted People, 1803-1843.* Cincinnati: Robert Clarke & Co., 1879.

McPherson, James M. *Battle Cry of Freedom*. New York: Oxford Univ. Press, 1988.
————. *For Cause & Comrades: Why Men Fought the Civil War*. New York: Oxford Univ. Press, 1997.
————. *What They Fought For 1861-1865*. Baton Rouge, La.: Louisiana State Univ. Press, 1994.
*Monterrey is Ours! The Mexican War Letters of Lieutenant Dana 1845-1847*, ed. Robert H. Ferrell. Lexington, Ky.: Univ. Press of Kentucky, 1990.
Morris, Roy, Jr. "I Am Dying Egypt, Dying." *Civil War Times* 25 (6): 24-31 (October 1986).
————. *Sheridan: The Life and Wars of General Phil Sheridan*. New York: Crown Pub., 1992.
Nevins, Allan. *The Emergence of Lincoln: Douglas, Buchanan, and Party Chaos 1857-1859*. New York: Scribner's, 1950.
————. *The Emergence of Lincoln: Prologue to Civil War 1859-1861*. New York: Scribner's, 1950.
*Official Roster of the Soldiers of the State of Ohio in the War of the Rebellion, 1861-1866*, 12 vols. Cincinnati: Wilstach, Baldwin & Co., 1886-1895.
Pendleton, Charlotte [Charlton], *Songs of the Year and Other Poems*. Cincinnati: Robert Clarke & Co., 1875.
Perko, S.J. "To Enlighten the Rising Generation: School Formation in Cincinnati, 1821-1836." *Queen City Heritage* 43 (1): 33 (Spring 1985).
Ramage, James A. *Rebel Raider: The Life of General John Hunt Morgan*. Lexington, Ky.: Univ. Press of Kentucky, 1986.
Reid, Whitelaw. *Ohio in the War: Her Statesmen, Her Generals, and Soldiers*. 2 vols. Cincinnati: Moore, Wilstach, and Baldwin, 1868.
Remini, Robert V. *Henry Clay: Statesman for the Union*. New York: Norton & Co., 1991.
Rosebloom, Eugene H. *The Civil War Era 1850-1870*, vol. 4. *The History of the State of Ohio*, ed. Carl Wittke. Columbus: Ohio State Archaeological and Historical Society, 1944.
Ryan, Paul J. "Ohio in the Mexican War." *Ohio Archeological and Historical Publications* 21: 277-99 (1912).
Sifakis, Stewart. *Who Was Who in the Confederacy*. New York: Facts on File, 1988.
————. *Who Was Who in the Union*. New York: Facts on File, 1988.
Sloan, Mary Rahn. *The History of Camp Dennison, Ohio 1796-1956*. 1956. Reprint, Cincinnati: Blue Ash Office Supply, Inc., 1987.
Starr, Stephen Z. "Camp Dennison, 1861-1865." *Historical and Philosopical Society of Ohio Bulletin* 19 (3): 166-90 (July 1961).
Stevens, Linda Walker. "Old Nick: Cincinnati Winemaker." *Timeline* 13 (2): 24-35 (March/April 1996.)
Taylor, William R. *Cavalier and Yankee: The Old South and American National Character*. New York: Harper & Row, 1961.
Tucker, Louis Leonard. "Cincinnati during the Civil War." *Publications of the Ohio Civil War Centennial Commission* 9: 3-42 (1962).

————. "Cincinnati: Athens of the West, 1830-1861." *Ohio History* 75: 11-25 (Winter 1966).

————. "Hiram Powers and Cincinnati." *Cincinnati Historical Society Bulletin* 25 (1): 21-49 (January 1967.)

*War of the Rebellion . . . Official Records of the Union and Confederate Armies.* 128 volumes. Washington, D.C.: Government Printing Office, 1880-1901.

Wimberg, Robert J. *Cincinnati and the Civil War.* Cincinnati: Ohio Book Store, 1992.

Winders, Richard Bruce. *Mr. Polk's Army: The American Military Experience in the Mexican War.* College Station, Tex.: Texas A&M Univ. Press, 1997.

# Index

# For Honor Glory & Union

THE MEXICAN & CIVIL WAR LETTERS
OF BRIG. GEN. WILLIAM HAINES LYTLE

*Ruth C. Carter, Editor*

Cincinnati native William Haines Lytle
volunteered for service in the Mexican
War in late 1847. By 1861 the fervent
pro-states' rights Democrat with strong
family ties to Kentucky slaveholders was
in personality and temperament more a
Southern cavalier than a Yankee. But, like
his father and grandfather before him, he
believed strongly in the preservation of the
Union.

Lytle's Civil War letters detail the
intensity of the battles in the western
theater and illuminate the activities of the
Army of the Ohio and the Army of the
Cumberland in the early years of the war.
Because he liked to participate in society,
his writings also offer glimpses of the
interaction between Union officers and
Southern civilians in Kentucky, Tennessee,
and Alabama.

During the Mexican War, Lytle primarily served garrison duty. An ardent nationalist and partisan Democrat, he supported President Polk's policies to expand U.S. territory. Little has been recorded about garrison life during the Mexican War, but it was there Lytle learned to deal with troops and to handle periods of inaction and unpleasant situations. These skills would prove invaluable to him in the Civil War.

Lytle became known for his courage under fire and his devotion to his troops. He rose quickly through the ranks, participating in combat at Carnifex Ferry and Perryville. Lytle was killed at Chickamauga while leading a valiant charge to stop Confederate troops storming through an opening in Union lines.

Ruth C. Carter is head of the Archives Service Center and curator of Historical Collections for the University of Pittsburgh Library System.

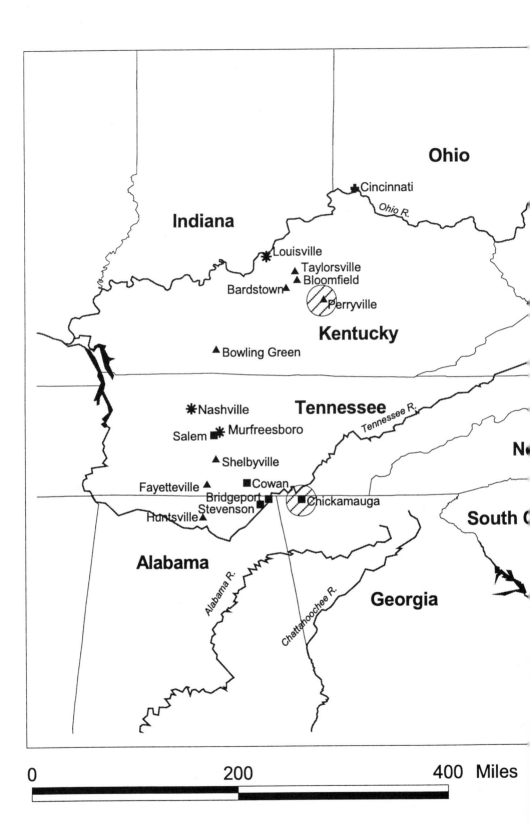